A Natural History of Conifers

A NATURAL HISTORY

of

CONIFERS

Aljos Farjon

Foreword by William G. Chaloner

TIMBER PRESS

Published in 2008 by
Timber Press, Inc.
The Haseltine Building
133 S.W. Second Avenue, Suite 450
Portland, Oregon 97204-3527, U.S.A.
www.timberpress.com

For contact information regarding editorial, marketing, sales, and
distribution in the United Kingdom, see www.timberpress.co.uk.

Printed in China

Library of Congress Cataloging-in-Publication Data

Farjon, Aljos.
    A natural history of conifers / Aljos Farjon.
        p. cm.
    Includes bibliographical references and index.
    ISBN-13: 978-0-88192-869-3
  1. Conifers. I. Title.
    QK494F36 2008
  585—dc22
                                        2007036730

A catalog record for this book is also available from the British Library.

To Shahina

Contents

Conifer Geography

Conifers and People

Conifers and Conservation

Foreword

THIS DELIGHTFUL VOLUME gives us a picture of a fascinating group of plants which, perhaps more than any other living organisms, have contrived to survive the ups and downs of Earth history through some 300 million years of moving continents and changing climate. They made their first evolutionary appearance as a very trivial element, alongside the giant club-mosses and horsetails that dominated the coal-forming swamps, which were to give us the fuel for the Industrial Revolution. By the time the dinosaurs had become the dominant components of the land fauna, the conifers were playing a comparable role in the forests that covered much of the Earth's surface of that time. When the flowering plants appeared, shortly before the chalk was laid down over much of western Europe, many older groups of plants succumbed to the aggressive ecological success of the newcomers. But the conifers survived this challenge and have held their own to the present day, still dominating vast tracts of the Northern Hemisphere's high latitudes.

Despite their retaining a remarkable ecological versatility, the conifers are poorly represented in Britain's native flora. Since the ice retreated off Britain at the end of the last glacial period some 10,000 years ago, only three species of conifer became successfully established here. Happily, three attributes of the human inhabitants of these islands have made up for that deficiency. These are an inclination to explore the far corners of the Earth and to bring back the botanical spoils of such expeditions; to grow softwood timber in plantation; and to decorate our gardens and landscapes with graceful trees that retain their charms round the year.

Aljos Farjon, recently retired from the staff of the Royal Botanic Gardens, Kew, is a renowned world authority on conifers. His several recent books dealing with conifers are scholarly and definitive works, warmly received by botanists all over the world. But this one is different: it is written for a wider audience and presents the subject from a much broader perspective. Farjon explores their distribution, both geographically and in the time dimension of geology, and more enterprisingly, in their interaction with human beings. The latter ranges from the uses to which conifers have been put, in horticulture and in landscape, from paper to furniture, and to the larger scale of their use as building material. The broad brush of Farjon's natural history takes us into conifer territory that few of us, even conifer specialists, had ever contemplated. But the enthusiast should not be put off by any suggestion that its treatment is a dumbing down of conifer science. For though intelligible to a wide readership, this book still contains new treasures and insights, especially of evolutionary relationships, which make it a unique and valuable contribution to our understanding of this rewarding corner of plant science.

WILLIAM G. CHALONER FRS, Professor of Botany,
Geology Department, Royal Holloway, University of London

Preface

WRITING A POPULAR SCIENCE BOOK about the subject that one has studied professionally for many years is a challenging but—as I discovered—enormously gratifying experience. Here is the chance to write up those stories that you have sometimes communicated at the coffee table in the staff room of your institute, but that would not have been allowed through by the editor of a scientific journal. They are often the things that make science exciting, but excitement is not allowed in those journals, at least not explicitly. You have to stick to the data and the results, and storytelling is frowned upon as unscientific. "Factual information, please, and no frills" is the message to authors in such journals. One of the challenges with popular science writing is that the author has, of course, to stay within the limits of science, separating facts from fiction and knowledge from conjecture. The journalistic temptation to simplify and exaggerate the knowledge of science for a good story, so often seen in newspapers, has to be avoided. I am a scientist with a reputation at stake, but just as important, one should not deceive the readers. When something is not entirely certain, one must say so, even if it would be more exciting if it was a fact. That is what I have tried to do in this book. However, I could only do that and still tell good stories if I were really on top of my subject. And that has led to another good thing I experienced in researching and writing this book. Many botanists consider me to be the world expert on conifers, but I discovered aspects of conifers I did not know much about when I started this book, so I studied and learned a good many things before I wrote about them.

This book has arisen from a desire to explore, with the reader, one of the most interesting kinds of plants on earth. When Timber Press approached me for ideas about a book on conifers, it was immediately obvious to me that I should try to approach the subject from as many angles as my knowledge and abilities would permit. While most of my scientific output on conifers has been taxonomic, I have always had a broad interest in the natural history of these plants. I use the term in the fullness of its meaning, the one Darwin would have understood. It includes what some scientists today seem to wish to separate as the only "real" science—for example, the research into phylogeny using DNA sequence data—as well as topics ranging from evolutionary history to geographic distribution. To me there is no true difference from other data, methods, and enquiries, as long as we test the results and are prepared to change views in the light of better evidence.

I explore the conifers from the basic question of what they are, through their evolution and taxonomy, their ecology and distribution, to human uses and issues of conservation. One of my aims has been to try to counter a rather negative and simplistic image of conifers that seems to prevail especially in the Northern Hemisphere. Negative because certain species, or hybrids, have been widely planted for limited purposes that only benefit their egocentric owners, afflicting urban living space and countryside alike. Such cases have not only led to bad press, but to litigation and hence enmities that have cast a shadow over the word *conifer*. This book will, I hope, dispel that prejudice. I shall have succeeded if at the end of it, you will realize how little conifers as a group of plants resemble hedges grown out of proportion or monocultures admitting little wildlife under their dense, light-shutting canopies.

This book starts with a question, "What are conifers?" It seems an easy question to answer, but it is not. I thought it was a good way to introduce the complexity of systematics in biology, by which we can only attempt to answer the question. To further introduce conifers, I explain the image problem and how to solve it, which leads into the issue of diversity from both taxonomic and ecological points of view. You will find that there is more to discover, even for specialists, than we thought.

The systematics of conifers has been a subject of investigation for more than two centuries. I review some of that, but I also felt I must try to explain what taxonomy is about in more general terms. Taxonomy is, very unfortunately, a discipline in trouble, and I hope to encourage renewed interest in it. This section culminates in an evolutionary classification of conifers that is in fact new, in the sense that I present it here for the first time. These chapters may be somewhat technical, but I have tried to explain the jargon both in the text and in a glossary, if needed.

We then come to review the past. Conifers as a group are extraordinarily ancient, much older than the flowering plants. As I have pointed out in previous chapters, without the fossils of often-extinct conifers we will not understand their evolution. And this past, as you will see later, helps to explain the present, as it always does in history.

Another of my favourite subjects is ecology, and I was a plant ecologist before I became a taxonomist. Few plant ecologies are more fascinating than those of conifers, which have succeeded to persist in so many parts of the world for so long. They have seen catastrophic extinction events as well as the rise of formidable competitors, the angiosperms or flowering plants. The stories of how conifers coped are some of the most thrilling in plant lore (scientific lore, of course).

Far from being evolutionary losers, conifers have succeeded extremely well in many places. Scarcely less remarkable is how conifers got to occupy, with only 630 species, every continent, ranging from the high latitudes to the tropics. Their distribution, past and present, involves all the questions biogeographers can possibly ask about this aspect of biology. Here, too, we will encounter a remarkable fact not earlier published with the backing of data: more than half of all the species of conifers encircle the Pacific Ocean.

It is true, conifers are important to people. In this section, I shall highlight the uses human societies have made and make of conifers, and you may find some unexpected as well as better-known connections between conifers and people. Natural history will often come peeking round the corner of commonalities such as dwarf conifers for the garden and wood for furniture.

Finally, there is the issue of conservation. We live in a world that is increasingly dominated by humans at the cost of other forms of life, and conifers do not escape from this threat to their continued existence. It is easy to paint a bleak picture without exaggerating the facts. More importantly, we should address the problems, and to be able to do that, building awareness is a first and necessary step. That is also an aim of this book: if conifers are appreciated for what they really are, we may find more support to protect them.

Without the help and support of others, this book would not have been realized. I began it almost from the day in March 2006 when, due to a regrettable government rule still in force at the time, I had to retire from the Royal Botanic Gardens, Kew, on turning 60 years of age. This meant I had to seek grant money. A modest but important grant was received from the Bentham Moxon Trust to complete my research of the genus *Araucaria*, which was left unfinished at retirement; this has helped to write up chapter 32 in particular. I am most grateful to a private donor, Philippe de Spoelberch in Belgium, for a generous grant towards this project. My former Director at Kew, Sir Ghillean Prance, has acted as my ambassador on this and other occasions, and I am indebted to him for his support. I also express my gratitude to the Keeper of the Herbarium at Kew, Simon Owens, for support of a different kind in giving me undiminished access to the facilities at Kew. In the writing of the book, discussions with colleagues and specialists about certain topics I had no first-hand knowledge of have helped me improve the text of certain chapters. I particularly value and acknowledge the time Derek Spicer gave to introduce me to the intricacies of growing dwarf conifers at his nursery in Leicestershire, England. Several of his photographs on the subject adorn this book. Dan Nickrent of Southern Illinois University corrected me on some issues with dwarf mistletoes and provided me with a very good photograph of one of the species. Pim van der Knaap of the University of Zürich noted several errors regarding the past migration of spruces in Europe and pointed me toward new research on the subject.

The publisher and I decided to have illustrations throughout the book to illuminate the text. Therefore, as I wrote the chapters, I inserted tentative captions for illustrations whenever I thought it would be good to have one, regardless of whether I already had that illustration. About 20 per cent had to come from others, often unknown to me at the time. I have been very fortunate with both the quality of these illustrations and the willingness to help from many sources. I am particularly grateful to Bob Van Pelt, who generously helped me to illustrate the chapter that deals with his speciality, giant conifers. My conifer colleagues Martin Gardner and Chris Page provided photographs on request with their customary generosity, as did others whose photographs are credited in the captions. Gar Rothwell of Ohio University read the text of some of the chapters on fossil conifers and granted the use of illustrations from some of his publications. Very generous permission to use illustrations of fossil conifers from the Triassic of South Africa was given by John Anderson. The photograph of a coniferous fossil was supplied by Lutz Kunzmann of the Museum für Mineralogie und Geologie in Dresden, Germany. When I realized I needed a picture of a young, pot-grown Norfolk Island pine to compare with one of the earliest conifers known, the Royal Horticultural Society's garden at Wisley had exactly what I wanted, and their staff were kindly helpful with my attempts to photograph it. I am particularly pleased with a photograph of a prehistoric amber necklace from the Drents Museum in Assen, The Netherlands. For this Jan-Albert Bakker, an archaeologist who I have known since my early teens, acted as a mediator. The Internet and Google have become indispensable tools for finding pictures and their sources. In this way I found excellent photographs of the two animals about which I wanted to tell stories linked with conifers, and I am grateful to their photographers, Jiri Bohdal and Gary Nefis, who provided them. The Field Museum, Chicago, allowed me to use an image of their famous diorama of a Carboniferous coal forest. Timber Press has been helpful with everything I asked of them throughout the preparation of this book, and I thank Jane Connor, Dale Johnson, and Anna Mumford for their assistance and support in making this book a reality.

This book was a great pleasure to write. My enthusiasm must have been apparent to colleagues and friends, and some of them may once in a while have thought, "There he is again with his conifers." But there is one who never got tired and even read the whole manuscript when it was finished, Shahina Ghazanfar. I dedicate this book to her.

Introduction
to Conifers

1 What Are Conifers?

AT FIRST SIGHT, *most people would think that the answer to this question is straight-forward. We are all familiar with conifers, or so we believe. The meaning of the term, cone-bearers, appears to describe at least one characteristic common to all conifers: they produce cones, which are the more or less woody, scaly fruits that contain seeds. We also know that conifers are woody plants, usually trees, and that most are evergreen and have needles instead of flat leaves. So far, so good, it seems. But do all conifers have these familiar characters? Or, with the argument turned round: Are all plants with one or more of these characters conifers? If I tell you that the answer to both questions is no in more than a few cases, confusion appears to reign. Well, I hope that in this chapter I can present a clearer picture of what makes conifers distinct from other plants. The answer has to do with evolution and phylogenetic relationships. The characteristics that define conifers are the result of evolution and indicate these relationships. Here is how this story unfolds.*

▲ ▲ ▲

Early classifications, or scientific groupings of plants, oversimplified in an attempt to bring some logical order to what seemed a chaotic diversity. The best-known example is the system devised by Linnaeus in the first half of the 18th century. I call these classifications "scientific" merely to distinguish them from still earlier, mostly utilitarian systems; for instance, one can group plants according to their uses, such as food, medicine, for clothing, or tool making. Of course, knowing a plant's use is science insofar as all knowledge is science. But scientific classifications aim at something more, to discover a natural order of things that is thought to exist independent of our own purposes. Linnaeus, as a scholar of the Enlightenment, tried to achieve this natural classification in his great work *Systema Naturae* (1735 and later, much enlarged editions). Although the system he devised for flowering plants based on their sexual characters was admittedly artificial—or more clearly, arbitrary—it remained in use for a long time. Under such a system, if another character is used as the basis, you are likely to get a different grouping or classification, and there is no objective way of deciding which one is better or true. The purpose of artificial systems is to aid in recognition or naming. We use them today, for instance, in identification keys in Floras. Linnaeus' sexual system for flowers seemed to work reasonably well, at least for the plants then known. But did it work for conifers? Well, it couldn't. Linnaeus did not realize that, however, and so he fitted them in somehow, as we can read in his most famous book *Species Plantarum* (1753 and later editions).

Do all conifers have cones, and if not, why are those that don't still classified as conifers? And why are other plants with cones not conifers? How do we distinguish between characters that give us the right signal and those that put us in the wrong direction? These questions don't have easy answers, and botanists have taken a long time to arrive at what we think is the correct answer. An early flash of insight came from Robert Brown in 1826. Brown was a noted botanist in London who sailed around Australia with Capt. Phillip P. King. In an appendix to King's narrative of that journey, Brown gave a lengthy account of a new plant genus that he named *Kingia*. This is not a conifer—it is in the family Xanthorrhoeaceae, known in Australia as "black boys"—but his detailed observations of the minute flowers, ovaries, and ovules led him to the analogy in the "female flower of Cycadae and Coniferae." Here he discovered that the ovules are not enclosed in an ovary. Brown became the first botanist to understand and describe the difference between angiosperms and gymnosperms. Angiosperms have flowers, which have ovaries with ovules in them that become, upon fertilization, fruits and seeds. Gymnosperms have ovules that become seeds, but they are not in ovaries that become fruits. Both cycads and conifers, as Brown demonstrated, are gymnosperms. That takes us a big step forward in understanding conifers, but mainly by exclusion: It tells us that seed plants with true flowers are not conifers, and by implication, that conifers do not have flowers. I speak, of course, as a botanist; in a more colloquial sense of the word *flower*, conifers are often said to flower when the young and often-colourful seed cones or the male pollen cones appear.

As Brown noted, cycads have similar female reproductive organs, and these, as well as the male organs, usually form cones. Yet cycads are not conifers. Here we come to more complex issues as we look at unique combinations of characters that now must distinguish natural groups among gymnosperms. If we carefully investigate seed plants that live today, it is not difficult to establish that they are gymnosperms. We must observe the female reproductive organs and especially their earlier phases of development. Invariably, the ovules are exposed, not enclosed. Seeds can be enclosed in cones, however, which has led Barry Tomlinson of Harvard University to say that we should in fact call these plants *gymnovules*, not *gymnosperms* (*gymnos*, naked; *ovula*, egg; *sperma*, seed). I think we are stuck with a well-known term, however, and it is true at least for a good many species of gymnosperms that ovules remain exposed as they become seeds.

In evolutionary terms, gymnospermy is clearly the primitive state and angiosperms derived from a gymnosperm, although we don't know which one. In the fossil record, all early seed plants are gymnosperms; angiosperms arrive relatively late, perhaps in the Jurassic but certainly by the Lower Cretaceous. Most groups of what we can recognize as gymnosperms became extinct, and those that remain are a small example of what once covered the Earth. Conifers are among the early gymnosperms and, of course, still exist as a group: we can classify them as the order Coniferales. The other extant groups are cycads (Cycadales), ginkgos (Ginkgoales), and the order Gnetales. The ranking as orders is arbitrary, and other taxonomists prefer a rank higher as classes, for which different names are in use. But it does not tell us anything essentially different, so we keep to orders.

Shortly after Brown's publication, everyone had recognized the cycads—which resemble palms to the layman—as truly distinct, even though they have cones. They have no obvious growth of secondary wood, and their leaves are pinnate as in some palms.

The cones of cycads are clearly simple, that is, consisting of simple fertile scales on an axis without any other appendages. The anatomy of cycads' stems and leaves is very distinctive from those of other plants, and so are microstructures such as leaf stomata and pollen.

Both conifers and cycads have seed cones, and cycad cones are simple. For much of the 19th and early 20th centuries, European botanists debated the nature of female conifer cones, and in particular whether they are simple or compound. A simple cone has an axis with one kind of appendage, whereas a compound cone has more than one kind, whereby one appendage is connected to the other. One problem to resolving this debate was that there are cones of conifers that seem to have only one kind of appendage. Let us take two commonly known examples. If you look at the seed cone of a Douglas fir (*Pseudotsuga menziesii*), you will see two very different kinds of appendages (I use a neutral term deliberately for now). One is thin and narrow and ends in three prongs, and the other is thicker, broad, and rounded. They are both spirally arranged around the axis, which is invisible inside the cone. No matter how much we strain our eyes as we look at a mature cone of a Balkan pine (*Pinus peuce*), we can see only rounded appendages. However, if you were to look at the very early stages of both cones, they would be quite similar. After fertilization of the ovules, the thin and narrow appendages in the Balkan pine cone grow no more, and in a mature cone you can hardly see their remnants at the base of the large scales. That was a relatively easy one. But when we move on to other conifers, it can become really difficult to find evidence at any stage of two kinds of appendages, let alone how they are or are not connected.

The debate was not helped either by the confusing terminology used. Most botanists tried to describe cones in terms of flowering plants. The question became: Is a cone a flower (in German: *Blüte*) or is it an inflorescence (*Blütenstand*)? In fact, it is neither. All kinds of evidence for or against were put forward, such as the anatomy of vascular strands by Strasburger and van Tieghem, which in the end proved little as we now know. At times the gentlemen could become quite excited and even started to doubt

Seed cone of *Pseudotsuga menziesii*, Douglas fir

Seed cone of *Pinus peuce*, Balkan pine

each other's mental capabilities, as in the exchanges between Čelakovský and Eichler. Then, at long last, a botanist came up with the solution. His name was Rudolf Florin.

Florin was a Swedish palaeobotanist, someone whose primary subject is fossil plants. In a series of brilliantly researched papers, he described and interpreted fossil plant remains from the later Palaeozoic (Carboniferous and Permian) that had belonged to woody shrubs or trees with needle or scale leaves and appeared to have had primitive seed cones. His first paper was published in a Swedish botanical journal in 1939, but his better-known work on this subject was published in the 1950s. Florin observed in these fossils a more or less gradual evolution from the earliest forms almost until modern cones. Clearly, the earliest forms all had compound systems, usually much more open and diversified than any cones at present. Ovules or seeds were on short branch-like appendices, and these were accompanied by small scale leaves. The whole structure was subtended by a long bifurcated leaf, and these were in turn spirally arranged around an axis. In later forms, the numbers are reduced, with fewer appendices and scale leaves per unit; they also become wider and flatter and begin to fuse into one scale with one to three seeds each, depending on the species. The bifurcated leaf subtending each fertile unit remains, but its apex changes to a single point. In conifers from the later periods, the Triassic and Jurassic, we essentially have types that still exist, at least if we look at the classic concept of a conifer cone as given for the Douglas fir and Balkan pine above. Although later studies, based on more and sometimes better fossils, have amended Florin's insights here and there, his basic concept is still valid. The female conifer cone is a compound structure that is unique to this group and derived from ancient and more complex structures that originated in the Carboniferous about 310 million years ago. They are not to be compared with inflorescences or with flowers and consist of an axis with two types of appendices: a bract (the subtending leaf) and a scale bearing the ovules or seeds derived from a fertile dwarf shoot.

With this we have a unique and unifying character to distinguish all conifers from other gymnosperms. Well, not quite yet. The difficulties that the 19th-century botanists had were not all imaginary. Florin himself could not discover any trace of a compound cone in yews (*Taxus*) and its allies (Taxaceae). Thus, he insisted they were not conifers (Coniferales) and placed them in an order of their own (Taxales), especially after some fossil evidence indicated their relatively ancient origin in the Triassic. Florin knew, of course, that in that distant past many kinds of gymnosperms had existed that we would not call conifers, and taxads might have evolved from one of these.

The invention of the scanning electron microscope has made it possible to magnify—to almost unlimited levels, if neces-

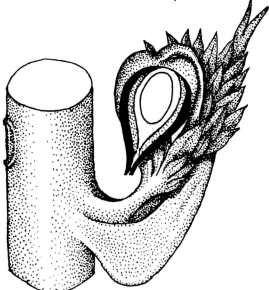

Reconstruction of a segment of the compound cone of *Emporia*, an early conifer, showing a bifurcated bract and fertile shoot with a reflexed seed. From Stewart and Rothwell (1993); reprinted by permission of Cambridge University Press

sary—morphological structure in three-dimensional photographic images. This has opened a whole new world of characters and their development through early stages. Most recently, the next very important step has become possible: we can start to link this development to the DNA (genes) responsible for the changes. This branch of biological science is called "evolutionary developmental biology," a mouthful that no one wishes to remember, so it has become known as "evo-devo." In the last two decades many conifers have been put into the scanning electron microscope. Florin could not discover separate bracts and seed scales in the Cupressaceae and thought that they were fused together, as is the case in the monkey-puzzle tree (*Araucaria araucana*), in which the distinction between the two remains more or less visible. These electron microscope studies have now revealed a more complicated story of development. Because we know more about the phylogeny of conifers, we can say something about which forms are likely to be primitive and which are more derived. We also know more about the genes and how they work to change morphology.

From this we can infer what could have happened in the evolution that led to cones

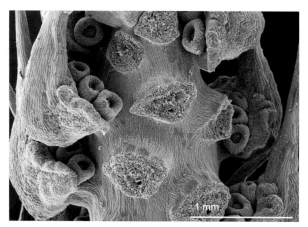

Cone axis with bracts (outer) and ovules (cup-shaped structures) of the seed cone of *Sequoia sempervirens*.

Juniperus virginiana cone apex with single ovule (centre) surrounded by bracts.

without seed scales. Species with initially two appendages—bract and seed scale—evolved into species in which the seed scale does not appear during development, and the bract alone now forms the cone scale. (Genetically, much of the development in morphology appears to be controlled by relatively few genes that have hardly changed in evolutionary history and are known as homeotic genes. They determine both where something appears and when in the embryological development.) During the evolution of species in the Cupressaceae, it appears that the ovules moved off the seed scale to a position between the axis and bract. Once the seed scale became redundant, its development was switched off, while the bract took over the formation of the cone scale. If this is correct, then species in that family with only one type of appendage (the bract) derived from a species that had both, and the compound cone remains the unique and unifying morphological character of conifers.

The Taxaceae are still a bit more difficult than the Cupressaceae to explain. The common yew (*Taxus baccata*) has a single seed at the end of a tiny branchlet, surrounded by a succulent aril. At least one recent and detailed German study of the branching systems associated with seeds in Taxaceae concluded that they represent an extreme reduction of a compound system that skipped the phase with a seed scale altogether (Stützel and Röwekamp 1999). Although not everyone is convinced, independent DNA evidence strongly indicates a very close relationship between taxads and conifers. Perhaps the fossil record will help us here, too, as it did for Florin in the 1950s, while evo-devo also promises a new way of looking at an old question. At present, it seems best to include taxads in the order Coniferales.

Are there any other unifying characters that help us to separate conifers from other groups? Wood anatomists can readily tell conifer wood from that of other groups. Conifer wood lacks vessels and instead has tracheids with large, bordered pits. The rays are always narrow, except those that contain radial resin canals. All conifers contain resin in the wood or in the leaves. In this manner, using a unique combination of characters, we can construct a description of conifers. From it, we can obtain further insight how to interpret coneless conifers such as *Taxus* and some species of *Juniperus*. Finally, there are unique and unifying characters in the DNA (molecular characters). All this together will define conifers. Now I can end this perhaps somewhat technical discussion with a concise definition of conifers, after which we will all agree what they are.

Conifers are shrubs or trees with secondary wood built of tracheids with large bordered pits in their walls and narrow rays. The leaves are simple and single or parallel veined. Resin is produced in the wood or in the leaves and is conducted through resin canals. The reproductive organs are separated into male and female, with male cones (pollen cones) simple and female cones (seed cones) compound or reduced. Conifers have only one copy of a large inverted repeat in the chloroplast DNA, whereas all other plants studied so far have two copies.

During the evolution of conifers that led to *Taxus baccata*, the common yew, a seed with a colourful, succulent aril is all that remained of a compound cone. Photograph by Henry D. Hooper

2 The Image Problem with Christmas Trees and Hedges

CONIFERS CAN EXCITE PEOPLE *in ways that are often quite disconcerting to a botanist who has made it a lifelong vocation to study them. At meetings and other functions, people often accost me with their most pressing question on the subject. The most commonly asked questions fall roughly into two categories: "Why is my garden conifer dying?" and "How big will the conifer in my neighbour's garden become?" My answers to these questions are invariably unhelpful, because I am neither a plant pathologist nor a gardener and do not wish to be involved in litigation issues. Less tricky are the ladies who want me to tell them which conifer would not drop its needles into their high carpet when taken indoors as a Christmas tree. And then there was this gentleman from Scotland who insisted that I advise him (gratis, of course) which of the Mexican pines he should plant on his land in the Highlands. He had found me when I worked in the Department of Plant Sciences at the University of Oxford on Mexican pines. He pursued me, with a very loud voice that caused me to hold the telephone receiver at a little distance, all the way through to my new position at the Royal Botanic Gardens, Kew. When I tell such people, politely, that I am not really qualified to answer their questions, they finally give up in disbelief. "So much for the conifer expert!" they undoubtedly think.*

▲ ▲ ▲

Conifers have an image problem. They are the most diverse, interesting, beautiful, and wonderful trees and shrubs in the world, I think, yet they conjure up images of dark, looming cohorts of plantation trees and the dull, towering hedge of your neighbour. And, indeed, when we take them into the house in midwinter to brighten them up with glittering ornaments and candles or lamps, the ungrateful things leave us their needles in the carpet. Do these impressions of conifers reflect ignorance? Well, yes, but the general public, who have not made a study of the subject, can hardly be blamed. Perhaps it is the fault of the media—always a fine target. Well, yes it is, but unless we experts come down from our ivory towers and start to provide some education, in a way that transfers our enthusiasm along with the knowledge, we can in the end only blame ourselves. It was this realization that encouraged me to write this book.

The view that people have of conifers is intricately linked with the way we use them in our European cultures. These uses are by and large determined by two major and related enterprises: horticulture and forestry. In contrast to such traditions in China and Japan, more ancient and traditional uses are rare in Western cultures. The Christian religion long ago banished the veneration of trees, which we can still observe in Asia, and only a few things have remained or crept back from our pagan days, such as the planting of yews in English churchyards. The Christmas tree in the house is a 19th-century German invention; the more traditional greenery that came into the house at this time consisted of hollies and mistletoes. Spruce trees are not native to much of northwestern Europe, and where they are, as in Scandinavia, spruces are so ubiquitous that they were never seen as harbingers or symbols of new life. Traditional medicine has mostly been replaced by scientific thinking about illness and diseases, and European conifers, being rather poor in taxonomic diversity, did not have much to offer anyway. As it turns out, even the common yew (*Taxus baccata*) has a lower content of Taxol, the biochemical basis for anticancer drugs, than several of the other species in the genus. But horticulture and forestry could and did flourish in Europe from the 17th century onwards. Of the two endeavours, horticulture has come up with a much greater diversity of conifers to use than has forestry. Yet horticulture can be accused of the same evil: It will only produce what sells, and the economics determine the available diversity.

Few tree nurseries can indulge in the propagation of new species on any scale that would make a difference without risking financial loss or worse. In forestry, these constraints are even stronger. This tendency to conservatism is enhanced by risk factors that can only be overcome through extensive trials, which are expensive and time consuming with plants that mature over many years. As a result, the number of conifer species commercially available is relatively small even in horticulture; in forestry it is really small. Cultivars have substantially increased the diversity as seen from a gardeners' viewpoint, although many are only slight variations on a theme centred on habit

A conifer hedge, grown out of proportion in a neighbourhood, does not help to give a positive image of conifers.

and colour of foliage, in other words garden architectural qualities. These selections add little to botanical interest and, I suspect, this is one reason why they are found to be boring. Collector gardeners may find conifers of interest, but to the general public they seem to have little to offer, which is reflected in the few selections available in most garden centres. The economics of forestry now limit even more than in the past what can be planted: it has to grow fast on poor soils with little maintenance. Sitka spruce (*Picea sitchensis*) and radiata pine or Monterey pine (*Pinus radiata*) are the results. For instance, go to large gardens and parks in New Zealand and see what and how they plant there. New Zealand has one of the most diverse and interesting native conifer floras in the world, but you will see few if any of them planted. It will look as if you were in England or Germany. In forestry, the New Zealanders have virtually replaced the native forests with plantations of radiata pine. The United States, with a huge native conifer flora more akin to Europe than New Zealand, still mostly plants what was developed and selected in Europe. Of course, these countries were predominantly settled by Europeans, who brought their culture and traditions with them, but that culture is now rapidly becoming global.

To begin to replace this gloomy picture of uniform boredom with something more exciting, I shall first give an overview of the true diversity and interest of the world's conifers. Ecological and evolutionary aspects play major roles in the causes of the diversity, but more detailed accounts of these will be given in later sections. Here I simply give a glimpse into the amazing kaleidoscope by contrasting extremes and comparing the common with the uncommon.

Conifers are the dominant trees that form the vast boreal forests in the Northern Hemisphere. This biome stretches around the Earth along the northern latitudes and is still largely intact despite inroads by loggers and increased incidence of fire. These are the conifers most people in Europe, Asia, and North America are familiar with. They consist of only a handful of species, almost all in the pine family (Pinaceae) and belonging to a few genera: *Abies* (fir), *Larix* (larch), *Picea* (spruce), and *Pinus* (pine). Shrubby junipers (*Juniperus*, Cupressaceae) often form part of the understorey. Only in some areas along the northern Pacific coasts are some other genera of Cupressaceae present at these latitudes. In general, the evergreen tree species of conifers in this zone tend to resemble each other in their narrowly conical habit, with only the deciduous larches being broad and open. The extreme climate in the boreal zone is a severe limitation to diversity. No equivalent great monotonous forests of conifers occur in the Southern Hemisphere. Conifers live on all continents except Antarctica, where they have been found only as fossils. Diversity in species and growth forms increases in the Northern Hemisphere towards the equator and is high at all latitudes where conifers occur in the Southern Hemisphere.

For some truly amazing conifers, let us first briefly visit the coasts of the Pacific Ocean at temperate northern latitudes. In the Pacific Northwest, ranging from British Columbia to northern California, the size of conifers is the dominating factor. Conifers of nearly all genera that occur here attain record sizes not found anywhere else. The tallest individual tree in the region, a coast redwood or sequoia (*Sequoia sempervirens*), has attained 112 m (367 ft). Douglas fir (*Pseudotsuga menziesii*), Sitka spruce (*Picea sitchensis*), grand fir (*Abies grandis*), and western red cedar (*Thuja plicata*) all have champions of 80–100 m (262–328 ft). Growing conditions for these conifers must be better here than almost anywhere else. A little to the south, in the Sierra Nevada of California, grows the most massive conifer (and tree) in the world: the big tree or giant sequoia (*Sequoiadendron giganteum*) that measures 90 m (295 ft). We know from fossil evidence that some of these giants were more widespread and occurred even in Europe; it could indicate that the optimal conditions for such monstrous trees are now very rare and may become rarer still. Japan and Taiwan on the other side of the northern Pacific have some giant conifers, too, such as *Cryptomeria japonica* (sugi) and *Taiwania cryptomerioides*. Both are monotypic, a term that means they are the only known species in their genus, and both are now classified in Cupressaceae. Like the sequoias on the other side of the ocean, they are the relics of a bygone age of giants that goes back to the latter days of the dinosaurs.

At the other end of the scale are dwarf conifers. I do not mean cultivars sold as dwarf conifers, which sometimes cheat their buyers by growing much larger than promised. I am talking about natural dwarfs. Perhaps the most diminutive species grows in the western mountains of Tasmania, Australia. *Microcachrys tetragona* (Podocarpaceae) is a creeping tiny shrub growing only 10–25 cm (4–10 in) tall. It has tiny scale leaves arranged in four rows along the twigs and very strange seed cones resembling raspberries. Some junipers are scarcely taller, but can spread wide over sand or shingle, such as *Juniperus procumbens* in the Japanese Ryukyu Islands. Shrubby growth habits are com-

This *Sequoiadendron giganteum*, the General Sherman Tree, is the most massive conifer in the world and grows in Sequoia National Park, California.

This creeping shrub of Tasmania, *Microcachrys tetragona*, is the smallest conifer in the world.

Dwarfing of conifers in nature can occur on very poor soils, as in this example of a diminutive Australian conifer *Callitris preissii* bearing a full-grown seed cone.

mon in both high altitudes and semi-deserts, and many conifer genera and species around the world have adopted this form to cope with a harsh environment. A variant on this tendency to reduce size is miniature trees, if we define trees as woody plants with single stems and several branches. These are common on extremely nutrient-poor soils, especially in warm climates. In New Caledonia are found dwarf trees such as *Dacrydium araucarioides* (Podocarpaceae) and *Neocallitropsis pancheri* (Cupressaceae) with a peculiar growth habit. The sparse, long branches spread out in whorls on the erect stem and are upturned at the ends, like the arms of a candelabrum. Interestingly, this habit is also seen in some angiosperms at the same localities. In California's Mendocino County, close to the Pacific coast, a dwarf form of Gowen cypress (*Cupressus goveniana*) occurs on hardpan or leached sand. At this locality this species is often not taller than 30 cm (12 in) but produces pollen and seed cones. Only a little distance away, on slightly better soil, the same species can attain 50 m (165 ft). In Western Australia I have seen the same dwarfing of *Callitris preissii* and *C. drummondii* (Cupressaceae), which can grow much taller. Two species from New South Wales, *Callitris monticola* and *C. muelleri*, are only known as dwarf trees.

The oldest individual trees in the world are all conifers. The record age, verified by ring counts of a tree stump (the central bit missing), is 4862 years, but the tree was estimated to have grown for at least 5000 years. Embarrassingly, this count was obtained from a stump of a felled specimen of Great Basin bristlecone pine (*Pinus longaeva*, Pinaceae); the oldest individual of this species counted and still alive is about 4600 years. Other record ages are all in the family Cupressaceae. One of the greatest ages obtained is a ring count of the outer part of a trunk of *Fitzroya cupressoides*, known as alerce in Chile and another of the giant conifers, of 3622 years (Lara and Villalba 1993). As in most large conifers growing in wet coastal climates, these trunks are often hollow because much of the heartwood has rotten away. We can only guess at how many years we must add to estimate the true age—similar problems bedevil the age estimates of oaks and yews in many countries. Perhaps there was a large conifer in Chile that was older than the oldest bristlecone pine, but we may never know it. Just recently I met Antonio Lara, and he told me that they had ring-counted a sawn stump of *F. cupressoides* with an intact core at 4080 years. Record ages of other extreme Methuselahs are *Chamaecyparis formosensis* in Taiwan, a tree that attains enormous girth like the sequoias but is not as tall, at 3000+ years; the big tree (*Sequoiadendron giganteum*) of the Californian Sierras, which is 3266 years old; the Nootka cypress (*Xanthocyparis nootkatensis*) of the Pacific Northwest, which was estimated to be 3500+ years old; a tree belonging to the species *Juniperus scopulorum* in Utah estimated at 3600+ years; and the redwood (*Sequoia sempervirens*) on the Californian coast, with a modest 2200 years. A thousand years is not very old for many conifers. The entire history of European civilization (if we start that with ancient Greece) is much shorter than the age of most of these individual trees. Yet we know from the fossil record that such trees have germinated, grown, lived to maturity and senescence, and finally died countless times in many parts of the world where they no longer occur today—unless recently planted. What babies are the giant sequoias in the parks and gardens of Europe, with a mere 150 years!

It may come as a surprise to hear that nearly a third of all conifer species occur

Dacrydium cupressinum, a New Zealand podocarp, growing as a tall forest tree.

in the tropics. Many are very different from our familiar conifers mentioned at the beginning of this chapter. The genus *Agathis* (Araucariaceae; one species from the tip of North Island in New Zealand is called kauri) consists of about 20 species of mostly very large forest trees with huge stems, an unconifer-like multicoloured bark flaking in jigsaw-puzzle patterns, and wide-spreading crowns emerging above the canopy bearing foliage of broadly ovate, multiple-veined leathery leaves. The compact, egg-shaped seed cones disintegrate on the tree, and the pollen cones are like miniature cones of cycads. These trees produce so much resin, which seeps into the ground, that it can be mined.

Also largely tropical, but spreading to temperate latitudes in the Southern Hemisphere, is the genus *Podocarpus*, after *Pinus* the most speciose genus of conifers. They range from decumbent shrubs to the largest trees, and both extremes can be found in New Zealand: *Podocarpus nivalis* and *P. totara*. Some species have the largest leaves of conifers, and these do not look like those of other conifers, except in their anatomy (see drawing in chapter 7). The cones of *Podocarpus* are very peculiar. They are strongly reduced at maturity so as to produce only a single, mostly uncovered seed. The bracts and seed scales of aborted ovules are fused, strongly inflated, succulent, and brightly coloured, forming a receptacle basal to the seed (see photo in chapter 12 and drawing in chapter 17). Birds, having colour vision, are the main dispersers, swallowing the whole cone, digesting the receptacle, and dropping the seed. This strategy is performed differently in some other genera of Podocarpaceae, such as

Opposite: *Pinus longaeva*, Great Basin bristlecone pine, in the White Mountains of California

Agathis australis, the kauri of New Zealand, attains massive size.

The jigsaw-puzzle pattern of the bark of *Agathis australis*

Podocarpus lawrencei, a Tasmanian podocarp that always grows as a low shrub

The New Caledonian conifer *Araucaria scopulorum* has small leaves that resemble reptilian scales.

The large and spiny leaves of the monkey-puzzle tree, *Araucaria araucana*

the African *Afrocarpus* and the South American *Prumnopitys*. There is no receptacle—everything except a single fertilized seed disappears—but a fleshy layer (epimatium) envelops the nearly globular seed, producing something remarkably similar to a cherry (see photo in chapter 17). The birds are certainly attracted and perform the same service as for *Podocarpus*. Whereas all conifers are wind pollinated, the Podocarpaceae have abandoned the conifer cone as a means to keep seeds before dispersal and pretend to have fruits like angiosperms. The species of Taxaceae do this in similar, but not identical, ways, as do those in the genus *Juniperus* (Cupressaceae). But few of these have attained such diversity and perfection in imitating fruits as have the Podocarpaceae.

Few conifers look more prehistoric than those in the genus *Araucaria* (Araucariaceae). One species from Chile and Argentina is *Araucaria araucana*, known as the monkey-puzzle tree in somewhat playful English. Some *Araucaria* species have broadly domed crowns but most are more columnar. The branches are covered in leathery leaves, ranging across species from very small like the scales of a snake to large and spiny. These trees do not shed leaves but rather whole branches. In several *Araucaria* species, new branches develop where the old ones fell, and these have very different, needle-like leaves. The fossil record tells us that members of the genus have seen the dinosaurs come and go and have not changed much in 200 million years. They were once spread worldwide but now have a very scattered distribution in the Southern Hemisphere, with more than half of the species on the island of New Caledonia. Araucarias poke their shaggy spires up from the coral reefs or above the lower trees, and a dinosaur nibbling on their foliage would not seem out of place there.

In fact, conifers more often than not remind us of the geological past, whether the deep past or not so long ago. In the winter of 2004–2005 I made a trip with some people to the centre of the Sahara, to see the great desert, not to see conifers, of course. Did I say "of course"? In southeastern Algeria on the Tassili n'Ajjer, a dissected sandstone plateau, we saw the famous tarout (*Cupressus dupreziana*), a large tree in a land without trees. At this place a few hundred of them survive over deep ground water, and the nearest other conifers are 2000 km (1250 mi) away. It is the last remnant of once verdant forests and savannas that attracted abundant wildlife and herdsmen as well as hunters, as the numerous prehistoric rock paintings in the area testify. To see this conifer among the rocks and the sand under a cloudless blue sky is about as remote from your neighbour's dark green Leyland hedge as you can get.

On another trip, my colleague and I were driving along the narrow country road across the Plaine des Lacs in the southern part of New Caledonia on our way to some location in the distant hills, where I hoped to find some of the araucarias I was studying. To our left appeared a new sign, neatly carved in some planks of the wood of a

Cupressus dupreziana, the loneliest conifer in the world, grows in the central Sahara in southeastern Algeria.

kauri: Reserve botanique de la Chûte de la Madeleine. "We can spare an hour or so, let's have a look," I said to my companion, and she agreed. We parked the car and paid a modest entrance fee to a friendly ranger. What we saw next was the most enchanted conifer wood I have ever visited. In view of the pretty waterfall grew the weirdest conifers northerners like us had ever seen. We were in an elfin forest of strange trees and shrubs. In the water, near the shore of the river, grew *Retrophyllum minus* (Podocarpaceae), an upturned turnip of a dwarf tree with flat, stubby leaves and grape-like seeds. It is a rheophyte (a plant with a life cycle in streams), the only one known in conifers. Next to it on the shore was a conifer almost as odd, with fluffy foliage, *Dacrydium*

Retrophyllum minus, a semi-aquatic conifer of the Plaine des Lacs in New Caledonia

guillauminii (Podocarpaceae) and only known from this locality. The dwarfish tree *Neocallitropsis pancheri* (Cupressaceae), with its strange upright, spiky-foliaged branches that litter the ground under it, was everywhere, but in its openness barely covering the rough volcanic lava flows and lateritic hills above the stream. The skeletal candelabrum arms of *Dacrydium araucarioides* rose above them in the near background. Across the river, on a ridge against the sky, stood the truly prehistoric looking *Araucaria muelleri*, with its long, bare arms ending in brooms of thick-foliaged branches. There were

Neocallitropsis pancheri, a weird member of the Cupressaceae in New Caledonia

The prehistoric-looking podocarp *Dacrydium araucarioides* grows only on the poisonous ultramafic soils of New Caledonia.

other plants than conifers, but they seemed to be insignificant. There were no grasses, even though the terrain was nowhere densely wooded. No grasses!

Some years ago, I had another phone call at Kew. It was a programmer from the BBC. "Dr. Farjon, can you tell me where in the world we should go to film our TV series 'Walking with Dinosaurs'?" Ah well, this sounded a bit more interesting. I explained that dinosaurs existed for 160 million years, and there were conifers, cycads, and ferns all that time and later also angiosperms. But there were no grasses—ever. Where could you now go for an open landscape with conifers and no grasses? I thought hard and finally suggested this place in New Caledonia, without having been there myself, and talked enthusiastically about the strange conifers there. I now saw it with my own eyes, and it is indeed the perfect place for Jurassic dinosaurs.

3 Diversity Upheld Against the Odds

THUS FAR, WE HAVE ESTABLISHED *what conifers are and that they are highly diverse and interesting, as I'm sure you will agree. But how diverse are they, really? What determines diversity and how do we define it? I have given some examples of the very large and very small, the very old, and the forms unfamiliar at least to most residents of the Northern Hemisphere. But that was a rather subjective account; there must be better ways to defend my case. As a systematic botanist, I should emphasize taxonomic diversity, perhaps. But ecologists might be more interested in how conifers have adapted to grow in many different habitats. And this diversity has a historical dimension, too. It came about through evolution and extinction. Well, let us take all three factors into account and see whether we can give my claim some scientific backing.*

▲ ▲ ▲

Taxonomic Diversity

When biologists consider taxonomic diversity, we basically count families, genera, and species, the three main ranked categories that taxonomists use to classify organisms. With eight families, 70 genera, and 627 species, the conifers are not very impressive in numbers. Many single families of angiosperms have numbers of species in the thousands, and there are some genera with 1000 or more species, such as *Acacia*. In the Northern Hemisphere, oaks (genus *Quercus*) number nearly as many species as all conifers, which as we have seen rank above family as the order Coniferales.

But taxonomic diversity is something more than species numbers. Many species are rather similar, whereas others are more distinct. Some biologists want to use an additional term for that, *disparity*. We need to make that visible and in fact the two following ranks do just that. By dividing 627 species by 70 genera, we have on average only nine species per genus. Eight families make for an average of 78 species per family, but when we know that the three largest families account for 547 species, that leaves us with 80 species in five families or just 16 species per family. Another way of looking at it is to see how many genera have only one species. Because genera are more distinct than most species, these species are more distinct than most others. In this way, we can establish better how great or small the taxonomic diversity of conifers is, as shown in Table 1.

First, we note that three of the eight families have only one genus, and one of these has only a single species. These three genera are likely to be distinct. I say "likely" because I am making the assumption that the classification reflects phylogenetic distinction as well, not just morphological disparity. They should be less closely related than are genera classified within a family. The same applies to species. Another strong indicator of unusual diversity is the number of genera with only a single species: 30 (nearly

43 per cent) of the total of 70 genera. Another 21 genera have only two to five species. The Cupressaceae have by far the highest number of these monotypic and paucitypic genera, 17 and 10, respectively. Let us now look briefly at the other end of the scale. Large genera (although modestly so) are a bit arbitrarily defined with 21 species or more, and they number only six. These large genera are obviously found in the three largest families; the Cupressaceae has only one, *Juniperus* with 52 species. The only two genera with more than 100 species are *Podocarpus* with 108 and *Pinus* with 109. Of these latter two, the genus *Pinus* is probably more diverse, with a larger number of disparate species, than the less-well-studied genus *Podocarpus*. Taxonomists have often felt an urge to split the pines up into several genera but have probably been deterred by the nomenclatural consequences, if not the howling derision from the rest of the botanical world. Despite their disparity, pines clearly should be treated as one genus. We can obtain a glimpse of the disparity versus the similarity among the species in the genus *Pinus* if we use a recent classification and compare the numbers, as shown in Table 2.

As in conifers as a whole, within *Pinus* we can see a similar separation into subsections with low numbers of species (one to four) and those with higher numbers.

Table 1. Taxonomic diversity of conifers divided over eight families, with numbers of genera and species. The genera are divided among those with one species (monotypic), two to five species, six to 20 species, and ≥ 21 species.

	GENERA	SPECIES	1 SPECIES	2–5 SPECIES	6–20 SPECIES	≥ 21 SPECIES
Sciadopityaceae	1	1	1			
Phyllocladaceae	1	4		1		
Cephalotaxaceae	1	11			1	
Araucariaceae	3	41	1		2	
Taxaceae	5	23	2	1	2	
Pinaceae	11	228	3	3	2	3
Podocarpaceae	18	186	6	6	4	2
Cupressaceae	30	133	17	10	2	1
Totals	**70**	**627**	**30**	**21**	**13**	**6**

Source: Data are based on Farjon (2001) with the addition of one new genus in Cupressaceae and a few species since published or relegated to synonymy.

Table 2. Taxonomic diversity within the genus *Pinus* counting the number of species in the subsections of the two subgenera recognized in most recent classifications

SUBGENERA	SECTIONS	SUBSECTIONS	SPECIES IN EACH SUBSECTION	TOTALS
Pinus	2	5	9, 17, 4, 14, 27	71
Strobus	2	7	1, 3, 3, 6, 3, 1, 21	38
Totals	**4**	**12**		**109**

Source: Data based on Farjon (2005a)

Most of the disparate species are in the subgenus *Strobus* and in particular in the section *Parrya*, which has four of the seven subsections, all with small numbers of species except one with six. In subgenus *Pinus* there is only one small subsection with four species, subsection *Contortae*, and it is a bit more speciose than the other small subsections, two of which are monotypic. Only four subsections have numbers of species in two-digit figures. The same trend emerges as in the conifers at large: relatively high numbers of disparate species and only a few groups with higher numbers of more similar species. The taxonomic diversity is much greater than would be expected statistically in a group of plants with only 627 species.

Ecological Diversity

The next measurement of diversity is provided by ecology, a subject I will discuss in more detail later. Here we will briefly look at the diversity of habitats in which conifers live. The worldwide distribution of conifers (see the map in chapter 21) indicates that their ecological diversity must be huge. But there are gaps on this map, and maybe they can tell us something about habitats not favoured by conifers. We need to establish what habitats exist in those areas without conifers. One approach is to list the major natural vegetation types of the world and see whether conifers live in them, as shown in Table 3.

Table 3. Major vegetation types in which vascular plants occur and the number of conifer families and genera that can be found in each

MAJOR VEGETATION TYPES	FAMILIES	GENERA	EXAMPLES
Arctic tundra	2	≥ 3	*Juniperus, Larix, Pinus*
Boreal coniferous forests	2	≥ 5	*Abies, Juniperus, Larix, Picea, Pinus*
Northern montane coniferous forests	4	> 10	*Abies, Cephalotaxus, Cupressus, Larix, Picea, Pinus, Sequoiadendron, Taxus, Thuja*
Southern montane coniferous forests	4	> 10	*Araucaria, Austrocedrus, Dacrydium, Libocedrus, Phyllocladus, Podocarpus*
Subalpine and alpine scrublands	4	> 10	*Athrotaxis, Diselma, Juniperus, Lepidothamnus, Microcachrys, Phyllocladus, Pinus, Podocarpus*
Northern Pacific temperate rainforests	4	> 10	*Abies, Chamaecyparis, Picea, Pseudotsuga, Sequoia, Taxus, Thuja, Tsuga*
Southern Pacific temperate rainforests	4	> 10	*Araucaria, Dacrydium, Fitzroya, Phyllocladus, Pilgerodendron, Podocarpus, Prumnopitys*
Temperate deciduous forests	5	> 10	*Araucaria, Juniperus, Nageia, Pinus, Platycladus, Taxodium, Torreya*
Temperate evergreen forests	5	> 10	*Amentotaxus, Cephalotaxus, Fokienia, Keteleeria, Libocedrus, Podocarpus*

Table 3. (continued)

MAJOR VEGETATION TYPES	FAMILIES	GENERA	EXAMPLES
Lowland tropical deciduous forest	2	≥ 2	*Callitris, Podocarpus*
Lowland tropical rainforest	0		
Montane tropical rainforest	6	> 10	*Afrocarpus, Agathis, Araucaria, Austrotaxus, Cephalotaxus, Dacrycarpus, Keteleeria, Libocedrus, Podocarpus, Sundacarpus*
High montane tropical cloud forest	4	> 10	*Araucaria, Dacrydium, Papuacedrus, Phyllocladus*
Mediterranean climate scrublands	2	≥ 5	*Actinostrobus, Callitris, Juniperus, Pinus, Tetraclinis, Widdringtonia*
Subtropical grasslands/ savannas	2	4	*Callitris, Cupressus, Juniperus, Pinus*
Semi-deserts and steppes	2	4	*Callitris, Cupressus, Juniperus, Pinus*
Deserts (hot)	1	2	*Cupressus, Juniperus*
Salt deserts	0		
Salt marshes	0		
Semi-aquatic vegetation	1	1	*Retrophyllum*
Submerged aquatic vegetation	0		

It is far easier to sum up where conifers do not occur than to list all the major habitats where we can expect them. Conifers don't like salt and they are not too keen to be submerged either. Salt is the enemy of the plant cell, and few plants have evolved means to expel it before it can do harm; conifers are not among them. Woody plants can grow in marshes as long as submergence is only incidental and of short duration; essentially they have to aerate their root systems and expose leaves to air. The swamp cypress (*Taxodium distichum*) grows in such wet places, but you cannot call it semi-aquatic. The only conifer that is semi-aquatic, a rheophyte we have already met, is the New Caledonian podocarp *Retrophyllum minus*. We can list a few conifers from hot deserts, such as *Cupressus dupreziana* in the Sahara, but these are special cases, too, and the great hot deserts of the world are largely devoid of conifers.

When talking about lifestyles, we should mention two other categories: epiphytes and parasites. Epiphytes grow on other plants (usually on trees) but do not take anything from them but support. Parasites grow on other plants and extract the products of photosynthesis from their hosts. Although conifers may germinate upon other trees, especially fallen ones, none are obligate epiphytes, so that is another habitat they do not really occupy. But there is a parasite among the conifers. It is a dwarfish shrubby tree in the Podocarpaceae, *Parasitaxus usta* (see photo in chapter 18), and it is endemic on the extraordinary conifer island of New Caledonia.

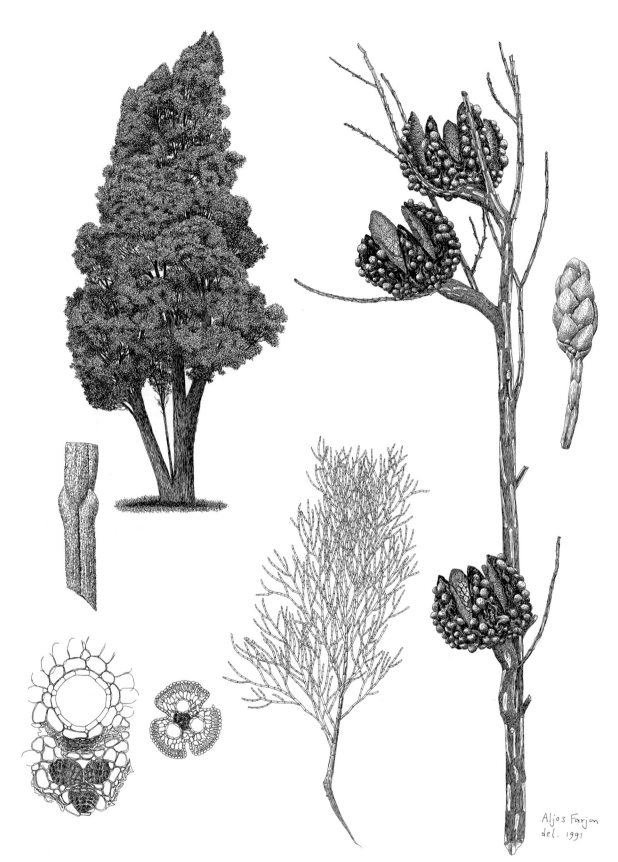

Callitris preissii (Cupressaceae), the Rottnest Island pine from Western Australia. The anatomy of the tiny scale leaves helps this tree to survive drought in its semi-desert environment.

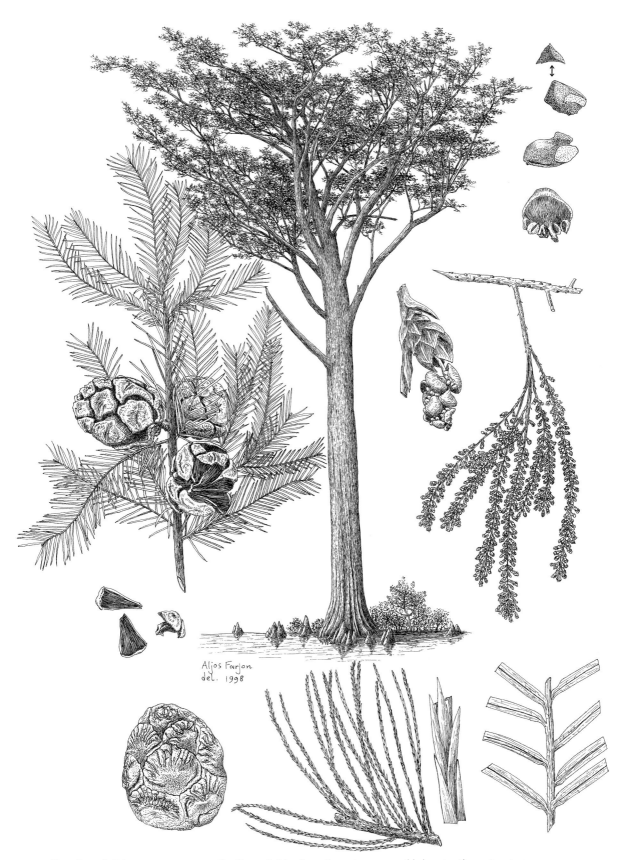

Taxodium distichum, swamp cypress; the "knees" rising from the water are possibly keeping the root system in contact with the air.

Taxodium distichum, swamp cypress, forms deciduous swamp forests in the southeastern United States.

Evolution and Extinction

As I introduce the third factor with a bearing on conifer diversity, history or time, you will begin to understand the extraordinary diversity that characterizes this ancient group of plants. We have seen that the conifers are a truly ancient group, having existed and evolved for more than 300 million years. During that enormous amount of time, continents have been separated, merged, and separated again, even though they move no faster than the growth of your fingernails. Mountain ranges have arisen and been eroded down, climates went from tropical to arctic and back again, forests became inland seas or deserts and forests once more. This time span is more than enough to become adapted or to become extinct. Thus, it should be no surprise that conifers now occur in so many of the major habitats, even though they are absent in some and may never have grown there in the geological past. When suitable habitats became available, there were often conifers around to take advantage. When this happened not too long ago, say within the past 25 million years, we will probably still see the results of such radiation into new habitats and territory. The large genera, such as *Abies, Juniperus*, and especially *Pinus* and *Podocarpus*, are examples.

The genus *Pinus* has been around so long that the other effect of geological time—extinction—has left its mark on diversity as well. The disparate species in their own little subsections may be the result of extinction: they are possibly the last survivors of once successful radiations into habitats that have changed or became rare. In fact, this is probably true for conifers as a whole. The only family that is virtually cosmopolitan, Cupressaceae, is also the most diverse ecologically; its species are present in almost all major vegetation types, and in some extreme places they have left every other conifer behind. Yet the family is filled with monotypic genera, many of them clearly relicts as the fossil record shows. So that is how this diversity in the conifers came to be: a combination of evolution and extinction throughout a long history. Diversity upheld against the odds.

I have to explain one last anomaly in Table 3, the absence of conifers in lowland tropical rainforests. These are some of the gaps shown on the map in chapter 21, most notably in the Amazon Basin and in the Congo Basin, the two areas in the world with the most extensive lowland tropical rainforests. These gaps represent the success of the angiosperms, the causes of which are complicated and again mostly historical. Conifers may have certain disadvantages compared to angiosperms. Over the long time of evolution, with so many species of angiosperms evolving, if the two types had to compete, the conifers in most cases had to retreat to habitats less suitable for their competitors. This was more easily done in mountains, on coasts, in high deserts, and where the climate was cold. The tropical lowlands are too uniform ecologically and at the same time very suitable for plant growth generally. Over time, the angiosperms have completely ousted the conifers from these habitats. If conifers had been able to become lianas or epiphytes, they might still be found in the Amazon Basin.

4 Will We Know All of Them?

I HAVE TO CONFESS SOMETHING to my readers. When I first became interested in the taxonomy of conifers in the early 1980s, I had no idea how I could myself contribute to this knowledge. I was developing this interest because I had begun to draw the species of Pinus *for a book that would depict most of them, each accompanied by a brief descriptive text (Farjon 1984, 2005a). Frans Stafleu, a professor at the University of Utrecht, encouraged me and helped find the publisher. With a background in floristic inventories and vegetation studies in the wetlands and woodlands of the Netherlands, I naively thought that all the species of* Pinus *and of other conifers were already known and that there was little one could really add to this knowledge. But as I continued with the study of conifers, now backed by the Institute of Systematic Botany in Utrecht, led by Frans and later by Paul Maas, I became a taxonomist and soon learned that even in this long-studied group of plants much remained unknown or only poorly known. I could indeed make a contribution.*

▲ ▲ ▲

It must seem astonishing to many people to hear the honest answer to an obvious question: How many species of plants are there in the world? That answer is that we do not know. Or perhaps I should say, we do not agree. Yet plants are one of the best-known kinds of organisms, receiving centuries of scientific attention from botanists, first in Europe and now worldwide. Only birds and mammals have received more attention and are more completely known as a result (there are also not as many of them). Plants are not in the same category of ignorance as fungi or nematodes, of which we only know a small proportion of the estimated large numbers of species that are actually out there. Plants are easy because they are conspicuous and they do not run or fly away. Yet recent estimates of the number of species vary by nearly 100 per cent, from 223,000 to 422,000, even though there is general agreement that botanists have probably named and described around 90 per cent of all the species that exist. How is that possible? Are taxonomists mad dilettantes who can't arrive at the same conclusion about something as basic as this? It is a very important question, because if we do not know how great the species diversity is in plants, then we have no idea how extensive the commitment will be to conserve them all. This is why the Convention on Biological Diversity has issued a Global Plant Strategy in which one of the targets, to be met in 2010, is to come up with an approved World Checklist of Plants. If botanists can agree, we may know by then how many plant species there actually are.

This extraordinary situation results from the history of taxonomic botany. This discipline, for a long time only practised by Europeans and their descendants, has been and for some still is a very individualistic activity. For instance, a botanist found or received what looked to him to be a new plant and proceeded to name and describe it in a publication. Of course, he had consulted some other works but did not find it described there. Thus, a new species was added to the list. However, in another country another botanist had found the same plant and named it already, but this remained unknown to the first botanist, who therefore was unknowingly not the first but merely the latest to describe the plant. Therefore, two names were given to what was actually one species. There are other causes for the proliferation of botanical names, such as excessive splitting of named and described species because specimens are found that differ somewhat from the species as originally circumscribed. All this has resulted in an estimated ratio of about 3:1 or 4:1 of published names of species versus real species. We all know this, but there is disagreement about that ratio of synonyms versus accepted names. Botanists know how many validly published binomials we have for plants, but the question is what proportion of these are synonyms. If we have 1 million names, a ratio of 3:1 gives 333,000 species and a ratio of 4:1 gives 250,000 species.

The only reliable, bedrock-solid way of finding out is a meticulous study of all named species, or what taxonomists call a revision, usually resulting in a monograph. A botanical monograph, as the word implies, treats a single unit or group of species, such as a genus or a family. Doubts about some species may still remain even after that, but the monographer admits this and points out what the difficulties are, so that later workers may pick up the problematic taxa when more is known or better techniques are available. This is a lot of work, and I have written monographs on the genus *Pinus* (in the Neotropics; Farjon and Styles 1997), the family Pinaceae (Farjon 1990), and the family Cupressaceae (Farjon 2005b). The latter work covers only 133 species, with 649 names, for a ratio of 4.9:1. Because more botanists have been interested in *Pinus* for a longer time, the ratio for this genus is 6.8:1 and there are also 23 names of uncertain application. More worrying is that some botanists persist in entertaining narrower or wider species concepts even after a recent monograph; one simply cannot impose a particular taxonomy. The circumscription and delimitation of a plant species are not straightforward much of the time. In addition, we simply do not have the resources to do revisions for all plants, so botanists must make choices and set priorities. Checklists fall far short of monographs in authority and half-life—the period after which only half of the contents of the work are still true—by which time it should definitely be revised. That is a real dilemma, and quick fixes are not going to solve it. I think the World Checklist of Plants should be compiled, and the more specialists are consulted, the better it will be. We botanists must also do the revisions but be selective and make this too a collaborative effort. This book can be seen as a plea for conifers to be considered worthy of selection for such in-depth attention.

Thus, you will now understand that the number of 627 species of conifers is not rock-hard science. For some taxonomic groups the number of species is pretty close to the true number, for others less so, and for some it comes nearer to an estimate that may turn out 10 per cent or even 20 per cent off the mark after revision. From here onwards, I shall use a round figure of 630 species, as I have done in lectures and other works. These figures come from work on a conifer checklist of the kind now proposed for all plants, plus a few recent revisions. They are bound to change if further revisions were undertaken, especially in the family Podocarpaceae. Some groups are very difficult, such as the genera *Agathis* (Araucariaceae) and *Taxus* (Taxaceae), and new approaches, such as DNA analysis, may be needed, although there is no guarantee that these will provide clear taxonomic answers. At present taxonomists are applying this approach to *Araucaria*, with promising results. Morphology and DNA seem by and large to agree, so we can learn how to tackle the more difficult groups. But while this work progresses slowly, other things are happening.

New species are continuously being proposed in the botanical literature. These fall roughly into two categories. The first are often based on known material, usually herbarium specimens, and most of the time constitute the splits alluded to above. These new species are often proposed by those who entertain, perhaps subconsciously, an essentialist or typological concept of species. To them, species are a category, an arbitrary construct of the mind, and each individual species has a set of essential characters. Variation, if observed, is seen as an aberration from the essential character, which is often described as the median value of a particular quantitative character, such as leaf length. The second approach sees species as realities resulting from evolution. They are populations of individuals—each individual genetically different from the other, at least in sexually reproducing populations—and demonstrate both cohesion within the species and separation from other species. Within a species, some characters may be highly variable and others are nearly constant, depending on selection pressures that may or may not eliminate mutants. Median or mean values of characters are meaningless to an evolutionary biologist. It is as Stephen J. Gould (1985) wrote, "species must be defined as ranges of irreducible variation," and a taxonomist must learn what Ernst Mayr (1988) called "population thinking." We have to look for discontinuities in characters, not statistically significant median values, because only the former can indicate the reproductive barriers between distinct species. Of course, this description is a very much simplified and therefore not entirely just appraisal of two ways of looking at species. But I hope it will be obvious that if you accept the evolutionary approach, a critical evaluation of many proposed species is necessary.

Does this mean that we have discovered all the existing species of conifers and that to arrive at the true number we only need to do the evaluations? No, it is not as simple as that. Although most conifers are large trees or shrubs, there are still species hidden away in inaccessible places such as deep canyons or steep mountains, densely covered in impenetrable vegetation. Recent discoveries have proven the case; for instance, *Wollemia nobilis*, or Wollemi pine, was discovered in Australia in 1994. Quite a few new conifers were found recently in Vietnam, and I was involved in some of these. In this country a few very good and industrious botanists, including Dr. Nguyen Tien Hiep and Prof. Phan Ke Loc, have taken on the huge task of the inventory of their nation's flora, with government support. From time to time they invite foreign specialists to join them on trips to very remote locations where botanists have not been before. In 2003 it was my turn, and I was asked to check out two recent finds that were exciting enough for any conifer enthusiast, let alone for the one who was finalizing a monograph of the family Cupressaceae, to which these two appeared to belong. One was the discovery of a new locality of an already known, but rather special, conifer, *Taiwania cryptomerioides*. The other involved what I had recognized from herbarium specimens sent to me to most probably be a new genus and species, *Xanthocyparis vietnamensis*.

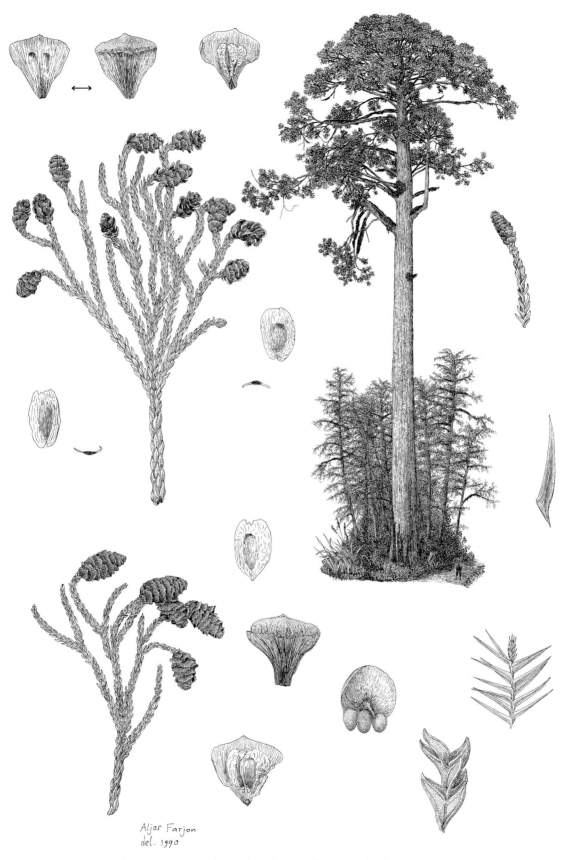

Aljos Farjon
del. 1990

Taiwania cryptomerioides (Cupressaceae) is known from three widely separate localities in Asia.

Taiwania cryptomerioides growing in the Hoang Lien Mountains of Vietnam, where it was discovered in 2002.

We knew of two certain locations of *Taiwania cryptomerioides*, a very large conifer first described from Taiwan by the Japanese botanist Bunzo Hayata in 1906. Ten years later it was discovered far away in the mountains bordering Yunnan Province of China and Myanmar (then known as Burma), by the Austrian botanist Heinrich von Handel-Mazzetti. This species had been planted in various other places in China, perhaps long ago and without known records of the deed. So we were suspicious about this first report from northern Vietnam, submitted by a junior botanist in 2002.

We arrived with a small party on the back of motorcycles at the very end of a primitive road terminating in montane tropical rainforest. From there we started, with the help of porters and guides, to haul our luggage and equipment up the lower slopes of the Hoang Lien Mountains on a poorly defined, very slippery trail. After a hard day's work we were in the middle of the forest, but nowhere near the conifers we wanted to see. Our guides built a shelter with freshly cut bamboo and a tarpaulin to eat under, for it had started to rain. For me they had put up a tent, for themselves they would sling up hammocks under the shelter after the fire had gone out. Some of the porters just made themselves a bed of bamboo leaves, not worried by the creepy-crawlies of the forest. I did not sleep for a long time because of the rain and the incredible chorus of at least five different kinds of frogs.

The next afternoon we finally arrived at the *Taiwania* trees. My first conclusion was that there was no doubt about the botanical identity. After three days of surveying, we

Very steep limestone mountains in North Vietnam are the habitat of the newly described conifer *Xanthocyparis vietnamensis*.

had found nearly 100 trees and some seedlings and saplings, and I was convinced that this was a natural population, many hundreds of kilometres distant from the nearest in Yunnan. We also knew that it was in acute danger of extinction, because on the far side of a nearby mountain ridge is a broad valley with villages of the Hmong people, who have been in the business of cutting trees and burning off the forest. We visited the villages and talked to the headman of the main village, which became the start of a community-based conservation programme for this remarkable conifer.

In the far north of Vietnam, right on the border with China, you will find some of the most rugged mountains in Southeast Asia. It is a karst landscape, stretching far into China, built of thousands of tower-like mountains interspersed with tortuous valleys. Ancient Palaeozoic limestone has been uplifted and deeply eroded, and the limestone is now hard as marble and forms knife-sharp edges and ridges. The ridges and summits are riddled with holes and fissures, but support very little soil, and it is here that more than ten species of conifer have been found, among them the new genus and species, which I named *Xanthocyparis vietnamensis*. This species was serendipitously discovered in 1999 by my colleague, the great orchid specialist at Kew, Phil Cribb. These peaks are an orchid paradise, and he was looking for rare slipper orchids (*Paphiopedilum*) in the company of Vietnamese and Russian botanists. Sitting under this unfamiliar conifer high up on a ridge, Phil took a small branch and presented it to Nguyen Tien Hiep, one of Vietnam's leading botanists, asking if he recognized it. Nobody recognized it, so they took some photographs and a specimen, and Phil gave them to me back in Kew with the same question. There was not much to go by, so I thought it was perhaps an aberrant specimen (poor growing conditions) of a well-known conifer in the region. But more material was collected so I could compare it better. The tree had, strangely, two very different types of leaves on the same branches, juvenile and adult. These are normally separated between seedlings and mature trees. The small seed cones were also unusual, but reminiscent of a well-known species on the northwestern coast

Xanthocyparis vietnamensis, Vietnamese golden cypress, is a newly described genus and species in the family Cupressaceae.

On mature trees of *Xanthocyparis vietnamensis*, both juvenile and adult foliage exist on a single branch.

of North America. Another expedition, led by Dan Harder, then at the Missouri Botanical Garden, went to the area. This time they collected plenty of material and I could do some serious work. We eventually jointly published the finding in the journal *Novon*: a new genus and species in Cupressaceae (Farjon et al. 2002).

In 2002 there I was, clambering up these ridges myself and trying to keep up with my much more surefooted Vietnamese companions without breaking a leg in a sharp-edged hole. It took some imagination, as I had no specimen to demonstrate to the local Hmong guide which of the ten conifers I was most interested to see. At one point I luckily found a small dead branch but no tree, which had probably been cut and taken some years ago. With that in hand, it took the guide a mere twenty minutes to come back with a green branch. The Hmong people don't know Latin names and classifications, but they do know their trees. The next day he walked us through a labyrinth of valleys with maize plantations in red earth and little hamlets with naked children and shy women to a towering mountain, where we stopped for some lunch. When the climb began, I sometimes could not tell if I was walking and holding onto rocks or only plants. Orchids, mosses, and ferns were everywhere, dense fog alternated with sunshine. And, suddenly, there it was: a large, contorted tree. One of my Vietnamese companions went up into it, perched above the abyss, to collect my specimens. I was very happy. When we were down below again, I saw some of the little children and crouched down to show the fresh, fragrant foliage to them. They all suddenly burst into loud crying. Apparently, they had never seen a man with a beard so nearby, and our guide had to come back to give them some sweets.

The Systematics
of Conifers

5 Who Is Related to Whom?

MY MIDDLE BROTHER *has a long-standing interest in the genealogy of our family, and he has travelled across good parts of Europe to find out more about it. Our family name, Farjon, is from French Huguenots who apparently hailed from near Montpellier in the south of France as long ago as the early 16th century. At the beginning of the 18th century one of them came to Amsterdam, and, my brother tells me, all the Farjons in the Netherlands (plus him in Germany, our youngest brother in Switzerland, and me in England) derive from that single ancestor. Is this a biological fact? I am afraid it is not. He is forgetting the mothers and their fathers and mothers.*

▲ ▲ ▲

It is true that some genes in him and me will be the same as were present in that ancestor, but they are very few indeed. With every new generation only half of the genes are passed on from the father, the other half coming from the mother, who is unrelated (we should hope) every time. I have $1 \times \frac{1}{2}$ of my father's genes and $1 \times (\frac{1}{2})^2 = \frac{1}{4}$ of one of my two grandfathers' genes. If there are roughly four generations in a century, then after 450 years I have only 0.00038 per cent of my genes in common with that earliest known Montpellier father. From the man who came to Amsterdam some 300 years ago I will have a bit more, 0.098 per cent (after 10 generations or 250 years). All the rest comes from all sorts of other people, both fathers and mothers. The genetic relationships through time of sexually reproducing individuals are like a network, not like a tree. Genealogical trees of people trace a name though a history of liaisons between males and females and their offspring. In our culture this is the name of the males, but not genetic relationships. Every one of us has an uncountable number of unrelated ancestors.

When we talk about the genetic relationships of species, the situation is entirely different. Species normally do not interbreed, they separate. Because their genes are not recombined with those of other species, the relationships among species are not a network, but a branching system. We have seen in the introduction that taxonomists should attempt to produce classifications of species with their evolution in mind, because that will produce natural groups as opposed to artificial ones. The genetic relationships among species are a key factor to inform us about possible natural classifications. We must therefore find methods to discover what are referred to as phylogenetic relationships. A key concept, first clearly formulated by the German entomologist Willi Hennig in 1950, is that of the shared derived character. When two species are more closely related to each other than to any other species, they share a unique common ancestor, from which they inherited a shared derived character. This character is present in the ancestor, who acquired it, and in its descendants, but not in any other species or ancestors. Together they form a branch, or clade: ancestor plus two species descended from it, indicated by the shared derived character. Other characters present in the two species may also be found in other species. They tell us nothing about the phylogenetic relationship of these two species, but may indicate relationships within a more inclusive clade. In that case, they are shared ancestral characters at the level of the two species (known as synplesiomorphy), but shared derived characters of the species in our more inclusive clade, including its common ancestor (known as synapomorphy). The search is for as many synapomorphies as can be detected in a given dataset of characters and species.

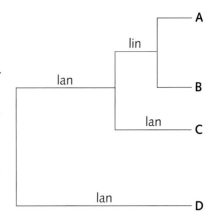

A simple cladogram showing the phylogenetic relationships and shared derived characters of the hypothetical species A–D. Character states are lanceolate leaves (lan), the ancestral state, and linear leaves (lin), which arose in the common ancestor of A and B. Species A and B are within the same clade, and species A, B, and C are within a more inclusive clade.

This basic principle—comparison of characters to find the shared derived ones indicating phylogenetic relationships, which are illustrated in branching diagrams or cladograms—has grown into a methodology within systematic biology called cladistics. Algorithms have been found to do the comparisons, which with even a few species and characters quickly accelerates into gigantic calculations best done by computers. Of course, characters are often not as well behaved as we would like them to be. A particular character may be present in nearly all species of a clade but missing in one, or appear in all species of one clade and again in a species that came out in a different clade based on other characters. Such characters do not seem to give off a clear-cut phylogenetic signal. Only by analyzing many characters does it become possible to recognize these aberrant ones for what they probably are: losses or reversals (or parallelisms), characters that evolved independently twice. Or it may be that we want to re-examine them to see if we did not interpret them wrongly in the first place, an activity called character coding in the jargon. Using morphological characters can be informative but is often beset with such problems. Analyzing DNA sequences does seem much more straightforward, as there are only four nucleotides and the way they pair up is very simple and fixed. But DNA sequences have their own problems, into which we shall not venture here. The important thing to remember is that cladistics has become a very powerful methodology to analyze characters, in particular certain DNA sequence characters, with the aim to infer phylogenetic relationships between taxa.

In the practice of cladistics another principle is introduced, which is called parsimony. The number of mathematically possible ways characters can be distributed on cladograms is very large, resulting in numerous trees from which it would be impossible to choose objectively which one represents the most plausible phylogeny. The assumption behind parsimony is that a phylogeny is more plausible if it requires fewer evolutionary changes in characters (coded as character states). The introduction of an algorithm that calculates the most parsimonious cladograms greatly reduces their number.

Finally, we would want to know something about the branching sequence or the time dimension of cladograms the analysis produces—the tree has to be rooted. In a given group of species and their inferred phylogenetic relationships, what is the position of the deepest common ancestor, or root? The distinction between the derived and the ancestral characters used gives the answer. Remember that only synapomorphies define clades, so the more inclusive ones, defining the larger clades in the tree, mark the clades nearer to the root and the algorithm arranges the species accordingly. We can also infer from this procedure in what direction a character might have evolved. If we find that lanceolate leaves mark a lower node in the tree while linear leaves mark a higher node, as shown in the figure, we can assume that the ancestral state was lanceolate and that linear leaves evolved from that shape.

How does all this apply to conifers? Who is related to whom? And are inferred phylogenetic relationships all we need to construct a satisfactory classification of conifers? Can we do it on the basis of the species that still exist, or do we have to look into the distant past and consider all the extinct forms as well? Some answers to these questions will be given in the next chapter.

6 The Fragmented Tree of Life, or Phylogeny Without a Past

IN THE PREVIOUS CHAPTER *I explained the basics of phylogenetic analysis, or the investigation into the genetic relationships of taxa. Applying these cladistic methods to the existing species of conifers may tell us, with reasonable confidence, how closely or remotely related these species are to each other. I keep a deliberate qualification in this statement because, for one, there is as yet some incongruence in the results with the application of the same methods to different data. If the data were unambiguous, they should be expected to give the same results, but they do not. What this means is that the same set of species is likely to give different results about their inferred phylogenetic relationships when different morphological or molecular data are used to do the analyses. In other words, the inferred relationships of characters do not appear to be congruent with the actual relationships of taxa.*

▲ ▲ ▲

Combined analyses using various datasets tend to give improved results that are more likely to be congruent. The datasets tend to become more extensive with time, and we can therefore expect to get better results that we can have more confidence in than at present. We are not there yet, and I for one wish to remain sceptical about results that seem to flagrantly contradict established wisdom derived from detailed studies of plant morphology and character evolution. One notorious recent example is the finding based on molecular data that the Gnetales (an aberrant group of gymnosperms) are most closely related to Pinaceae and therefore must be conifers (Coniferales). Often such conclusions are based on a limited study, while the advocates of these conclusions seem to allow no doubt: The objective cladistic analysis tells the truth! It is only the truth within the paradigms of cladistics and, of course, the constraints of the data used. In good science, it is never more than a hypothesis. A hypothesis is there to be falsified, preferably by refutation of a consequence that logically follows from the hypothesis. A hypothesis without falsifiable consequences is not scientific. Statistical support for the hypothesis, often quoted in cladistic publications, is only internal evidence.

Let us assume that for conifers as circumscribed in the introduction we can eventually discover the real genetic relationships among all 630 species. Of course, we will discover groups of species recently evolved and closely related that do not influence the overall branching order (or topology) in the phylogenetic tree. We can reduce these to a few representatives, a procedure that makes the tree less complicated. But is that phylogenetic tree informing us adequately about the evolution of conifers that actually happened? The answer very much depends on what we know, or do not know, about the evolutionary history of conifers. Phylogenetic relationships inferred for extant taxa are only relative relationships: A is more closely related to B than either is to C. Most cladists will argue that this is all we want to know; we do not know the ancestor of A, B, and C, as ancestors remain forever hypothetical. Phylogenetic analysis never discovers ancestors, only relationships between taxa. Willi Hennig, the originator of cladistics, expressed it succinctly: "The task of the phylogenetic system is not to present the result of evolution, but only to present the phylogenetic relationships of species and species groups" (Hennig 1966). For conifers, this appears to me unsatisfactory, resulting in knowledge with little information content. We have seen how fragmented the remaining conifers are in this respect. If we could, we would like to fill in the gaps now apparent in the surviving conifers with these extinct groups of taxa. It would give us a much more complete and perhaps evolutionary phylogeny, but can it be done?

To do a proper phylogenetic analysis, you need good characters assigned to species. This is difficult but possible with morphological characters for extant species; in principle, we can obtain all the data required. In addition, we have the DNA of these species. If we desire to include data from fossils, however, we will encounter almost insurmountable problems. For a start, there is normally no DNA, the few very fragmentary bits that have been preserved notwithstanding. The popular novel and movie *Jurassic Park* is indeed an intriguing but impossible scenario that belongs within the realms of science fiction. Anatomical and morphological data are present in fossils, sometimes exquisitely well preserved. But there is a major problem with fossils, especially those from trees and shrubs. They are always small fragments, never whole plants. We give them the names of genera and species, but they are not that, they are organ taxa based on wood, leaves, or cones. We may find leaves and cones together in the sediment and suspect that they belonged to the same plant, but if they are not organically connected, they may as well have come from very different species. All sorts of debris can end up washed together in the mud. Thus, with few exceptions where whole plant reconstructions have been possible on the basis of many different remains, the fossil species cannot be compared with the living ones in terms of character data sufficient for a phylogenetic analysis. This is not entirely true at the level of higher taxonomic ranks, where we may have enough knowledge from the fossils to compare them with present families or sometimes genera. When I discuss the relationships of conifer families in chapter 9, we will return to this and see if the inclusion of extinct families gives us more information about evolution and phylogeny than the extant families alone.

To illustrate the scale of the problem, there are eight extant conifer families (Araucariaceae, Cephalotaxaceae, Cupressaceae, Phyllocladaceae, Pinaceae, Podocarpaceae, Sciadopityaceae, Taxaceae) and 12 extinct families (Cheirolepidiaceae, Doliostrobaceae, Emporiaceae, Ferrugliocladaceae, Geinitziaceae, Majonicaceae, Palissyaceae, Pararaucariaceae, Thucydiaceae, Ulmanniaceae, Utrechtiaceae, Voltziaceae) that have been reasonably well established in the palaeobotanical literature and are recognized by the present specialists in the field. It is impossible to know how many genera and species these extinct families would have had, at any one time or in total, but some must have been very diverse even on the basis of what has been found and identified so far. In addition, there are numerous fossils that are so fragmentary that it is not possible to assign them to one of these families. The names given in the past to fossil wood often fall in this category of *incertae sedis*, as do many for leaves and twigs. Some of this material may represent families as yet insufficiently known. As more fossils are found, taxonomic concepts change and families can be merged as well as erected. Unusual conifers or conifer-like gymnosperms are also known from the Permian Angara flora in Siberia, researched by Sergei V. Meyen, and from the Triassic Molteno flora of South Africa, described by John and Heidi Anderson. The affinities of these plants remain uncertain so they have not been included here.

From all this it should be clear that our conifer tree of life is going to look like a tree with many branches lopped off if we base it on the extant families only, as is done by those who work with molecular data and cladistics. It does not mean anything significant in terms of evolution to debate whether Pinaceae or Podocarpaceae are basal in the cladogram or which family is within the same clade as (that is, sister to) Cupressaceae. In the *real* tree of evolution, which we do not and perhaps cannot know, there were many other families involved.

In such a tree there is indeed the question of ancestors. The likelihood of identifying an ancestor to a particular species is vanishingly small. But at the higher ranks, it may well be informative to speculate (there is evidence but no proof) about ancestors. Most palaeobotanists are pretty sure that if we were to identify the nearest common ancestor to all the species of Cupressaceae, we would classify it in the Voltziaceae. With cladistic analysis we would not arrive at such a conclusion. As we have seen, phylogenetic relationships are found by comparing shared derived characters. Shared ancestral characters play no role in phylogeny reconstruction. However, they may indicate ancestors, which after all existed. Darwin emphasized that evolution is descent with modification. The modification used in cladistics is only of the kind that tracks descent; the shared ancestral characters are ignored, yet they too are shared because of a common evolutionary origin. For groups of species without much evidence of extinction, perhaps phylogeny equals classification. For the conifers, however, this would present an impoverished picture of evolution, a phylogeny without a past.

7 More Genera, Fewer Species

AS TIME GOES BY, *more and more species are discovered, described, and named. We have visited this obvious fact in the introduction when I asked the question, "Will we know all of them?" In this chapter, we will consider how to classify these species into families and genera. We will also consider whether there are consequences particular to an ancient group of plants, such as the conifers, with regard to species recognition or delimitation. We need to touch on a bit of history in this chapter, but I shall not bore you with a review of all the classifications that have been proposed—it would fill a book. Instead, I want to discuss the trends leading to the current understanding of the diversity of conifers in taxonomic terms.*

▲ ▲ ▲

The starting point for most of botany's plant names is the two-volume book by Linnaeus, *Species Plantarum*, published in 1753. Based on sexual characters, Linnaeus placed the conifers he knew in two separate groups. As we have seen, however, he admitted that these were artificial groups, and botanists have long ago abandoned them. More interesting, in a book Linnaeus believed to be a fairly complete inventory of the world's plants, he only included 26 species of conifers. His contemporary Philip Miller, the famous head of the Chelsea Physic Garden, recognized 58 species. Thus, there was disagreement almost from the start. Linnaeus was not terribly good at conifers. Later editions of his book greatly expanded the number of plant species, but the conifers remained for a time nearly the same.

The sexual system of classification devised by Linnaeus was soon followed by more natural classifications, grouping plants according to perceived affinities based on a variety of characters. The most influential classification of this kind, recognizing orders (our families) and within them genera and species, was published between 1824 and 1873 by the Swiss-French de Candolle family (father, son, and grandson). It was expanded and amended by George Bentham and Sir Joseph Hooker at the Royal Botanic Gardens, Kew, and towards the end of the 19th century included nearly 100,000 species of plants in 202 families. The great herbarium at Kew, now with 7 million specimens of dried plants, is still arranged according to the classification system of Bentham and Hooker. With the publication of *The Origin of Species* by Charles Darwin in 1859, the rationale of biological classification changed completely. The systems that now developed were based on evolution, the theory of descent with modification. It was at first in Germany that evolution was explicitly incorporated into botanical classifications, of which those by August Wilhelm Eichler and his famous successor at the Berlin Botanic Garden, Adolf Engler, were the most influential. However, because many different views on how evolution had proceeded in plants were developed, many different classification systems followed from them. General progress of understanding was therefore slow, and many questions could not be resolved for lack of agreement.

During most of the 19th century and into the 20th century, the conifers were recognized as a single family. Eichler had placed them, following Robert Brown's insight, in the Gymnospermae, which he correctly considered a more primitive group in evolutionary terms, from which the Angiospermae have evolved. That was a major step forward, and it took a long while before it was followed in the English-speaking part of the botanical world. Geopolitics apparently did play a role in science and in this case not a progressive one, as it blocked exchange of information and collaboration. This discussion largely took place in the German and sometimes French languages. In the early part of the 20th century this was made good for the English language by the American botanist C. J. Chamberlain in his brilliant work on the structure and evolution of gymnosperms. While conifers (usually still including *Ginkgo*) were recognized as a natural group, it now became clear that there were substantial differences among them that warranted recognition at a level above genus. Different families came to be recognized among the conifers, eventually leading to the eight families here accepted (Araucariaceae, Cephalotaxaceae, Cupressaceae, Phyllocladaceae, Pinaceae, Podocarpaceae, Sciadopityaceae, Taxaceae). Many more have been proposed and are being proposed.

As we have seen, conifers are a very diverse group of plants with a long history and many extinct forms that often differed substantially from what lives today. There are those who desire to express that diversity by assigning higher (more inclusive) ranks to each subdivision of conifers, elevating genera to families, families to orders, and these again to even higher ranks. We would then have the division Pinophyta (gymnosperms) with several classes (extant and extinct) of which conifers (Pinatae) are one. The rationale behind this is the evolutionary history of plants. Conifers are a major group of gymnosperms, and the latter were for a very long time the only seed plants around and much more diverse than what is left today. Therefore, palaeobotanists often use these higher ranks in their classifications (such as Anderson and Anderson 2003). There is some merit in this desire to reflect that diversity in the ranking used for gymnosperms. On the other hand, without the ability to confidently fill in the gaps to reconstruct the phylogenetic tree of gymnosperms, such ranking remains largely arbitrary. In this book, I shall consider the extinct order Voltziales and the extant order Coniferales as conifers in a broad sense and use only the (familiar) family names for the formal groups at one rank below orders. There is a consensus developing in the botanical community. My *World Checklist and Bibliography of Conifers* (Farjon 1998, 2001), which takes a consensus approach, is now being used as the standard reference by several major organizations,

The seed cones and foliage of dawn redwood, *Metasequoia glyptostroboides* (Cupressaceae)

The seed cones and foliage of Arizona cypress, *Cupressus arizonica* (Cupressaceae)

including IUCN (The World Conservation Union), the Royal Horticultural Society, and botanic gardens with global collections. However, the taxonomy in the checklist is not the law, as such notions are not valid in biology.

In the classification of conifers, the most important development of the last 50 years or so has been the greater subdivision of families, creating more genera. This has been most prolific in the family Podocarpaceae, which went from just seven to 18 genera. The podocarp genera *Dacrydium* and especially *Podocarpus* have been split into several separate genera, mostly containing from one to a few species only. The family Cupressaceae now has 30 genera, more than any other conifer family. A few splits have occurred here, too, but the increase is mostly due to the merger of Taxodiaceae with this family, adding nine genera. That is not really an increase in the number of genera recognized in conifers. New discoveries have contributed to the increase in genera, but these were relatively few. Since 1950 the genera *Cathaya*, *Wollemia*, and *Xanthocyparis* have been newly described, and *Metasequoia* was found just a few years earlier. It seems that a consensus at this level is now also within reach, and that most of these genera do stand up against testing by phylogenetic analyses as well as more detailed morphological investigation. New splits continue to be proposed from some quarters, but these are increasingly based on the excessive importance (weighting) attributed to certain microcharacters (such as the micromorphology of seeds), and sometimes on DNA sequence data. Taxa should always be based on an analysis of all available evidence.

Some taxonomists from time to time feel an urge to split the genus *Pinus* into two (or perhaps three) genera. The pines are perhaps more diverse than any other genus. Does it make sense? It is important to appreciate that diversity as such is not a valid criterion to split up a natural group that is clearly based on common descent of its members. Spreading into a wide geographical range with many different habitats can lead in time to greater diversity. There are many unique characters that unite all pines and separate them from species in other genera of the Pinaceae. We can recognize groups of pines within the genus at lower ranks, such as subgenus. Remember that the ranks of taxa are largely arbitrary (which is why a minority wants to abolish them). The rank of genus, however, has consequences for names. If we split *Pinus* into two genera, all the species combined within the new genus will have to change names. I can hear the uproar that this will create even from the quiet seclusion of my home. Pines are economically more important than all other conifers combined, and users of botanical names see no merit in having them changed. This is, apart from scientific considerations, a good reason for constraint in the further splitting of some genera.

What are the consequences, if any, for species delimitation? I shall try to explain it using the example of the genus *Podocarpus*. With the exclusion of several species now classified in other genera, each with distinct characters of their own now no longer considered those of *Podocarpus*, the circumscription of that genus has been narrowed. The species of *Podocarpus* all have terminal buds; spirally inserted, elongated, flat leaves with a single central vein; and seed cones that develop an inflated, succulent, and coloured receptacle subtending a single, naked seed. There are a few other distinctions, but these are the main ones uniting all species that have this combination of characters in the genus *Podocarpus* and excluding those that don't. In the context of an evolutionary species concept, we still need to look for distinctive character states (discontinuities) to delimit species. With fewer characters, that has now become more difficult. If we can't find these distinctions, there is little ground for the recognition of separate species. With 108 species, the genus *Podocarpus* is the second largest of the conifers. Are they all good species? I shall try to give some general answers to this question in the next chapter.

Botanical characters of some species of *Podocarpus*

8 The Winnowing Task of the Monographer

IN 1950 C.G.G.J. VAN STEENIS, *professor of botany at the University of Leiden and director of the Rijksherbarium, embarked with a few collaborators on one of the most ambitious Flora-writing projects ever undertaken.* Flora Malesiana *aims to describe all the vascular plants that occur between the Malay Peninsula and New Guinea, or the tropical region known among biologists as Malesia. This multi-volume project still continues, long after his death. Van Steenis once famously said that it is the task of a plant taxonomist not to discover how many species there are, but how few. But are taxonomists not rightly known as the experts to discover and describe new species? Are there not many new species yet to be discovered and described? Whenever we hear about the world's biodiversity, it is stressed that there are so many unknown species, especially in the tropics. Some estimate that 10 or more times the numbers already known are hidden out there in the jungle. Yet here was this botanist, more than 50 years ago, talking about fewer species. Surely, he must have had it wrong. In fact, I believe Prof. van Steenis had a very good point.*

▲ ▲ ▲

When we hear these estimates about millions of species still to be discovered, it is rarely mentioned to what general taxonomic groups these unknown creatures are believed to belong. Rather few of them are vascular plants. Mammals, birds, and amphibians are even less likely to be among them, for we know almost all the mammals and birds already. Other large and conspicuous (or interesting) animals are not very far behind. Thus, these "missing" species include insects, especially beetles, spiders and their ilk, nematodes and other small creepy-crawlies in the litter and canopy, and fungi, lots and lots of fungi. I don't even mention unicellular organisms such as bacteria. Biologists should be honest when they talk to the press: the millions still unknown are unknown for a good reason. There are certainly a good number of plant species still to be discovered, especially in the tropics and in regions like Malesia, where large islands such as Borneo and New Guinea are still not fully explored botanically. However, the great majority of plant species has already been discovered and described, and it was this situation that Prof. van Steenis was referring to.

When taxonomists contribute to a project such as *Flora Malesiana*, they do not start from scratch. They have to look at what has already been described and named from the region they are covering. Usually, taxonomists tackle a group, such as a family, by gathering all the new descriptions of species for that area. A monographer treats the whole family, wherever it occurs, in the same way. These new descriptions often have a long history, but fortunately there is a starting date: anything described prior to 1 May 1753, when Linnaeus published *Species Plantarum*, can be ignored. Once collected, these descriptions are compared with the plant specimens they were based on (the types) and with other specimens. Soon, doubts about some of the species will arise. It would seem as if two botanists, at different times, independently described and named one and the same species. Then the revising taxonomist must investigate the matter in more detail. He or she must compare more specimens ascribed to the two species, search for variation in the characters described, and attempt to find other characters that were not mentioned but may distinguish the species. It is usually a lot more work to disprove a species than it was to erect it. Because a Flora writer, and especially a monographer, will see many more specimens of more species than the botanist who erected and described one or a few of the species in a family, greater experience and knowledge of the variation that exists within the group is gained. Both field and laboratory work again increase that knowledge substantially—the monographer becomes an expert. Modern techniques, not available to past botanists, can be applied to all species. More complete species descriptions can be drawn up and characters determined that really separate them. The final result is almost always fewer species, not more. That reduced number can of course still include new species not recognized before. These will result from a better overall comparison of the material and sometimes from new discoveries in the field.

Van Steenis was a conservative taxonomist who disliked splitters, people who wish to name species on the slightest differences in characters found in specimens. Rather he advocated lumping, the combining of similar species into one. Such attitudes and decision-making are ultimately arbitrary. If species are based on morphological (or chemical or molecular) differences, then there are no hard-and-fast rules to delineate where a species should be recognized. Characters indicate species, they do not define them. This is why species should be based on multiple lines of evidence, including morphology, DNA, reproductive barriers, phenology, ecology, functional relationships with animals, phylogenetic reconstruction of evolutionary lineages, and more. That is not always easy. Plants lack the behaviour of animals that often reveals which individuals belong to the same species—and indeed, often also to what sex. While working on a Flora or a monograph of a genus or family, a taxonomist cannot investigate all these aspects for all the possible species in that group. If the group is well studied, there may be publications about some of these aspects for a few species, but the taxonomist still does not know if they differ among all the species. Therefore, judgements will have to be made. From a competent, experienced monographer, we may expect that these are informed judgements. The species accepted in a well-researched monograph usually stand the test of time, and such publications have a long half-life in scientific terms.

What does all this mean for conifers? I have written monographs on two of the largest families of conifers, Cupressaceae and Pinaceae, and the latter more or less in bits and pieces. Of course, other taxonomists have worked on these and other families as well, but some of that work is now out of date, incomplete, or both. Especially the family Podocarpaceae, the third of the large families, lacks a comprehensive and thorough modern revision. Since the last revision, published in a series of papers by J. T. Buchholz and N. E. Gray between 1948 and 1962, generic concepts have changed substantially and numerous new species have been described. David de Laubenfels, a later student of podocarps, added much new taxonomy, including a treatment of the family in

Flora Malesiana, but a monographic revision is now what is most needed. Some groups, such as the genus *Taxus*, may be too difficult for more traditional, morphological methods alone and need the multiple-evidence approach. Some preliminary work has been done with my *World Checklist and Bibliography of Conifers* (Farjon 1998, 2001) in which the results of modern monographic work, revisions for critical Floras, and a consensus taxonomy were combined to produce a list of accepted species in the conifers.

The statistics of this bring home the point made in this chapter. Currently, in my Botanical Research and Herbarium Management System (BRAHMS) conifer database there are 4441 names of taxa and only 812 of these are accepted names; the others are nearly all synonyms. That is a ratio of 5.5 synonyms for every accepted name at the ranks of species, subspecies, and variety. These figures are unevenly divided among the families, reflecting both the number of taxonomic studies applied to them and the results, or the lack of, recent monographic revisions. For the Cupressaceae, recently revised in a monograph, the total number of names in these ranks is 1076, of which 182 are accepted, giving a ratio of 5.9 to 1. The Podocarpaceae have only 634 names in my database, of which 191 are accepted, for a ratio of 3.3 to 1. These two families are roughly equal in the number of presently accepted taxa, yet the number of names in the Cupressaceae is nearly 70 per cent higher. The more taxonomic attention a family of plants has received over time, the more names there will have been published. Much of the synonymy in Cupressaceae relates to European taxa, going all the way back to Linnaeus. Podocarpaceae are largely restricted to the Southern Hemisphere, where attention was focussed much later and by fewer taxonomists. Fortunately, we therefore have fewer names to consider. Thus, it is likely that the final ratio of names against accepted names will not rise much above the average of 5.5 to 1.

Nevertheless, there is still some capacity for winnowing even in a well-studied group like the conifers. To give just one example: Traditionally, three species of *Abies* were recognized in northern Turkey, *Abies equi-trojani, A. bornmuelleriana*, and *A. nordmanniana*. They occur in disjunct populations from west to east; the first two are much smaller than the last, which spreads beyond the Turkish borders into the Caucasus. If you compare the specimens from northern and western Turkey, you will find that there are no distinct characters and that the differences, where they seem to exist, are gradual. The geographical separation is real, but it can be explained by climate change since the last ice age. Perhaps they are better classified as subspecies or varieties of *A. nordmanniana*, the earliest name. That was the situation when I did my research for my book on Pinaceae (Farjon 1990). I could see slight differences between specimens from the Caucasus and those from further west, but none between the populations in the west. This agreed with the findings of some other authors on the subject. Therefore, I recognized *A. nordmanniana* and one separate subspecies. When, much later, I was able to see some of the trees in the wild, this observation was confirmed. Eventually, we may be able to give an accurate answer to Prof. van Steenis's question: How few species of conifers are there?

Is the Caucasian fir (*Abies nordmanniana*) one species or three?

9 A Classification Attempted Once Again

WHAT SHOULD A CLASSIFICATION *of the conifers look like? What information do we want to infer from it? From what I have argued in the previous chapters, it appears that it should tell us something about phylogenetic relationships, possible ancestors, and modification of characters through evolution. The classification should tell us which branches on the phylogenetic tree became extinct and which survived to the present, as well as give an indication of species diversity within each branch. Based on all this information, we can draw an evolutionary tree with thin as well as inflated branches alongside a time scale, as often seen in books about palaeontology. These diagrams are not phylogenetic trees or cladograms, although the results of cladistic analyses will have helped to construct the conifer evolutionary tree at the level of families.*

▲ ▲ ▲

When attempting to account for extinct taxa from the fossil record, the classification at ranks below family becomes much more difficult. It would be a very fragmented classification, and many fossils could not be placed with confidence. A classification down to the genera of the extant families of conifers is presented in the appendix. For the purpose of this book, it would go into too much detail to take it any further down the taxonomic ranks; I will instead refer to some specialist literature for examples in the appendix. We will have an opportunity to review some of the fossil genera and species later.

Eight extant families and 12 extinct families of conifers are recognized. Rather than just giving the classification and evolutionary tree I wish to propose here, I should like to take you through the reasoning by which we may arrive there. Let us take a first look at how we can sort this out by putting the families in a chronological order, from first appearance in geological time to their extinction or to the present (Table 4).

The first important fact to note is that what palaeobotanists call basal conifer families had all become extinct by the end of the Palaeozoic (Upper Permian) 245 million years ago (Ma). The only family from that time that continued to exist into the Mesozoic (Triassic to Lower Jurassic [Lias]) is the Voltziaceae. Another notable fact is that the Podocarpaceae is the oldest extant conifer family, closely followed by the Araucariaceae. Several families that appeared at the same time or later than these two became extinct a long time ago. The Pinaceae is relatively late in appearance, in fact the latest of the extant families save the Phyllocladaceae. Despite the uncertainties of the fossil record, there are some important generalizations to be made for an evolutionary classification of the conifers. The first is that the early Mesozoic conifers, which include some extant families, evolved from Palaeozoic ancestors or from Voltziaceae, the one family that extended from the Upper Permian into the Jurassic. The second generalization is that the later Mesozoic families probably derived from Mesozoic ancestors, because by the Jurassic all basal conifer families had become extinct.

Table 4. The 20 extinct and extant families of conifers, with their approximate first and last appearances in geological time

FAMILY	FIRST APPEARANCE	Ma	LAST APPEARANCE	Ma
Thucydiaceae (✖)	Pennsylvanian (Stephanian)	300	Pennsylvanian (Stephanian)	295
Emporiaceae (✖)	Pennsylvanian (Stephanian)	300	Pennsylvanian (Stephanian)	290
Utrechtiaceae (✖)	Pennsylvanian (Stephanian)	295	Lower Permian	280
Ferrugliocladaceae (✖)	Lower Permian	285	Lower Permian	270
Majonicaceae (✖)	Upper Permian	270	Upper Permian	245
Ulmanniaceae (✖)	Upper Permian	260	Upper Permian	245
Voltziaceae (✖)	Upper Permian	250	Lower Jurassic (Lias)	200
Podocarpaceae (▲)	Middle Triassic	240	present	
Cheirolepidiaceae (✖)	Late Triassic (Carnian)	225	Upper Cretaceous (Turonian)	95
Palissyaceae (✖)	Late Triassic (Rhaetian)	210	Lower Jurassic (Lias)	190
Araucariaceae (▲)	Late Triassic	220	present	
Pararaucariaceae (✖)	Middle Jurassic (Dogger)	175	Middle Jurassic (Dogger)	165
Taxaceae (▲)	Middle Jurassic (Dogger)	175	present	
Sciadopityaceae (▲)	Middle Jurassic (Dogger)	170	present	
Cephalotaxaceae (▲)	Middle Jurassic (Dogger)	170	present	
Cupressaceae (▲)	Upper Jurassic (Malm)	160	present	
Pinaceae (▲)	Upper Jurassic (Malm)	150	present	
Geinitziaceae (✖)	Upper Cretaceous (Turonian)	90	Miocene	30
Doliostrobaceae (✖)	Upper Cretaceous (Maastrichtian)	70	Oligocene	40
Phyllocladaceae (▲)	Upper Cretaceous (Maastrichtian)	70	present	

Note: ✖, extinct; ▲, extant; Ma, million years ago

The next step is to see if we can discover the phylogenetic relationships of these families, both extinct and extant, based on the published results of cladistic analyses. Again, this is difficult for fossils because we have few characters of which we can be confident, and DNA is not available. For reasons to do with algorithms and statistics, it is possible to analyze only a few taxa at one time if only a few characters are available. In a recent cladistic analysis of basal conifers, Rothwell et al. (2005) found Thucydiaceae to be the sister taxon to both "walchian" and "voltzian" conifers. The Gondwanan family Ferrugliocladaceae is still lower on their cladogram; this enigmatic group with its simplified fertile dwarf shoots is perhaps an early branch off the evolutionary tree leading to true conifers. Emporiaceae and Utrechtiaceae are in a walchian clade that is sister to a voltzian clade with Majonicaceae and Voltziaceae. Other analyses gave different relationships to these four families; in the cladogram presented here the relationship between Ulmanniaceae, Utrechtiaceae, and Majonicaceae remains therefore unresolved. In an analysis researching the origin of modern conifer families, Charles Miller (in Beck 1988) obtained a cladogram in which Voltziaceae and Ulmanniaceae are basal to a clade with the two subclades Pararaucariaceae + (Araucariaceae, Pinaceae) and Cheirolepidiaceae + (Podocarpaceae, Cephalotaxaceae). That result fits well with the timing in the fossil record, but the relationships of the extant families found by Miller are more doubtful. The palaeobotanist Ruth Stockey (1994) demonstrated a relationship of the tiny family Pararaucariaceae with Pinaceae, not with Araucariaceae, and so I shall place it accordingly. The enigmatic and highly diverse extinct family Cheirolepidiaceae, well described by Joan Watson (in Beck 1988) who did not wish to speculate about its relationships, is here placed as the sister group to the clade (Sciadopityaceae, Cupressaceae, Doliostrobaceae, Geinitziaceae). Watson, like many palaeobotanists, maintained the family Taxodiaceae, but it is firmly embedded in Cupressaceae based upon all available evidence (Farjon 2005b). The Cheirolepidiaceae shares numerous characters with Cupressaceae *sensu lato* and only differs substantially in its characteristic pollen.

Let us now look at some results of phylogenetic analyses using DNA data of extant conifers. In most of these publications, the Pinaceae form a clade basal to the rest of the conifers used in the analyses, which is not in agreement with the fossil evidence. Perhaps the chloroplast DNA and nuclear (ribosomal) RNA have evolved more slowly in that family than in others. The molecular analyses do agree with the geological time record in grouping Podocarpaceae and Araucariaceae in one clade, usually basal to but at least separate from Cephalotaxaceae, Cupressaceae, and Taxaceae. We must use that arrangement instead of Miller's based on morphology, because he had to invoke an unlikely reversal of an important character to place Cephalotaxaceae with Podocarpaceae.

Where do we place the Pinaceae? Both molecular evidence and morphological analyses conclude that their characters are mostly primitive in comparison to the more derived states in other Mesozoic conifers, including all or most extant families. Yet the earliest fossil evidence for this family is from the Late Jurassic. Fossils assigned to *Pseudolarix* begin to appear in strata deposited at this time. There are also some Jurassic fossil seed cones assigned to Pinaceae that could belong to an unknown family if we had knowledge of the rest of these plants. The oldest unambiguous fossil of a pine (*Pinus*) is known from the Lower Cretaceous (Albian) of Belgium, 110 Ma. Will we find older fossils? It is not impossible, but until then the placement of this family in an evolutionary classification remains ambiguous. The remaining extinct families, although not included in any cladistic analyses, can be tentatively placed according to their affinities inferred from their descriptions in the palaeobotanical literature.

The next step is to look at possible ancestors at the level of families. Could some families have given rise to others? This is tricky and borders on speculation. One option is to say that Mesozoic or modern conifers (Coniferales) arose from Voltziales, a catch all at the ordinal rank for the basal conifers including Voltziaceae. But that is almost self-evident and really tells us nothing much about a common ancestor at all. The Voltziaceae had many genera with relatively advanced seed cones, from which Rudolf Florin and others after him inferred the structures seen in most extant conifer families. With the exception of *Araucaria* and *Dacrydium* (Araucariaceae and Podocarpaceae, respectively), which have foliage very similar to the basal conifers of the Permian, most extant conifers with generalized (not specialized) leaf types resemble those found in

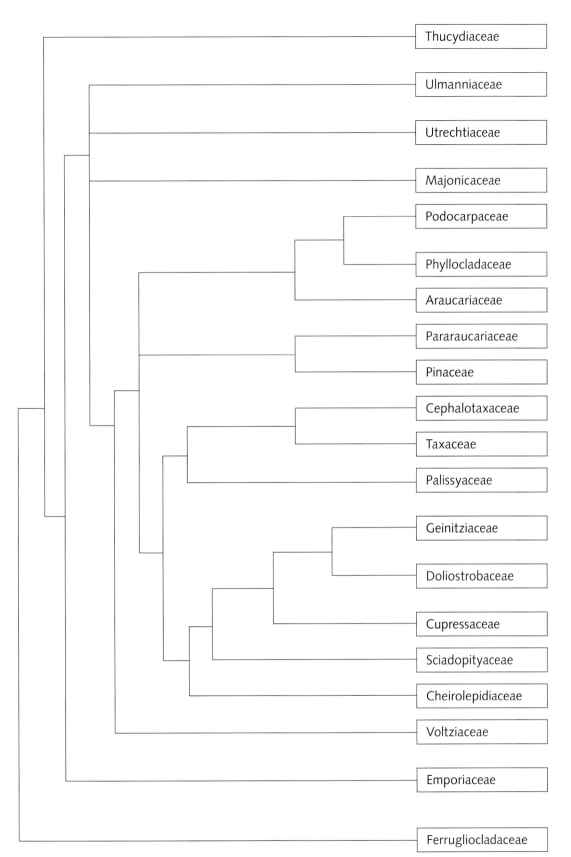

A hypothetical phylogeny of the 20 extinct and extant conifer families based on their appearance in the fossil record, published phylogenetic analyses, and relationships inferred from comparative morphological studies.

the Voltziaceae as well. I think we may consider this family as having provided the ancestor of most of the later conifer families except Araucariaceae and Podocarpaceae. Going a phase back in the evolution of the conifer seed cone, we could follow Florin and the majority of his successors once more and consider the Majonicaceae and Ulmanniaceae as derived from Utrechtiaceae (walchian conifers of Florin). Doliostrobaceae and Geinitziaceae seem to have evolved from basal and more advanced members of Cupressaceae, respectively, so I have placed them as derived from this family. Phyllocladaceae is a specialized family with a single recognized genus derived from Podocarpaceae (and included in it by some). Other possible ancestors among the 20 families would be more speculative, so we must place them according to their inferred phylogenetic relationships instead.

Finally, we should place the families along the geological time scale and indicate how diverse in terms of genera and species they were. That is difficult again, because we know many of them by only one or a few genera, while we know all or most of the genera in the extant families, including several that became extinct. To include species would create even more bias towards extant families. We may be allowed to speculate here a little, too, and allow greater diversity for some extinct families where at least a good number of taxa have been described in the palaeobotanical literature. The result of all this gives us a classification of conifer families through geological time.

What can we infer from this hypothetical evolutionary tree? First, the basal conifer families known from the Permian did not last very long in comparison to most of the families that originated later. Second, the conifers really began to diversify in the Triassic (as shown by the numerous branches that arise on the evolutionary tree), reaching at least 11 families in the Jurassic and the greatest abundance of species in the Cretaceous. By the Tertiary, and certainly after the Eocene, only the present eight families were left and all gradually lost species diversity (as shown by the narrowing of the branches). The Voltziaceae and/or its immediate ancestors were a pivotal group of conifers from which later lineages and families arose. Much of this evolution took place in the Triassic, and it is clear that to understand this evolution better, palaeobotanists should concentrate their studies of fossil conifers on that period in the history of life.

Opposite: A hypothetical evolutionary tree showing origins, relationships, duration, and diversity of the 20 extinct and extant conifer families. The geological time scale is given in intervals of 10 million years in the column on the left, with the era, periods, and abbreviated names of epochs or stages (Alb, Albian; Apt, Aptian; Ber, Berriasian; Brm, Barremian; Cen, Cenomanian; Cmp, Campanian; Con, Coniacean; Eoc, Eocene; Hau, Hauterivian; Maa, Maastrichtian; Mio, Miocene; Nam, Namurian; Oli, Oligocene; Pal, Palaeocene; Ple, Pleistocene; Pli, Pliocene; San, Santonian; Ste, Stephanian; Tur, Turonian; Vlg, Valanginian; Wes, Westphalian). The relative diversity of families is represented by the width of each branch on the tree. The length represents the duration, and the termination when each family became extinct (if it did). Diversity is based on evidence from the fossil record and is in all cases incompletely known, as is the duration of most of the extinct families.

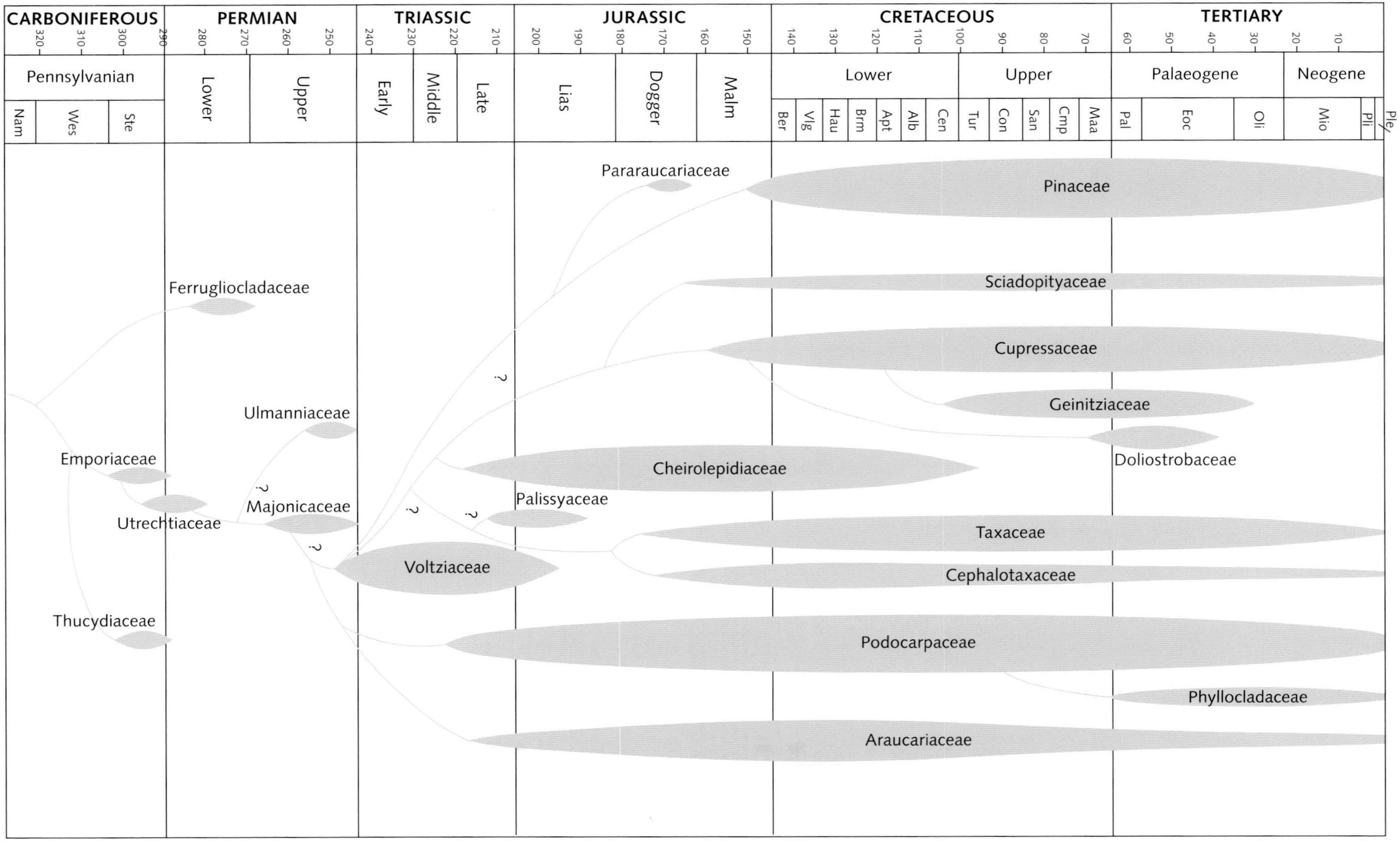
CARBONIFEROUS
PERMIAN
TRIASSIC
JURASSIC
CRETACEOUS
TERTIARY
320
310
300
290
280
270
260
250
240
230
220
210
200
190
180
170
160
150
140
130
120
110
100
90
80
70
60
50
40
30
20
10
Pennsylvanian
Lower
Upper
Early
Middle
Late
Lias
Dogger
Malm
Lower
Upper
Palaeogene
Neogene
Nam
Wes
Ste
Ber
Vlg
Hau
Brm
Apt
Alb
Cen
Tur
Con
San
Cmp
Maa
Pal
Eoc
Oli
Mio
Pli
Ple
Pararaucariaceae
Pinaceae
Ferrugliocladaceae
Sciadopityaceae
Cupressaceae
Geinitziaceae
Ulmanniaceae
Doliostrobaceae
Emporiaceae
Cheirolepidiaceae
Majonicaceae
Palissyaceae
Utrechtiaceae
Taxaceae
Voltziaceae
Cephalotaxaceae
Thucydiaceae
Podocarpaceae
Phyllocladaceae
Araucariaceae
?
?
?
?
?
?

Conifers of
the Past

10 All or Nothing About Ancestors

EVOLUTION IMPLIES ANCESTORS AND DESCENDANTS: *one species giving rise to another. Because ancestors exist, it is legitimate to ask who they are in relation to descendants. In several cases of recent speciation we know the answer to this question; both the ancestral species and its descendant are living species and their genetic relationships and subsequent separation and divergence have been studied in detail. Examples of well-known ancestors are mostly found in species of animals and plants that are of economic importance to mankind, such as wheat (Triticum species), tomato (Lycopersicon species), and pigeon (Columba species). The descendants of these ancestors were domesticated millennia ago and thereby evolved into distinct species. If the same process has happened without human interference by genetic separation and natural selection (instead of artificial selection), ancestors can be inferred from genetic and morphological as well as geographical and ecological evidence, but it becomes more difficult to prove. Two species that are closely related could be parent and daughter species, or they could be sister species with a common ancestor. Phylogenetic analysis, as we have seen, cannot answer the ancestor-descendant question, it only finds (closest) relationships between taxa. The ancestors are the anonymous nodes of a cladogram—if that cladogram is interpreted as a phylogenetic tree. If we want to put names to these ancestors, we have to follow other paths of investigation.*

▲ ▲ ▲

By investigating the evolution of conifer families through geological time, we have seen that evolutionary lineages began modestly and then diversified. The taxonomic unit of evolution is the species; from it a population of individuals (or even a single individual) separates, multiplies, genetically diversifies, and evolves to become a separate species. The separation can be geographical (allopatric speciation) or only ecological or even behavioural in animals (sympatric speciation). In plants, hybridization is also a source of new species, but this is relatively uncommon in conifers. The nearest ancestor of a group of species, such as a genus or family, was therefore a species. Can we discover that species? Is *Archaeopteryx lithographica*, the famous fossil bird from the Upper Jurassic (Malm) limestone of Bavaria, the nearest ancestor of all birds? It was certainly a very primitive and reptilian bird and, despite some rather dubious claims for other fossils, still the earliest one known. It is also likely to be closer to the true ancestor of birds than the similarly dubious, but due to cladistics now "unassailable" claim that some Late Cretaceous theropod dinosaur is the ancestor of birds. Whatever the eventual outcome of this controversy, it is extremely unlikely that we can pinpoint the real ancestor of a group of species, such as a family. Can we therefore say nothing about ancestors?

In the fossil record of plants, in particular, we are almost always confronted with little fragments, and most of these are leaves. Conifers are usually represented by fragments of foliage branches, because leaves often do not detach from twigs but fall with them. It is also quite common to find seeds, and at a microscopic level, pollen. Cones are less common but not unusual, but to find them attached to foliage branchlets is already stretching your luck. Pieces of wood, even large parts of logs, such as the famous stone trees in Petrified Forest National Park in Arizona, turn up in geological strata with some frequency.

To get an idea of what the fossil record has to offer, you may take a walk in a forest with conifers and observe what lies on the ground. Imagine that some of this debris gets washed into a river by heavy rains and ends up at the bottom of a lake after having been in the water long enough to sink. Subsequent floods bury it in mud and silt, and if all goes well these lake deposits eventually turn into sedimentary rock. Millions of years later this rock, once buried deep underground, is lifted up by tectonic forces and exposed by erosion. A palaeobotanist splits open the shale or limestone with a hammer and finds plant fossils. They are bits and pieces of all kinds of plants, often only preserved as impressions or turned into some form of coal or other mineral. On rare occasions the fragments are not or are only slightly compressed and the mineral is hard. Plant cell tissue has been replaced by silica or calcite and is anatomically preserved. This happens more often to wood, with its sturdy cell walls of lignin and cellulose, than to soft plant parts. The often prolonged time that plant fragments remained in contact with air and water before they were buried, as well as their rough transport in the river, have not helped to preserve the delicate structures. The fossil logs in the Late Triassic Chinle Formation of Arizona, although beautifully preserved and colourfully mineralized, were transported a long distance in a turbulent river before they were deposited in a large delta near a sea coast. Probably the sea tossed them about for a time as well. They were thereby stripped of all leaves, branches, bark, and most roots and none of these parts are found in the sediment with the logs.

Fossil logs of large conifers from the Triassic have been freed from sediments by erosion in the Painted Desert at Petrified Forest National Park, Arizona.

The anatomy of these logs is beautifully preserved, and wood anatomists have studied them intensively. Do we know to what species of conifer they belonged? Names have been given, but in palaeobotany, as we have seen, that often does not tell us what we would like to know. The most common type of wood, producing the biggest logs to be found in this desert, is known as *Araucarioxylon arizonense*. This name means *Araucaria*-type wood from Arizona. Does that mean that these trees were Triassic araucarias? Of present-day conifer genera, only the three that constitute the family Araucariaceae (*Agathis, Araucaria*, and *Wollemia*) display all the characteristics of this type of fossil wood. Among fossil gymnosperms, however, it appears that a whole range of trees, conifers as well as other gymnosperms, had this type of wood, some of it dating back to the Carboniferous and Permian, when there were no araucarias. The conclusion has to be that aucarias have a primitive type of gymnospermous wood compared to other extant conifers (remember, not a single leafy branch or cone has been found with these trees in Arizona). The name *Araucarioxylon* is ambiguous, and some have proposed to abandon it and use *Dadoxylon*, a name for very similar fossil wood, instead. This suggestion has not been taken up widely; in botanical nomenclature the literal meaning of names is irrelevant. We should not assume an araucaria tree when we find such wood in the fossil record, unless it is of an age in which we know that all other contenders had become extinct. The age of these logs, Upper Triassic, does not exclude the possibility that they belonged to the earliest representatives of *Araucaria*, the earliest appearing genus in Araucariaceae. But we cannot at all be certain of this, and we cannot consider them as an ancestor of the Araucariaceae.

Could our chances of identifying ancestors to extant—or extinct—families of conifers improve if we knew the anatomy and morphology of a whole plant? Undoubtedly. However, even with such an exquisite fossil as *Archaeopteryx lithographica*, a dream for a palaeobotanist, the matter can remain contentious. Attempts at reconstruction of whole fossil plants are now becoming feasible and more common. Jason Hilton, an expert in this field, explained in a recent lecture on the subject all the pitfalls and difficulties; it is a lot of painstaking detective work and takes years to complete. But a number of relatively complete plant concepts have been developed for Palaeozoic conifer taxa, several of these by Gar Rothwell of Ohio University and his collaborators. By careful comparison of these taxa, taking account of all characters known and emphasizing character combinations not found in other genera and families of conifers, higher taxa such as families can be more precisely circumscribed. Phylogenies can be reconstructed for more taxa that have thus been recognized. Taxonomic classifications informed by phylogeny are predictive: we can expect shared derived characters in certain groups (clades) where we do not actually observe them for lack of material. Generalizations about characters not found in some taxa can further help to reconstruct whole plants. These concepts of whole plants are partly hypothetical—they are themselves generalizations—but they can be used as visualizations in an evolutionary tree. If it is likely that the ancestor to extant conifers belonged to Voltziaceae, we will have a concept of what this ancestor might have looked like. That is as close as we can possibly get to the discovery of the real ancestor, which undoubtedly existed but cannot be known precisely. I am going to discuss some of these potential ancestors in the next chapter.

11 The Earliest Conifers

WHEN I WAS IN MY EARLY TEENS *my parents gave me a book for a birthday present, which in hindsight may have been one of the decisive instruments that shaped my future. It was the second edition of* De Geschiedenis van het Leven op Aarde *(The History of Life on Earth, 1952) by Professor of Geology G. L. Smit Sibinga at the University of Amsterdam. I read it from beginning to end and then again and again. The professor was an acquaintance of my father, and one day I was invited to visit as I had found a molar of a mammoth in a sandpit on the heath. I dreamed about life in the distant past and being a palaeontologist myself. Not long afterwards, my parents took the family to the south of the province of Limburg, and there I saw in a museum the plant fossils from the coal mines and a diorama of a coal forest in the Carboniferous. Now I wanted to become a palaeobotanist! Later, I wanted to do several other things, of course, and it took quite a while before I could call myself anything. My interest in the deep past has remained, and perhaps I turned to conifers because these represent a link with the ancient past more than most plants. The dioramas and paintings of the Carboniferous coal swamps and their weird vegetation conjure up a remote and yet vaguely familiar world, when life on land became prolific and luxurious for the first time. The period is most famous for its giant lycophytes, now only represented by smallish herbaceous forms popularly called club-mosses, but it was also during this time that the first seed plants appeared. Among these were trees known as cordaites.*

▲ ▲ ▲

Rudolf Florin considered the Cordaitales to be the ancestor of conifers. Unlike the more numerous and dominant lepidodendrons and sigillarias, giant relatives of today's diminutive club-mosses (lycopods), the cordaites were trees with coniferous wood. There are some anatomical differences, such as a wide pith, at least present in young branches, but the mature wood is very similar to fossil wood described under the name we have already encountered, *Araucarioxylon*. Cordaites could be tall trees up to 30 m (100 ft) or more with a fluted stem base and some species had stilted roots, adaptations to a life in swamps. The enormous, strap-shaped leaves were unlike those of any true conifer known. Some attained a length of 1 m (over 3 ft) and as much as 15 cm (6 in) in width, with numerous parallel veins that occasionally dichotomized. The fossils give the impression of a leaf that was leathery. The reproductive structures of cordaites (separate female and male, as in conifers) were branched systems, usually axillary to the strap-shaped leaves. On these branches, some dwarf shoots with scale-like leaves bore fertile scales at the tips. Whole plant concepts have been developed in recent years, and several species of cordaites are now well known.

The cordaites were more or less contemporaneous with the earliest conifers. They originated in the Westphalian or Namurian phase of the Pennsylvanian, about 10–20

Reconstruction of a coal swamp forest as it may have appeared in Carboniferous times, in the famous diorama at the Field Museum of Natural History, Chicago. Species of cordaites are represented top left and middle. Reprinted by permission of The Field Museum (no. GEO85637c)

million years earlier, and lasted until well into the Permian. Could the family Cordaitaceae contain the ancestor of conifers? In broad terms, Florin emphasized the evolution of the conifer cone from a branching system and he envisaged a gradual reduction of the leaves as well as the fertile branches into bracts and cones. In cladistic

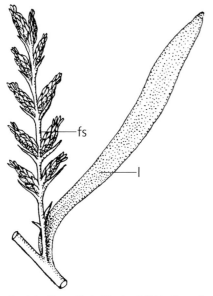

analyses the two are sister groups, but it is not easy to see how the cordaites could have given rise to the conifers, given the fundamental differences in the arrangement and structure of reproductive organs. It remains unexplained how the large, strap-shaped, and multiple-veined leaves of the cordaites could have transformed into the acicular, *Araucaria*-like leaves of the walchian conifers. On the other hand, broad, though smaller, multiple-veined leaves exist in extant conifers such as *Agathis* (Araucariaceae) and *Nageia* (Podocarpaceae); both are ancient families. Some of the cordaites had similar, ovate leaves. It is well possible that the evolution leading to conifers will show a grade in character transformations, as exemplified by

Cordaianthus with fertile shoot (fs) in the axil of a leaf (l). This is the commonly accepted reconstruction of the cordaitean strobilus. From Stewart and Rothwell (1993); reprinted by permission of Cambridge University Press

the recently described fossil species *Barthelia furcata* from the Late Pennsylvanian of Kansas (Rothwell and Mapes 2001). This fossil, neither a cordaite nor a conifer, combined characters of both and cannot be classified as either.

What did the early conifers look like? Recently discovered abundant remains of an Upper Carboniferous (Stephanian) conifer in Ohio have made a reconstruction of one of these possible. This conifer was named *Thucydia mahoningensis* and was classified in its own family, Thucydiaceae (Hernandez-Castillo et al. 2003). This conifer was a small tree not taller than 2 m (7 ft) and looked surprisingly similar in habit to a young *Araucaria heterophylla*, a conifer you can buy in a pot as a houseplant.

The erect stem of *Thucydia mahoningensis* had pseudo-whorls of spreading foliage branches at regular intervals. On these branches two rows of slender branchlets spread horizontally and bore S-curved needle-like leaves. At the top of this little tree branches were more erect and could divide twice; the leaves there were broader and of varying size. The fertile shoots were placed on the upper part of the erect stem and unbranched, about 10 cm long, with male and female reproductive units probably on separate plants. The reproductive units are both compound structures, with leaves acting as bracts in a fertile zone, in the axils of which are sporophylls as well as sterile scale leaves on short shoots. *Thucydia mahoningensis* did not form compact cones as in later conifers. The female shoots begin and end as a sterile shoot with normal leaves; the male shoots were probably fertile along the entire length. It is very interesting to note that the pollen cones of this early conifer were compound; in all extant conifers they are simple, that is, there is no subtending bract to the fertile structure or microsporophyll. *Thucydia mahoningensis* shared a compound male fertile shoot with the Cordaitaceae, the putative ancestor of conifers. Whereas the habit and foliage of this extinct conifer looked familiar enough, its cones were unlike any extant conifer and much more primitive.

 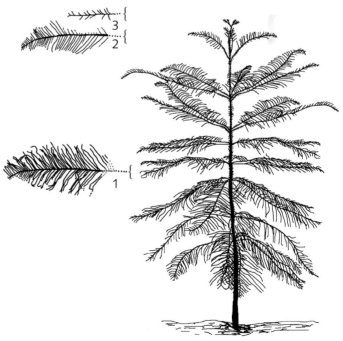

A pot-grown juvenile tree of *Araucaria heterophylla* (Norfolk Island pine) and a reconstruction of the 300 million-year-old conifer *Thucydia mahoningensis*. Latter from Hernandez-Castillo et al. (2003)

Still, some similarities remain, albeit as an exceptional occurrence. In several conifers we can sometimes find proliferating seed cones. A cone is a shoot with bracts, in the axils of which form seed scales. Occasionally, this formation of seed scales is retarded and the shoot reverts to vegetative growth, with the bracts turning back to leaves (needles) and the shoot apex forming winter buds for next year's vegetative growth. These proliferating cones reminds us of the fertile female shoot of the long extinct conifer, *Thucydia mahoningensis*. Such abnormal growth or teratology can thus teach us not only about the homologies of cone parts, but even give us a reminder how conifer cones started in evolution, as has been demonstrated in these remarkable fossils from an abandoned strip coal mine in the United States.

Of the Lower Permian conifers, *Utrechtia floriniformis* is relatively completely known from stems, foliage branches with branchlets and leaves, pollen cones, and seed cones. Rudolf Florin's names for this conifer and its parts (*Lebachia*, *Walchia*) have been found problematic, and one only survives in the informal category of "walchian conifers" for the Lower Permian Voltziales. Again these conifers resembled the slender, conical araucarias such as the Norfolk Island pine but in a more adult form than we have seen in the earlier *Thucydia mahoningensis*. A tall erect stem bore pseudo-whorls of five to seven horizontally spreading branches, gradually becoming shorter towards the top. These branches had pectinate rows of foliage branchlets covered in spirally arranged, decurrent, and needle-like S-curved leaves. Some of these branchlets terminated in short pollen cones, while higher up in the tree branches could have elongated seed cones proximally (nearer the stem) and leafy branchlets distally. Both male and female cones occurred on the same tree. The pollen cones were simple, with leaf-like microsporophylls on short stalks that were turned upwards and bore numerous pollen sacs on the stalks. The seed cones of *U. floriniformis* were compound; they had helically arranged forked bracts, in the axil of which a flattened dwarf shoot with small scale-like leaves around the base bore a single seed. Both male and female cones were

The normally developed seed cones of *Abies koreana*, with well-defined bracts and seed scales in a regular arrangement, and the abnormal proliferation of a cone of the same species, showing a return to leaves and vegetative shoot.

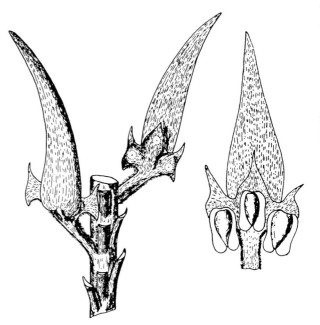

A more mature tree of *Araucaria heterophylla* (Norfolk Island pine), representing what the habit of *Utrechtia floriniformis* may have looked like, and reconstructions of parts of this extinct conifer from the Lower Permian. Latter from Stewart and Rothwell (1993); reprinted by permission of Cambridge University Press

considerably more compact than those from the earlier period described above, and we can easily recognize true conifer cones in them. Nevertheless, the seed scale is still a leafy short shoot and only shows the beginnings of a scale as can be seen today in pines or firs.

At the end of the Permian, a mass extinction event took place that was probably the most severe in the long history of life. Vincent Courtillot, author of the book *Evolutionary Catastrophes* (Cambridge University Press, 1999), has called it "the mother of all extinctions." Almost all the Palaeozoic continents had come together to form one great supercontinent, which geologists call Pangea ("all-earth"). Marine regression was very substantial, leaving few shallow seas between the deep ocean and the continent. Much

Fossil cone fragment and scales of the Early Triassic conifer *Cycadocarpidium pilosum*. From Grauvogel-Stamm (1978)

is known about groups of marine animals that went extinct during this event, but far less about terrestrial animals and plants. Few deposits on land from this period survive on the surface for inspection by palaeontologists. Erosion prevailed, and deserts were very extensive at this time. Massive flood volcanism in Siberia and China was linked

Leaves of *Podozamites lanceolatus* from the Jurassic (Lias). From Stewart and Rothwell (1993); reprinted by permission of Cambridge University Press

with disruptive climate change and coincided with two extinction crises, the greatest at the Permian–Triassic boundary and another 8 million years earlier.

Did this extinction event affect the conifers? From the evolutionary tree in chapter 9, we can see that only a single family, the Voltziaceae, appears to have made it across the boundary into the Triassic period. Let us now look at a representative of that family, a survivor of the extinction crisis, the genus *Cycadocarpidium* and especially the species *C. pilosum*, fossils of which were found in the early Triassic sandstones of the Vosges Mountains in France. I shall give a description of this conifer, while borrowing a bit from other species in the same genus described from later geological strata. The genus *Cycadocarpidium* is used for female cones or parts thereof with helically arranged leaf-like bracts on very short or longer stalks, at the base of which were reduced, lobed seed scales bearing two or three inverted, winged or wingless seeds. The bract-scale complexes are often found as single units in the sediment, which means that the cones fell apart at maturity. Often associated with these are broadly lanceolate, multiple-veined leaves that are known under the organ genus name *Podozamites* and are thought to have belonged to the same plant. They are similar to some slender leaf shapes found on young, shaded trees in the genera *Agathis* (Araucariaceae) and *Nageia* (Podocarpaceae). In the past these remains were thought to have affinities with cycads, but they are now clearly understood as conifers. Several species have been described; they existed from the Early Triassic until the Jurassic (Lias) and were distributed from present-day England to Iran. These unusual conifers were presumably large trees, but as we will always only find fragments and no trunks attached, this can never be proven beyond doubt. By working from analogy, we know that extant conifers with these broad leaf types are both big trees and evolutionarily ancient.

12 Conifer Heyday: The Age of Conifers

THE MESOZOIC ERA (245–65 million years ago [Ma]) is often hailed as the Age of Dinosaurs, and there can be little argument about it from our animal point of view. As Francis Hallé noted in his book In Praise of Plants *(2002), we humans are biased. We relate to animals naturally, and the kids all want to see the dinosaurs in the natural history museums—not the big trees in the arboreta. It is only through learning more about the natural history of plants, and especially of conifers (I am biased twice), that we will realize that they are just as amazing, but for other reasons, of which Hallé gave numerous examples. Of course, neither the dinosaurs nor humans would have existed had there been no plants. If we accept that place of primacy for all things vegetative, there is sound reason to call the Mesozoic (Triassic, Jurassic, and Cretaceous) the Age of Conifers. As a final blow to the superiority of the dinosaurs, conifers did not at all go extinct at the end of the Cretaceous.*

▲ ▲ ▲

During the Triassic, the losses of the great extinction event at the end of the Palaeozoic in terms of species diversity were gradually made good by new evolutionary radiation from those groups that had survived. The supercontinent had begun to break up into a northern landmass, Laurasia, and a southern landmass, Gondwana, divided by a widening ocean known as Thetys. Other seaways had begun to open as well. The climate improved from the "ice-house" conditions of the Upper Permian to the "hot-house" conditions of the Middle Triassic. These warm conditions with abundant rainfall prevailed throughout the Mesozoic and into the Tertiary (Palaeogene) and are in fact the normal global climate. When warm and humid climate is limited to the tropical latitudes, as it is at present, the Earth is in an ice-house condition, characterized by ice ages with polar icecaps and glaciers on mountains at middle latitudes. These cold periods are much shorter than the warm ones and usually last for less than 10 million years. The hot-house climate of the Triassic created ideal conditions for plant growth, and by the Late Triassic the flora may have reached one of the great peaks in diversity of past geological time. This diversification is reflected in the evolutionary tree of conifer families presented in chapter 9, with the first extant conifer families or the lineages leading to them appearing during this period.

The palaeobotanists John and Heidi Anderson from South Africa have earned world renown for their life-long study of the plant fossils in the Upper Triassic Molteno sandstone, shale, and chert beds in the vast Karoo Basin, deposited on river floodplains 220 Ma. Their book *Heyday of the Gymnosperms* (Anderson and Anderson 2003) described the fossil gymnosperm taxa (mostly fructifications) based on what must be one of the most comprehensive collections of fossil plant material from a single formation ever assembled. This collection approaches 30,000 specimen slabs, pieces of stone with fossil remains. About half of these belonged to gymnosperms, the other half to plants that do not produce seeds, such as ferns, horsetails, and lycopods. Not a single fossil can be assigned to an angiosperm or flowering plant. It would appear that these had not yet evolved, although the Andersons believe that something might be found one day that will change our understanding of their beginnings. Huge as their collection may be, the Andersons say that they have barely scratched the surface of this vast treasure house of fossils.

An early angiosperm in the Molteno would indeed be the find of the century, but meanwhile the gymnosperms are amazing enough. There are strange forms among them, such as the pendulous seed cone *Dordrechtites elongatus*, which apparently dispersed its T-shaped seed scales with the seeds firmly attached. It is not a conifer under our definition (the female cone is simple while not reduced), and it is unfortunate that no affiliated foliage is known with certainty. A very large pollen cone, *Fredianthus maysiformis* (the specific epithet compares it with a corn cob, *Zea mays*) could have belonged to a primitive voltzian conifer. If that is correct, at approximately 22 × 5 cm (9 × 2 in) it would be the largest conifer pollen cone known. However, the number of microsporangia (little sacs that contain the pollen) on each scale is much higher than in any known conifer, and this, as well as their position, is similar to cycads. Again, no foliage or seed cones are known of this plant, and with only two fossils found it must have been very rare indeed. Conifers produce numerous pollen cones and discard them freely

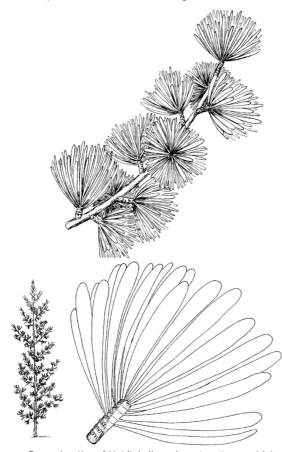

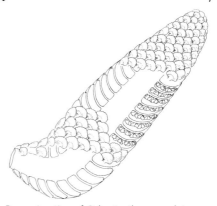

Reconstruction of *Odyssianthus crenulatus* (pollen cone). From Anderson and Anderson (2003); reprinted by permission of the authors

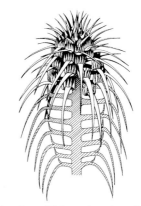

Reconstruction of *Heidiphyllum elongatum* (tree and foliage). From Anderson and Anderson (2003); reprinted by permission of the authors

Reconstruction of *Telemachus elongatus* (seed cone). From Anderson and Anderson (2003); reprinted by permission of the authors

after pollen dispersal by wind. Cycads produce very few pollen cones, which remain on the plant but can break off, while beetles disperse the pollen. Fossils of beetles are numerous in the Molteno beds, but the pollen of this fossil cone was not preserved.

More securely coniferous is a small tree that grew on the floodplain and formed dense thickets. It had fairly large (10 × 1 cm; 4 × 0.4 in), strap-shaped, multiple-veined leaves borne in tufts on short shoots, as in *Larix*; compact pollen cones to 7 cm (3 in) long; and an erect seed cone with long, recurved, spiny bracts. This tree can be assigned to the family Voltziaceae, but because the three organs have only been found detached, each has a separate name (organ taxon): *Heidiphyllum* for the foliage, *Odyssianthus* for the pollen cone, and *Telemachus* for the seed cone. Odysseus, the Homeric hero of the Odyssey, was the father of Telemachus, and Heidi and John Anderson gave these names to the fossils when it was discovered that they were affiliated. Another palaeobotanist had named the foliage after Heidi before its cones were identified. That these parts belonged to the same plant is inferred from the fact that they are consistently found together in numerous localities.

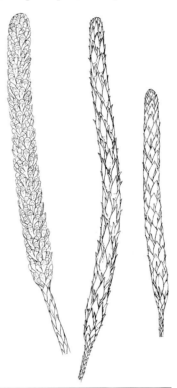

Early members of the family Podocarpaceae have also been discovered in the Molteno formation; the foliage is known as *Rissikia*, the pollen cones as *Rissikianthus*, and the seed cones as *Rissikistrobus*. These

The small seed cones with multiple scales of *Saxegothaea conspicua* remind us of the longer, but similar fossil cones of the Triassic podocarp *Rissikistrobus* found in the Molteno formation of South Africa. Reconstruction of fossils from Anderson and Anderson (2003); reproduced by permission of the authors

The seed cone of *Podocarpus macrophyllus* is reduced to a single seed, covered by a tough skin (epimatium) and subtended by a swollen, succulent, and colourful receptacle to attract birds.

seed cones were elongated and had numerous seeds, unlike those of most of the extant genera in the family, in which only one seed develops. A few present-day genera do remind us of these earliest podocarps by having retained cones with multiple scales and seeds, even though the cones are very small. These are *Saxegothaea* and *Microcachrys*, the latter of which is the smallest of the extant conifers (see *M. tetragona* photo in chapter 2). Both have but a single species left from what was presumably a greater diversity. The typical Gondwanan relict distribution, with *Saxegothaea* in southern South America and *Microcachrys* in Tasmania, supports this notion. The later success of the Podocarpaceae involved specialization of the female organs for bird dispersal, which was achieved by drastic reduction of the number of seeds to one and by supplementing this with an edible, colourful attraction.

Numerous other gymnosperms are represented in the Molteno, some belonging to orders that still exist, such as cycads and ginkgos, but many to orders wholly extinct. By using statistical methods and extrapolation, the Andersons estimated that the flora of this floodplain environment in the Triassic could have contained 250 genera and 2000 species of nonflowering plants, half of which were gymnosperms. Thus, very high species diversity seems to have been possible before flowering plants existed.

What was the situation elsewhere in the Mesozoic world? Rudolf Florin (1963) published maps with the distribution of fossil and living genera of conifers in a seminal paper on the subject. Although we can learn much from the maps about localities where fossil conifers have been found, they also tell us where palaeobotanists have searched for them. New discoveries are accumulating rapidly and help to correct the historical bias towards Europe, where palaeobotany began and the most promising sources for discoveries are now old museum drawers rather than stone quarries, most of which have been commercially abandoned. The Triassic Voltziaceae is now known as a family with as many species as the largest of the extant families. This family, although still mostly known from the Northern Hemisphere (once Laurasia), has increasingly been recognized from continents once united in Gondwana. Voltziaceae probably had a more or less worldwide distribution, like one of its descendants, the Cupressaceae, today.

In the Late Triassic, another important family arose, the Cheirolepidiaceae. This was a very morphologically diverse family; in fact, the only unifying character seems to be its distinctive pollen, known as *Classopollis* in palaeobotanical circles. If one is lucky enough to find a fossilized leafy shoot with a pollen cone that contains this type of pollen, we can be sure that the whole thing belongs to this family. In this manner, other organ fragments have gradually been recognized not to belong to Araucariaceae, Cupressaceae (including Taxodiaceae), or Podocarpaceae, but to the family Cheiro-lepidiaceae. Many of the names of these fossils still remind us of the earlier ideas about their affinities. The family Cheirolepidiaceae was not recognized in Florin's time, and many such fossils would have been incorrectly assigned to Cupressaceae. As far as we know, species in this family were mostly trees, some very large. The foliage usually has small, scale-like leaves but is of two general types, one with helically arranged leaves (*Brachyphyllum*) and another with whorled leaves that clasp the stems, giving them a jointed appearance (*Frenelopsis*). This variation is reminiscent of the Cupressaceae as presently circumscribed, which includes Taxodiaceae with helically arranged leaves. Not many seed cones are known, but they often had complex, lobed scales axillary to bracts in a helical arrangement. Two of the better-known species, *Frenelopsis ramosissima* and *Pseudofrenelopsis parceramosa*, have been reconstructed as shrubby and tree-

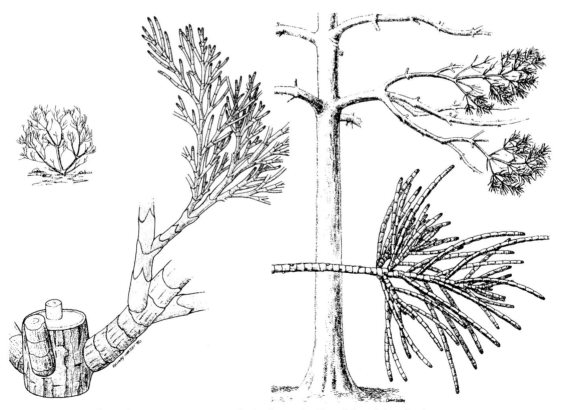

Reconstruction of *Frenelopsis ramosissima*, an extinct conifer belonging to the family Cheirolepidiaceae. From Beck (1988); reprinted by permission of Columbia University Press

Reconstruction of *Pseudofrenelopsis parceramosa*, an extinct conifer belonging to the family Cheirole-pidiaceae. From Alvin (1983); reprinted by permission of the Linnean Society of London

like, semi-succulent xerophytes. They may have grown in saline coastal mud flats or salt marshes of the Lower Cretaceous of Euramerica. (They were found in today's Maryland and Virginia, but during the Lower Cretaceous you could have walked from there into Portugal or Ireland, as the North Atlantic did not yet exist.) The plants' physiology to cope with salt may have been comparable to that of the morphologically similar angiosperm *Salicornia*, common in the shallow tidal zone of sea coasts today. If this ecological interpretation is correct, it would mean that in the distant past conifers did occupy habitats saturated with salt from where they are now totally absent, as discussed in chapter 3.

Other oddities among the conifers existed during the Mesozoic that are unheard of today. As previously discussed in chapter 3, there are very small conifers as well as very large (the largest) trees. However, in the Triassic of Europe there were herbaceous conifers that failed to produce secondary xylem (wood) in their stems. The best-known species, *Aethophyllum stipulare* from the Early Triassic *Voltzia* sandstone of the Vosges Mountains in France (another treasure trove of fossil gymnosperms), grew 1.5–2 m (5–7 ft) tall, with an erect stem at most 2 cm (0.75 in) thick at the base, virtually lacking xylem or wood cells. It had long and slender, strap-shaped leaves and few branches; the long pollen cones were at the top, and the compound, small seed cones were in groups together on lower branches. Entire seedlings and juveniles of this conifer have been found in abundance. *Aethophyllum stipulare* looked like a tall weed, and it was one. It was capable of fast growth, and grew in a floodplain of a river delta. It could produce cones at the same time as the onset of secondary growth, probably within a year. *Aethophyllum stipulare* was a ruderal plant, quickly invading and colonizing sections of the river delta that fell dry with the shifting of channels. Before the sand bars were flooded again, it had grown, "flowered," and set seed, by which it moved on to other suitable sites. The implications of this discovery are profound. Ruderal herbaceous plants today are restricted to angiosperms; no extant gymnosperms can behave like this. One of the common assumptions among botanists had been that this type of aggressive, quick colonization onto open, disturbed sites was responsible for the success of angiosperms. However, evidence now suggests that there were conifers that occupied that niche before there were any angiosperms. In the heyday of conifers, almost everything seemed possible. Are we going to discover an aquatic conifer next, or even a carnivorous one? It seems no longer wise to rule that out beforehand.

Reconstruction of the herbaceous ruderal conifer *Aethophyllum stipulare* from the Early Triassic *Voltzia* sandstone of the Vosges Mountains in France. From Rothwell et al. (2000)

All through the Jurassic and during the first part of the Lower Cretaceous the conifers remained the dominant tall, forest-building trees. Cycads and tree ferns could attain tree size, too, and there were *Ginkgo* trees (Ginkgoaceae), but they played a minor part in most forests and woodlands. A rough estimate has given a figure of 20,000 species of conifers for the Jurassic (Debazac 1964), contrasting with a mere 630 existing at the present time. The genus *Araucaria* occurred widely, both in the Northern Hemi-

Araucaria columnaris, a species restricted to the southeastern coast and some islands in New Caledonia, illustrates a habit of an araucaria just as likely for the Jurassic as the more familiar monkey-puzzle tree, *Araucaria araucana*.

sphere (Laurasia) and in the Southern Hemisphere (Gondwana), to where the last remnants are now restricted. Go to New Caledonia to obtain an impression of the landscape-forming importance of these architectural conifers during the Jurassic. Of a total of 19 *Araucaria* species, 13 occur there today. In otherwise undoubtedly accurate pictorial reconstructions of dinosaurs in the Jurassic landscape, the araucarias seldom fail to make an appearance, but they always look like the monkey-puzzle tree, *Araucaria araucana*. The araucarias of New Caledonia are rather different in their habits, and perhaps painters of Jurassic landscapes should take notice of these. Finding only fragments, we cannot learn much from the fossil record about the habit of large trees. Therefore, we take to the examples of their relatives that live today, which may not always be the trees we are most familiar with. We know that conifers in the Southern Hemisphere rarely look like the firs (*Abies*) and spruces (*Picea*) Europeans equate with conifers, the familiar Christmas-tree shape. There is no reason to believe that Mesozoic conifers looked like Christmas trees, either. Firs and spruces did not appear until the very end of the era or even later and then only in a few locations. Instead, the Mesozoic landscape would have been dominated by huge trees, such as *Sequoia* (a close relative, *Austrosequoia wintonensis*, occurred in Australia during the Cretaceous), *Taxodium, Podocarpus, Dacrydium*, and *Araucaria*, and numerous smaller coniferous trees and shrubs. Cycads were common, as were ginkgos and ferns, of course, including tree ferns. Later in the Lower Cretaceous, angiosperms such as magnolias appeared in the forests, while water lilies had begun to add splashes of flower colour to the dark waters of ponds.

Many people assume that the rise of the angiosperms meant the near demise of the gymnosperms. Is this true? Does the fossil record give us that impression? Let's investigate this doom scenario a little closer and see if we can agree or must disagree. We do not know exactly when the angiosperms evolved or from what kind of gymnospermous ancestor, but we do know that they became more abundant and therefore noticeable in the fossil record from the middle of the Lower Cretaceous (Barremian to Aptian) onwards. That is about 125–120 Ma, with most of the extant conifer families at their optimum in addition to the family Cheirolepidiaceae, which we have seen may even have contained salt-tolerant shrubs and trees. At first, angiosperms remained rare, but within a few million years they became abundant. Was there a decline of conifers at this time? From an ecological point of view, where plants must compete for light, space, and water, this must seem self-evident. If angiosperms were on the increase, unless more space became available at the same time, this could only have happened at the expense of non-angiosperms, conifers likely among them. A shift in habitat preferences must have occurred during the Cretaceous, whereby conifers gave way to angiosperms in those environments where the latter had a competitive advantage. Most conifers are light demanding and will not grow well in the shade of broad-leaved trees. The ecology of conifers will be discussed later, but it is obvious that conifers had to give way and lose their dominance gradually to the ever-multiplying and ever-diversifying angiosperms. On the other hand, with a nearly global warm or mild climate, almost all the land surface was available for abundant plant growth. Therefore, those

Opposite: *Araucaria araucana*, the monkey-puzzle tree of Chile and Argentina, always serves as the example of araucaria trees in paintings of dinosaurs in their environment. We do not know if all Jurassic araucarias looked like this or more like *Araucaria columnaris*. Photograph by C. N. Page

habitats most suitable for conifers were not at a premium, especially in mountains, on nutrient-deficient soils, and in any habitats that remained relatively open to sunlight reaching the ground. Some of the greatest mountain systems known to have existed, the American Cordilleras and the Himalayan chain and its ramifications, originated in the Tertiary. Thus, we do not see a decline in the numbers of conifer genera and families through the Upper Cretaceous and Palaeogene. Intriguingly, there is no evidence of an effect on conifer diversity of the mass extinction event at the so-called K–T boundary, which purportedly wiped out the dinosaurs at the end of the Cretaceous 65 Ma. Conifers were no longer the only tall, forest-forming trees—and in many forests angiosperms had largely replaced them—but they were still very abundant and diverse. In the later part of the Tertiary, the Neogene, that situation was going to change.

13 Decline to the Present

AXEL HEIBERG ISLAND *is a bleak place. It is a large island just to the west of the even larger Ellesmere Island, both without permanent settlements, in the Canadian High Arctic around 80°N. You cannot get there by ship, as the waters around the island are permanently covered in ice, with only brief, local summer leads opening. The land looks totally barren at first sight, a veritable cold desert. There is some plant growth, but the plants are all in miniature and very sparse, barely sustaining small herds of wandering musk oxen, which in some years do not take the trouble to come up to this far northern place at all. Everything is permanently frozen a few centimetres below the surface even in summer. Despite these conditions, Axel Heiberg Island is famous among palaeobotanists for its plant fossils buried in the Eocene Buchanan Lake formation.*

▲ ▲ ▲

If you went back 45 million years ago (Ma) to the Middle Eocene and paid an imaginary visit to this northern land, a totally different scene would unfold. At the Buchanan Lake you would be in a forested swamp stretching far in all directions, with some moderately high mountains seen in the distance. The temperature in summer would be warm, the air humid. An incredibly rich mixed forest would surround you, with ferns, gymnosperms, and angiosperms. You would see one species of *Ginkgo*, six genera of Pinaceae (*Larix*, *Picea*, *Pinus*, *Tsuga*, *Keteleeria*, and *Pseudolarix*), seven genera of Cupressaceae (*Metasequoia*, *Sequoia*, *Thuja*, *Taxodium*, *Glyptostrobus*, *Chamaecyparis*, and *Taiwania*), and some unidentified taxodiaceous conifers. The swamp forests would be dominated by the deciduous conifers *Metasequoia* and *Glyptostrobus* on the wetter, peaty sites, with horsetails (*Equisetum*) and ferns (*Osmunda*) covering the forest floor. Forests of drier sites on higher ground would be more diverse, with a greater participation of angiosperms, such as birches (*Betula*), alders (*Alnus*), and members of Fagaceae and Juglandaceae, mixed among the various conifers. Spruces (*Picea*) and pines (*Pinus*) would be growing at a greater distance in the uplands.

What was the climate here in the Eocene? Many of the nearest living relatives of the fossil species on Axel Heiberg Island occur in virtually frost-free environments. Although probably not situated at 80°N, this locality would still have been in the High Arctic above 70°N, with several months of darkness in winter and perpetual daylight in summer. Despite the dark winters, severe winter frosts would have been rare (McIver and Basinger 1999), and the climate was mesothermic and moist. Such conditions (except the winter darkness) and forests are now found around 30°N in the southeastern parts of China and the United States, where indeed most of the living relatives of these Eocene fossil trees grow.

Although the Buchanan Lake formation on Axel Heiberg Island is very rich, with often exquisitely well-preserved remains, many other localities have yielded similar fossils from the Tertiary. Another High Arctic locality is Spitsbergen in the Svalbard archipelago north of Scandinavia, where conifers occurred from the Early Cretaceous to the Eocene (Florin 1963). Conifers occurred in Greenland during these times as well. The world was still in the long hot-house climate phase, and forests extended almost to the poles. Antarctica, now covered under several kilometres of ice, was forested at least in most of the localities where nonmarine sedimentary rock of this time is exposed above the ice at present and plant fossils can and are being found. Many of the now-relict conifer genera had very wide distributions, although by the end of the Cretaceous a division between northern (Laurasian) and southern (Gondwanan) floras

The seed cone and foliage of *Keteleeria davidiana* (Pinaceae), a Chinese conifer that had a wide distribution during the Tertiary

was well established and would remain with the drifting apart of the present continents. Examples are *Sequoia, Sequoiadendron, Glyptostrobus,* and *Taxodium,* abundant in Europe and North America until the Pliocene; *Metasequoia,* in North America and Asia and across the Arctic until the Miocene; and *Sciadopitys,* in Europe until the Pliocene. In the Pinaceae, genera such as *Cathaya, Keteleeria,* and *Pseudolarix,* now (very) limited in eastern Asia, were widespread in North America, Europe, and Asia in the Tertiary. The conifer flora of Europe during the Tertiary must have been amazing; all the extant 11 genera in the family Pina-

The clustered pollen cones of *Pseudolarix amabilis.* From the Late Jurassic to the Pliocene (150–15 Ma), this unique genus and species in the Pinaceae occurred across Eurasia and North America.

ceae have been found there, as well as most of the Northern Hemisphere genera in the Cupressaceae. The fossil record from the European Tertiary demonstrates a diversity of pines (*Pinus*) comparable to those of the eastern United States or California today.

Global warming on a huge scale occurred after the end of the Cretaceous, with humid tropical or subtropical conditions extending between latitudes 70°N and 70°S. Many conifer genera, such as the ones just mentioned, thrived under these optimal climate regimes, reaching their greatest spread and species diversity in the Eocene, one of the warmest periods in the history of life. Others, such as the pines (*Pinus*), had greater difficulty competing with the angiosperms and retreated to mountains and the High Arctic

The seed cone and foliage of the Japanese umbrella pine (*Sciadopitys verticillata*), a unique conifer classified in its own family Sciadopityaceae, which was still abundant in the Tertiary forests of Europe but is now a rarity restricted to Japan. Photograph by C. N. Page

(Millar 1993). Orogeny (the building of mountains) created many habitats where angiosperms were at a disadvantage, and conifers have largely retreated to these refugia, particularly in the tropics. In lowlands, conifers became increasingly associated with marginal habitats like swamps; many Tertiary conifer remains are found in peat turned to lignite or in deposits from sluggish rivers flowing through these swamps. (There is some element of circularity in this reasoning that I should point out. Fossils are almost always found in sediments deposited by or in water; it is almost their only chance of nondestructive rapid burial. For terrestrial organisms, including almost all plants, this means there is a strong bias in the fossil record towards those that lived near water. With an increasing distance from it, the chance of getting into the fossil record rapidly decreases. Our knowledge of upland floras of the geological past is therefore much more limited than our knowledge of what grew on the banks of lowland rivers and their deltas and in swamps.)

Some conifer families that evolved, probably from cupressaceous ancestors, in the Upper Cretaceous of Europe still persisted during the Palaeogene. The family Geinitziaceae has been recently erected (Kunzmann 1999) for evergreen conifers with both scale-like and needle-like leaves in a helical arrangement and with oblong seed cones with peltate scales and small, flat, and round seeds with a narrow circular wing. The species *Geinitzia formosa* from the Upper Cretaceous (Santonian) of Germany had long seed cones with up to 90 scales. According to Kunzmann, this family stood morphologically between Taxodiaceae and Cupressaceae. The species of Taxodiaceae are basal members of Cupressaceae, and it is likely that the Geinitziaceae were derived from an extinct species that would fit there taxonomically (see the evolutionary tree in chapter 9). The Geinitziaceae flourished in western Eurasia but became extinct at the end of the

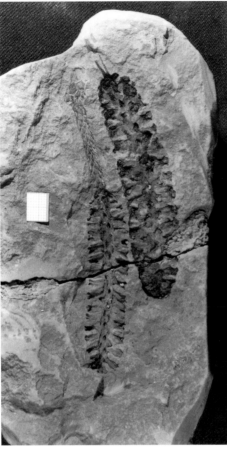

Fossil seed cones of *Geinitzia formosa* (Geinitziaceae) from the Upper Cretaceous (Santonian) Heidelberg formation near Quedlinburg, Germany. Photograph by Lutz Kunzmann

Phyllocladus aspleniifolius, in Australia known as celery pine, has transformed its branchlets to act as leaves and virtually lost its true leaves.

Palaeocene. The Doliostrobaceae had similar foliage, but the seed cones of *Doliostrobus taxiformis* had numerous cupped scales terminating in a cusp and broke up at maturity; each scale had one or two seeds with an asymmetrical wing. This family probably arose from a still more basal member of the Cupressaceae, but its species only appeared towards the end of the Cretaceous (Maastrichtian) in Europe and disappeared during the Oligocene about 40 Ma.

In the Southern Hemisphere, Phyllocladaceae evolved from a podocarpaceous ancestor at the end of the Cretaceous. The genus *Phyllocladus* is the only genus, and its most conspicuous character is the transformation of branchlets into flattened, leaf-like phylloclades ("leaf-branches") that contain chlorophyll and take on the function of leaves. The true leaves are reduced to tiny scales, which soon fall off. The small cones appear on the edges of the phylloclades or at their base and develop only a single seed partly surrounded by a soft aril (as in *Taxus*). The species of this genus spread throughout Australia, New Zealand, possibly New Caledonia, and into Malesia from New Guinea to Borneo and the Philippines and perhaps beyond. With the drying of Australia, *Phyllocladus* retreated to cooler and wetter Tasmania and New Zealand. If the genus occurred in New Caledonia it disappeared there later, and in Malesia it retreated to the high mountains. At present there are only four *Phyllocladus* species left.

The cold came on the sly, probably sometime near the end of the Oligocene. It started far away in Antarctica. This polar continent had now become isolated—the last landmass to separate from it was the southeastern corner of Australia with

The European larch, *Larix decidua*, still common in the Alps and Carpathians of Europe, is one of the few conifers to have survived the ice ages there.

Tasmania. As the Southern Ocean widened, a cold current developed that encircled Antarctica and blocked currents of warm ocean water coming south from the equatorial regions along the western margins of the Pacific and the widening Atlantic Ocean. Antarctica had been over the South Pole for millions of years, and the long winter nights now became really cold. The forests could not cope with the dark and the cold at the same time and disappeared to be replaced by tundra vegetation. When winter snow on the mountains no longer melted away in summer, it accumulated and glaciers formed. The refrigeration of Antarctica began about 15 Ma in the Miocene. Glaciers became icecaps, and by 10 Ma the continent was virtually frozen. Continental movements in the north enclosed the Arctic Ocean and blocked the access of warmer ocean water there. Because there was no continent over the North Pole, however, the refrigeration took longer and only became serious about 2 Ma, with the first formation of local icecaps in Greenland, Canada, and Scandinavia. The world had entered another ice-house phase. The broad vegetation belts from polar to tropical zones that we are familiar with—tundra, coniferous forest, broad-leaved deciduous forest, steppe, desert, and tropical forest—developed, most notably in the Northern Hemisphere where landmasses are widest longitudinally. The global space for trees became reduced, and as a consequence trees retreated. Few conifers could cope with long, cold, and snowy winters, which is why the great conifer-dominated forests of Canada and Siberia today have so few species.

When the extensive glaciations began in Europe about 1 Ma, the effects on tree species were disastrous. Whereas in North America and eastern Asia trees could migrate south during glacial periods, a similar escape route was blocked by mountains in Eu-

The growing cones of *Larix decidua* are quite colourful in early summer; later they turn dull brown.

rope. There, the glaciers expanded from the north as well as from the south, and few species found routes of escape to refugia in lands around the Mediterranean Sea. The ice ages were interrupted by warmer periods (interglacials) when the icecaps melted again (not in Antarctica), but these lasted on average only a tenth as long as the cold periods. Every successive interglacial saw fewer species of trees in Europe, and nearly all the conifer species that had thrived here until the end of the Tertiary disappeared. The exceptions that held out in Europe outside the Mediterranean Basin were a few species of pines (*Pinus cembra, P. mugo, P. nigra, P. pinaster, P. sylvestris*, and *P. uncinata*), one species of larch (*Larix decidua*), one of spruce (*Picea abies*), one of fir (*Abies alba*), all in Pinaceae, a juniper (*Juniperus communis*; Cupressaceae), and the common yew (*Taxus baccata*; Taxaceae). From perhaps the richest region for conifers in the temperate zones, Europe had become the poorest. The Mediterranean Basin, which includes the northern coast of Africa, fared somewhat better. It developed a climate with cool, moist winters and hot, dry summers. During the glacial periods the hot summers moved south, but the climate stayed tolerable for trees. Here some species found refuge and others evolved and adapted to the climate that bears the region's name.

The thinning of the ranks during the Pleistocene, the period of glaciations and short warm intervals, happened elsewhere as well. Complete extinctions were less common than in Europe, and often a species managed to hang on somewhere. That is how the sequoias became restricted to California, the dawn redwood to a few localities in China, and why the Wollemi pine (*Wollemia nobilis*) exists only in a steep sandstone canyon in New South Wales.

The Ecology
of Conifers

14 Conquering Armies and Vast Empires

IN AUGUST OF 1983, *my friend Pieter Bogaers and I floated down the Porcupine River to study the vegetation along this slow river in the far north of Yukon Territory and Alaska. Our journey in a small inflatable boat brought us from the tiny village of Old Crow to the mighty Yukon River just below the Alaskan village of Fort Yukon. In addition to a month's provisions, we were surrounded by plant presses, equipment to mark out transect lines and plots, and camping gear as well. We were travelling through uninhabited country for 300 km (190 mi), as we flew in from Fort Yukon in a small chartered airplane, but we would cover many kilometres more on the river as it meandered through the Yukon Flats. The trip entailed many days of hard rowing to make some progress, because head winds almost neutralized the effect of the current that should have taken us downstream more easily. We had no outboard motor, for we were not in a hurry and we did not want the din of an engine to disturb the tranquil peace of the wilderness.*

▲ ▲ ▲

The boreal conifer forest surrounded us on all sides. We went to the Porcupine River to study how the vegetation develops, after disturbance by the river, back to the conifer forest, going through phases of pioneer herbs on sand bars, willow thickets, poplar woods, and mixed forest. As the river meanders, it digs away forest at cut banks on the outer bends and deposits the gravel, sand, and clay on the inner bends. Here, pioneer plants become established, preparing the new soil for shrubs and trees. As a routine, every morning we rowed, then stopped for lunch and a swim in the river, after which we looked for a suitable location to record a vegetation plot or two or lay out a transect. In the evening we camped on the shore, taking precautions with our food against the omnipresent bears. At this latitude, just within the Arctic Circle, we had almost 24 hours of daylight, so we could make long days and short nights. Over the month-long trip we saw only a single conifer species, the white spruce (*Picea glauca*), which forms the conifer forest in the Yukon Flats.

It is hard to imagine in August, with the river so low and tranquil, but in May and June, when the snow has melted and the ice has broken up, this river rises 10-fold to a raging current carrying hundreds of uprooted trees along. On the inner bends, Pieter and I found driftwood lodged halfway up sizeable poplars (*Populus balsamifera*) or deep into the open woodland far from the summer bed of the river. The conifers begin where flooding no longer occurs, at first appearing among the poplars and willows, then taking over completely. The white spruce in this area does not grow very large; a 20-m (65-ft) tree with 50-cm (20-in) diameter is a big tree. The winters in the Yukon Flats are long and cold, the summers brief, dry, and hot. Away from the rivers, natural fires from lightning are the disturbing factor, setting the vegetation back to a pioneer stage. This plant community then develops differently from what we find on the river floodplain but eventually leads to the same spruce forest. There the conifers grow even slower than on the better-drained sandy soils of the river. If there is waterlogging from permafrost, peat may form slowly, or shallow lakes develop. On the Yukon Flats peat is rare but lakes are numerous. The summers are too short for luxuriant growth of aquatic and semi-aquatic plants and too dry for the growth of *Sphagnum* moss well above the water table. The absence of peaty swamps is probably one reason why Pieter and I did not see black spruce (*Picea mariana*) or tamarack (*Larix laricina*) away from the river near the lakes. But we did not explore very far in that direction, it must be admitted. Only a little distance away from the river, the spruce forest becomes nearly impenetrable with fallen trees, tangled shrubs, and abandoned river channels, and it is impossible to see more than 10 m (33 ft) ahead at any time. Pieter and I once spent four hours in an attempt to return to the river and our camp, after giving up reaching a lake that was on the map less than 1.6 km (1 mi) from its northern bank.

This dense growth of a single conifer species covering vast areas is characteristic of the northern taiga. In the north, the taiga begins where the tundra ends; to the south, it merges with deciduous broad-leaved forests, montane coniferous forests, or steppes. In North America the broad-leaved forests are in the east, the montane conifer forests in the west, and the prairies in between. In Eurasia it is a bit more complicated, although the general pattern is the same. The taiga is not entirely homogeneous. It is interrupted by lakes and swamps and dissected by large rivers. Furthermore, the constituent species are different on the two continents, although closely related. The genera involved are even fewer than the species: *Abies* (one species on each continent), *Larix* (three species), *Picea* (four or five species), and *Pinus* (four or five species), all in the

The only conifer to be seen along the rivers in the Yukon Flats of Alaska is white spruce (*Picea glauca*), shown here on a cut bank above the Porcupine River.

Pieter Bogaers samples a plot in pioneer vegetation dominated by young willows (*Salix interior*) on the flood-plain of the Porcupine River. Eventually the white spruce will return here.

Laying out a transect for sampling through vegetation in which white spruce (Picea glauca) has become well established, but which still shows its pioneer floodplain past

family Pinaceae. One or two conifer species may occur in the shrub layer: common juniper (*Juniperus communis*, Cupressaceae) and the dwarf Siberian pine or kiedrovnik (*Pinus pumila*) in eastern Siberia. In some areas two or three of these conifers may occur together, but very often there is only a single conifer species forming the forest, as in the Yukon Flats. The species will change going from one type of substrate to another, especially in relation to drainage. The two species of *Abies* require well-drained sandy soils; the other genera have species adapted to both well-drained soils and waterlogged soils. All these conifers require some preparation of open soils by other plants and the establishment of mycorrhizal fungi, but after this they invade and conquer, tolerating no other trees than a few scattered birches (*Betula*) or poplars (*Populus tremula* in Eurasia, *P. tremuloides* in North America).

The taiga environment is dynamic, with natural disturbance often covering large areas. I once travelled on the Alaska Highway in the north of British Columbia and to the left and right of the road saw nothing but burnt forest for two hours. It had been mostly lodgepole pine (*Pinus contorta*) now destroyed by fire, with some white spruce in several places less completely burnt. Pines burn like torches, the flames raging through the canopy at high speed, leaving the stems standing like black sticks covering hills and plains as far as the eye can see. It looked very dismal, and from the point of view of a forester it was—there was little left of value to harvest. But ecologically, there was nothing wrong at all.

Disturbance by fire and flooding is an integral part of the taiga ecosystem. Storms are rare, but outbursts of defoliating insect plagues, often associated with freak weather

Lodgepole pine (*Pinus contorta*) has a well-chosen vernacular name. This conifer was used by the northern Plains tribes to build tepees or lodges, the familiar conical family tents with poles sticking out at the top.

A·Farjon del.

Dwarf Siberian pine (*Pinus pumila*) grows as a shrub in the taiga of eastern Siberia, while it forms extensive thickets above the tree line in mountains.

conditions, can lay waste to the forest as well. Few spots remain undisturbed for longer than a century. On the Porcupine River, Pieter Bogaers and I found maximum ages of trees to be around 120 years, and most trees in the taiga are much younger than that. Opposing the destruction is the capacity of the shrubs and trees of the taiga to spread quickly and widely, the conifers included. Willows and poplars have extremely effective mechanisms to keep their seeds airborne for effective dispersal. Conifers go a little slower, as they need to wait a while to let the pioneers do their work. However, all taiga conifers have small, light seeds with effective wings of which they can produce great quantities. These seeds do not rest on the soil or in the litter but germinate quickly. Within a few decades the conifer forest is coming back from seed, not from resprouting, as is more commonly the strategy in fire-prone vegetation types at warmer latitudes. None of the taiga conifers can be coppiced. In fact, few conifers can be coppiced, and all of these grow in warmer climates.

It was this capacity to conquer new land in great numbers that enabled these conifers to return and occupy the vast northern regions during the relatively short interglacial phases in the Pleistocene. Repeatedly pushed south by advancing icecaps and growing seasons even too short for them, the conifers returned each time the land again became free of the ice cover. Glacial till is an excellent substrate for plant growth, and many others would have tried this new space, too. But, as we have seen, the conditions are tough. The short growing season of the taiga requires fast growth to attain maturity within a few years, the vagaries of weather and of fire opportunism. In the far north, permafrost severely limits what trees can grow where, if any at all. During the Pleistocene, with numerous ice ages and short warmer phases, a great winnowing took place that left few species adapted to these conditions. Those that did survive formed the conquering armies of conifers that built the vast empires of the taiga forests in Eurasia and North America. These are the most extensive forests on Earth.

On another trip, I visited a remarkable outlier of the taiga in the middle of the Kamchatka Peninsula in the far east of Russia. Here, the mosquitoes attack in dense swarms. The forest floor is soft as a sponge with thick cushions of mosses and lichens. Small,

Taiga (boreal conifer forest) on the Kamchatka Peninsula in the far east of Russia

pretty flowers such as those of *Linnaea borealis* and the miniature orchid *Goodyera repens* protrude from the mosses. In this place grow a species of Asian spruce, *Picea jezoensis*; the larch *Larix gmelinii*; and the birch *Betula platyphylla*. Squirrels make chirping rackets, and the huge footprints of bear are evident. This stretch of taiga is small, only 200 km (125 mi) in length and much less wide. To the north of it stretches the Siberian tundra, to the south are only birch forests, and to the east and west are volcanic mountains and then the ocean. This little patch of taiga must have become isolated but survived during the migrations of conifers.

Does this place already have a distinct species of conifer? Isolation means speciation, given enough time. Well, there is a claim about a distinct species of fir (*Abies gracilis*) that would be an endemic of Kamchatka. It is known from one locality, but this is not in the taiga. In fact, *A. gracilis* grows in an unlikely place on the coast of the Pacific Ocean. A small grove with densely growing trees is all that was ever found of this species. It is not very distinct from the Sachalin fir (*Abies sachalinensis*), but that species, or any other fir for that matter, grows far away to the south. Is it another relict of the Pleistocene or even Pliocene? Some believe so, but others whisper that this fir was perhaps planted by people who sailed to Kamchatka from Sachalin. I am inclined to that opinion myself because this population would be azonal, well outside its climatic zone, but we need to do some serious research to answer the question how it got there. Even the taiga, so boring to many, may still have a few coniferous surprises in store.

15 The Fortresses of Poverty

ON THE FLAT, FEATURELESS ISLAND *of Great Abaco in the Bahamas, the sands are as white as the paper this book has been printed on. Here and there the old coral reefs protrude, weathered and barely recognizable. They are a bit greyer, like old skeletons. No plant could grow on this, it would seem. Where are the soil, the water, the nutrients? Yet, a pine forest exists on Great Abaco, and the trees are moderately tall, to 20 m (65 ft). True, the forest is rather open, in places more like a savannah, with grasses, shrubs, and a small palm (Sabal palmetto) as ground cover. The pine is Pinus caribaea var. bahamensis, the only substantial tree that grows naturally in the Bahamas. It is common on most of the islands, as well as on the Turks Caicos Islands a bit further south.*

▲ ▲ ▲

Along the coast of Mendocino County, California, lies a series of marine terraces carved by the waves of the sea since the early Pleistocene. Beyond them the forested slopes rise to the interior, sending down streams that traverse the terraces. The higher terraces have extremely impoverished, highly acidic podzolic soils and support a sparse vegetation. The two most common trees on these terraces are conifers, Gowen cypress (*Cupressus goveniana*) and lodgepole pine (*Pinus contorta*). Both grow extremely slowly and do not attain heights greater than 1–2 m (3–7 ft), yet they produce cones like their large cousins on the hills nearby. The conifers on these terraces were considered separate species in the past because of their consistent dwarfish habit, including smaller leaves or cones. But they are just ecotypes, forms caused by the extremely meagre supply of nutrients available from these leached sandy soils. This dwarfing is especially apparent in the Gowen cypress; in some localities where flooding happens frequently, the dwarf suddenly becomes 30–45 m (100–150 ft) tall, with a diameter at breast height of 1–2.5 m (3–8 ft), but a columnar crown. Organic matter accumulates in such localities, while it is very low on sites where the trees form a pygmy forest. In its other locale, the Monterey Peninsula, *C. goveniana* grows on similar but better-drained acidic soils and attains normal proportions.

The weathered peridotite and ironstone rocks of the southern part of New Caledonia have formed oxidized, ultramafic soils poor in nutrients necessary for plant growth and often extremely toxic. High concentrations of iron, manganese, nickel, chrome, cobalt, and other metals give the soil in many places a cast-iron appearance, with shades of red and brown dominating. Streams such as the Rivière des Lacs and its tributaries are laden with poorly dissolved metals and often have a milky turquoise colour. This plant-unfriendly kind of soil supports an astonishing 40 species of conifer, of which 28 are totally restricted to it. The dwarfish forest that grows here is aptly named *maquis minier* ("mining scrubland"). The small trees often have sparsely branched, candelabra-shaped crowns, both angiosperms and gymnosperms alike. They grow slowly and

Conifer woodland dominated by *Dacrydium araucarioides* on ultramafic soil full of toxic metals on the Plaine des Lacs, New Caledonia

stand well apart; in between are few plants, among which ferns and sedges are common but grasses rare. The New Caledonian conifers must be well adapted to these extraordinary conditions. On the Plaine des Lacs, plantations with pines (*Pinus*) have done poorly, with low or often no yield at all. Even for pines these soils are too depauperate and perhaps too toxic.

The Bat Dai Son limestone mountain system is located in the northwestern part of Ha Giang Province in northern Vietnam. It is a typical karst plateau of late Palaeozoic limestone that has been deeply dissected by millions of years of erosion. Numerous steep, columnar mountains rise above intricate valley systems with underground drainage. The limestone on the surface is hard as marble and weathered into numerous knife-edged ridges and sharp pinnacles. The deep red-brown soil only occurs in the valley bottoms and on some less-steep lower slopes. Where these sites are not used for agriculture, they are clothed in large-leaved, evergreen tropical forest completely dominated by angiosperms, some large palms among them. Only small-leaved trees and shrubs cling to the steep rock faces, narrow ridges, and summits. Among these are the 10 species of conifer known from the area, one of which is the newly discovered and described genus and species *Xanthocyparis vietnamensis* I mentioned in chapter 4. The largest tree on the ridges and summits is a conifer, *Pseudotsuga sinensis*, related to the Douglas fir, but much smaller and with a very different growth habit. All trees grow more or less stunted here, with broad, flat crowns, their trunks rooted in fissures and holes in the rocks. They are covered with epiphytes: mosses, lichens, ferns, and espe-

Pinus balfouriana subsp. *austrina*, the southern form of foxtail pine, on Mineral Peak in Sequoia National Park in the Sierra Nevada of California

cially orchids; these plants also cover the limestone rocks. There is ample moisture here, but no soil.

On a long ridge below Mineral Peak, at 3100 m (10,150 ft) in the southern Sierra Nevada of California, there is a pine wood. It is the most beautiful stand of conifers I have ever seen. The impressive, bright orange trunks are ornamented with squamate patterns like the back of an alligator, above them sturdy branches are clothed in deep green foliage looking like thousands of squirrel tails, all set against the bluest of blue skies. The purplish green cones are very resinous; flushes of young needles, lighter green than the older ones, tip the branches. These are foxtail pines (*Pinus balfouriana*), and they are the only trees around. In fact, hardly any other plants grow here, only some patches of a ground-hugging

Bark of *Pinus balfouriana* subsp. *austrina*, foxtail pine

species of manzanita (*Arctostaphylos*, Ericaceae). Almost everywhere the ground is covered in bare stones, broken by repeated heating in the sun and freezing at night. Again there is no soil, no humus, no litter. The winter snows must be deep here and last long, if not blown away by gales. Undoubtedly, the larger trees are all more than 1000 years old, and some may be twice that. The foxtail pines grow very slowly, and there must be many a season in which the weather hardly allows for any growth at all.

These examples of conifers with what seems to be a preference for localities with poor conditions for general plant growth are not exceptions but representative of a common trend. Conifers predominantly occur on soils or in climates that are suboptimal for plant growth. However, as we know well from plantation forestry and horticulture, there is no evidence that conifers prefer (grow better on) nutrient-poor soils or harsh climates. Many species that are in their natural habitat restricted to these poor conditions grow exceedingly well if planted on fertile soils. Monterey or radiata pine (*Pinus radiata*) has been planted on a large scale, especially in the Southern Hemisphere, and is one of the most productive trees in the industry. Yet its natural habitat is the same podzolic sand that supports the two cypresses *Cupressus goveniana* and *C. macrocarpa*. It appears then that conifers, in order to survive in nature, have adapted to these poor sites. It is the strategy of evasion. Perhaps most conifer species have adopted this strategy, but it finds its most extreme expression on these pockets of rock and soil that have little else to offer than a substrate to hold onto. What are these conifers trying to escape from that they have adapted to put up with such poor conditions? The answer is competition from angiosperms, in particular fast-growing, large-leaved herbs, shrubs, and trees.

Many studies about productivity in trees have shown that conifers can be more productive than broad-leaved trees (angiosperms) in terms of tons of carbon or wood produced per hectare. This is despite the fact that per unit the leaves and wood vessels of angiosperms are more efficient in their respective tasks than the needles and tracheids of conifers. Wood vessels transport water more efficiently, and the greater surface and more elaborate venation of angiosperm leaves allow higher rates of assimilation. How then can conifers, at least some of them, grow faster and taller? It is done by slow accumulation of total leaf surface. Evergreen conifers retain several cohorts (representing seasons of growth) of leaves, which eventually give a much greater total surface of foliage than that of the leafiest angiosperm. But conifers are indeed slow to attain this, and there lies one of their crucial disadvantages. It is not the inability to eventually outgrow angiosperms, but the slow start in comparison to many angiosperms that has driven the conifers into the fortresses of poverty. It was long assumed that the evolution leading to weedy herbaceous angiosperms caused the decline of conifers. This may still be true, even though we now know that this experiment has been performed by conifers, too. In chapter 12 we met with the Triassic herbaceous conifer *Aethophyllum stipulare*, which became extinct before angiosperms evolved. Perhaps there were other ruderal, weedy conifers, but if so, they have not succeeded to the present time and it was indeed only an experiment in evolutionary terms.

As we saw in chapter 14, on the floodplain of the Porcupine River the white spruce (*Picea glauca*) only appears after the establishment of pioneer vegetation dominated by angiosperms. The white spruce is not quick enough; it arrives later and grows initially slower. If it were not for the harsh climate with the very short growing season, this conifer would probably not succeed at all. Angiosperms, because they grow faster in the early phases of vegetation restoration after disturbance, would permanently exclude conifers. Grasses are particularly effective and have excluded conifers from the steppes in Asia and the Americas and probably from the savannahs of Africa. That conifers can grow well there is again demonstrated by plantation forestry. Overgrazing and fire prevention, which suppress the grasses, can lead to the return of conifers; this happens at present with junipers (*Juniperus*) on the rangelands of the American West. However, if the site conditions are poor for plant growth, the conifers have a natural chance. Once they are mature, conifers will persist because they now can compete with any angiosperm. The ecologist W. J. Bond has compared this strategy with the fable of the tortoise and the hare. The two started off together, but soon the hare was so far ahead that he lost sight of the tortoise. He thought he would wait a while and rest, upon which he fell fast asleep. Meanwhile, the tortoise plodded on and in time reached the finish, after which the hare woke up to find he had lost the race. Unfortunately for gymnosperms, most angiosperms keep running unless they are handicapped.

This still leaves the question of how conifers overcame the handicaps of nutrient-poor soils and short growing seasons. What are the adaptations that have allowed conifers to prosper under these limiting conditions? And why have angiosperms not developed these in like measure? We will look at the soil conditions first. A plant uses its root system to take up water from the soil in which minerals, among which the necessary nutrients such as nitrogen, phosphorus, and potassium, are dissolved. Root systems can be very extensive and provide as much plant surface underground as the crown with leaves provides aboveground. Yet, in nutrient-poor substrates extensive root systems are still not enough. The surface must be enlarged to take in enough of the very little nutrients that become available from weathering of rock and bacterial activity decomposing organic matter. This is done through the symbiosis of plant roots with mycorrhizal fungi (*myco*, fungus; *rhizo*, root). Fungi have extensive underground networks of hyphae or fine fungal threads. The hyphae of mycorrhizal fungi form numerous connections with the tips of roots, replacing the hair roots, the smallest roots of a shrub or tree responsible for water and nutrient uptake. These fungi greatly extend the root length and surface—in some experimental trials with pine seedlings by 10,000 times. The hyphae handle the task of taking up water and nutrients from the hair roots. This results in greatly increased growth rates of the seedlings, despite the fact that the fungus takes something in return, the biochemical building blocks (molecules) for growth. It leaves more than enough for the tree to grow faster than without fungi. Almost all conifers, and some other plants such as orchids, have mycorrhizae on which they totally depend. Although mycorrhizal symbiosis also occurs in angiosperm trees such as birches, beeches, and oaks, it is absent or poorly developed in many others. Generally, in fertile soils mycorrhizal colonization is much reduced, so that most angiosperms did not evolve the ability to form these symbiotic relationships. We can see lots of mushrooms and toadstools (fungal fruiting bodies) in forests on fertile soils, but they are mostly not mycorrhizal fungi.

Schrenk's spruce (*Picea schrenkiana*), a forest-forming conifer in the high mountains of Kyrgyzstan

The other adaptation that has allowed conifers to survive in sites with nutrient-poor soils and short growing seasons is their small, evergreen leaves. The larger, more effective leaves of angiosperms come with disadvantages. They are excellent food for numerous animals, especially insects. Angiosperms' leaves expose so much delicate surface to the air in order to make maximum use of the sun's energy during the growing season. In the tropics and part of the subtropics, that is year-round; however, in the current ice-house climate, at higher latitudes there is a winter with frosts. We all know the problems with late frosts and trees flushing into leaves too early. Angiosperms at these latitudes have become deciduous; they drop their leaves in the autumn and shut down for the winter. Some northern conifers—or formerly northern conifers—are deciduous, too. This may have evolved not as an adaptation to cold but to lack of light in polar latitudes. Some larches (*Larix*) still occur within the Arctic Circle, whereas other deciduous conifers, such as *Metasequoia*, *Pseudolarix*, and *Taxodium*, have migrated south. The southernmost deciduous species, *Taxodium mucronatum* of Mexico and Guatemala, is only occasionally deciduous in connection with droughts. Most conifers, however, are evergreen and they retain several cohorts of leaves. These older leaves in the conifers of high latitudes and high elevations are resistant to frost. As long as there is daylight and water can flow, the leaves keep working, and that gives these conifers an edge over competing angiosperms. It is again the parable of the tortoise and the hare: by plodding on through the cold winters, the conifer wins the race. Therefore, conifers still dominate the forests of high latitudes, especially in the Northern Hemisphere, and of most of the high mountains.

16 Outlive Your Neighbour and Take His Property

ALTHOUGH IT IS THE MOST *widely applied strategy, not all conifers are escapists. As we have seen in the previous chapter, the critical time for conifers in the competition race with angiosperms is in the early stages of the life of a tree, from seedling to sapling and young tree. Once the forest canopy has been attained, most tree-sized conifers can take on any angiosperms that grow in the same habitat. It helps when the angiosperms, due to poor growing conditions, are slowed down themselves and conifers are carried along by mycorrhizae and evergreen foliage to attain that canopy height. That is why conifers have largely retreated to sites or regions where plant growth is constrained. But that cannot explain the success of the giant conifers, towering above all other trees, that we find in parts of the world where deep soils, abundant rain, and a mild temperate climate are most favourable to tree growth. These are the temperate rainforests at low to moderate altitudes that encircle the Pacific Ocean.*

▲ ▲ ▲

At the northern extremity of North Island, New Zealand, in the district of Northland is the Waipoua Forest. This nature reserve protects the largest remnant of pristine kauri forest, dominated by *Agathis australis*, which once covered both this district and the Coromandel Peninsula. In one of the most outrageous exploitation frenzies known in history, lasting only half a century until the kauris were almost gone, these magnificent trees were felled and carted off to the sawmills. There is healthy regrowth now in many areas, but only the Waipoua Forest and a few smaller reserves are left to give us an idea what it was like 200 years ago. When you enter this forest and walk the trails, you will see large trees all around. Chances are that you have heard about the large trees here and you may think you are already looking at them, until you come to stand in front of one of the true giants. These trees are as big as a lighthouse and look like one, if it were not for the mighty bush of massive branches that seem to sprout all at once from the top of the tower. The giants are really on a different scale from the other trees of the forest, although even these others are often bigger than any tree you could encounter in a European forest. If you explore further, you will find that the giants are few and far between. Could it be that most of the giants were cut here, too, and the forest has only grown back since the logging stopped? Not here: the Waipoua Forest escaped from the loggers and has never heard the ring of axes.

There are other trees in Waipoua Forest, too. This is a mixed angiosperm-conifer forest with an average of 20 tree species per hectare. The conifers include rimu (*Dacrydium cupressinum*), totara (*Podocarpus totara*), Hall's totara (*Podocarpus hallii*), and miro (*Prumnopitys ferruginea*), which are all Podocarpaceae, tanekaha (*Phyllocladus trichomanoides*; Phyllocladaceae), and kawaka (*Libocedrus plumosa*; Cupressaceae). Some of the angiosperms form canopy trees, such as species of the genera *Beilschmie-*

Kauri (*Agathis australis*), in the Waipoua Forest, North Island, New Zealand

dia (Lauraceae) and *Nestegis* (Oleaceae) and *Dysoxylum spectabile* (Meliaceae). It takes a bit more effort, but you could observe that the kauris, in particular, appear to occur in groups, sometimes to the exclusion of other large trees. It looks as if these groups are composed of trees of the same age and size. Outside these groups, the forest is more diverse, while the giants stand within or near the kauri groves. They are hung with lianas and epiphytes forming huge subtropical gardens high above the damp forest floor. Some of them may be 2000 years old, although the maximum count so far is 1679 years. There is evidence that much bigger trees than the giants now alive were logged. Never touched by our destructive greed, it seems that at least this forest with its great trees has been growing here undisturbed for thousands of years. It must have been old long before any people ever visited these islands.

The Olympic Mountains in the state of Washington collect a lot of snow each winter. The snow accumulates and forms glaciers from which melt-water rivers descend to the Pacific Ocean through broad valleys clothed in deep forests. At the lower end of these valleys it rarely snows but it rains a lot, 500 cm (200 in) per year or more. All this water swells the rivers, which are rather big for their short length and can carry huge trees down into the ocean, which throws them back on the beaches. Tree growth here is perhaps the most spectacular on Earth. Everything is big, in true American spirit. The riverbanks and islands are covered in stands of large alders (*Alnus rubra*) and poplars (*Populus trichocarpa*), but away from the rivers the conifers dominate. Most common is western hemlock (*Tsuga heterophylla*), followed by Sitka spruce (*Picea*

One of the giant kauris in the Waipoua Forest is called Tane Mahuta (Lord of the Forest) by the Maori, and it is now a tourist attraction.

Leaves and seed cones of *Agathis australis*

Podocarpus totara (totara). A forest giant known as the Pouakani totara grows in young secondary forest near Mangapehi, North Island, New Zealand.

The enormous trunk of a giant Douglas fir (*Pseudotsuga menziesii*) in the rainforest of Olympic National Park, south of Quinault Lake. Called Tichipawa (Thunderbolt), it is the third largest tree on record of this species.

Pollen cones and foliage of *Podocarpus totara*

Seed cones and foliage of Douglas fir (*Pseudotsuga menziesii*)

sitchensis). Here and there are groups of western red cedar (*Thuja plicata*), and on slightly higher ground the forest is often dominated by Douglas fir (*Pseudotsuga menziesii*). Pacific silver fir (*Abies amabilis*) and occasional stands of yellow cedar or Nootka cypress (*Xanthocyparis nootkatensis*) usually grow higher up the valleys. Not many large angiosperms grow here; the only one that makes a frequent appearance is bigleaf maple (*Acer macrophyllum*). The largest of these trees are usually heavily hung with mosses and ferns. The smaller vine maple (*Acer circinatum*) is common as an understorey tree in the conifer forest, and there are numerous shrubs. Mosses cover the forest floor and fallen trees in thick green blankets and pillows. If you could only see them, the crowns of the conifers are festooned with hanging mosses and lichens. They are too high up for a good view, as these trees are really tall. On one of my visits to the Olympic Rainforest, I came upon a giant Sitka spruce that had fallen and bridged the Hoh River. Walking on its huge trunk for 50–60 m (165–200 ft), I came to the canopy area of its crown, which had smashed into the alders on the far side of the river. It was a lichenologists paradise. One species of *Usnea* (I did not know which) was 2–3 m (6.5–10 ft) long, like silver-grey beards hanging from the branches.

In this forest, too, the true giants are widely scattered. The biggest are *Thuja plicata* and *Pseudotsuga menziesii*, closely followed by *Picea sitchensis*, but the other species (except *Tsuga heterophylla*) can reach giant proportions, too. The record age is held by *Xanthocyparis nootkatensis*, with over 2000 years (in Alaska even more); both *T. plicata* and *P. menziesii* attain at least 1000 years. In most old

One of the giant trees of *Thuja plicata*, known as Big Mother Cedar, growing in Clayoquot Sound, Vancouver Island, Canada. Drawing by Robert Van Pelt

Forest dominated by alerce (*Fitzroya cupressoides*) in southern Chile. Photograph by Martin Gardner

growth forests on the Olympic Peninsula, there are only big trees and no or very few young trees. There is abundant regeneration, mainly growing on fallen trees, but it seems to be all *T. heterophylla* and only a few *T. plicata* or *P. sitchensis*. Some fallen logs support hundreds of little hemlocks, growing out of the bark, needle litter, and moss, and these logs are known as nurse logs. The moss cover on the ground is too thick for the seeds to reach the soil. Eventually, a few of the seedlings get their roots around the nurse log into the ground and can grow to trees, standing in a line or colonnade long after the nurse log has decayed.

In the coastal mountains of southern Chile occurs a type of temperate rainforest in which the dominant tree is *Fitzroya cupressoides* (alerce), belonging to the family Cupressaceae. There is not very much old growth left because here, too, exploitation in the past took no heed of the future. Giant trees no longer exist. A huge stump known as the President's Seat near the town of Puerto Montt is all that is left to remind us of these giants. The present alerce forests consist of fragmented remnants, some of which still contain large trees, if not giants, so we can obtain an impression of their magnificence before Europeans came with their axes and saws.

This forest grows on shallow, often waterlogged, acidic soils derived from highly weathered metamorphic schist in the Coast Range or on deeper soils from volcanic ashfalls in the Andes. The alerce forest is now nearly restricted to land above 500 m (1650 ft), but in the past it covered the lowlands as well. Rainfall in the region is from 200 to 400 cm (80 to 160 in) per year. *Fitzroya cupressoides* is the tallest tree in the for-

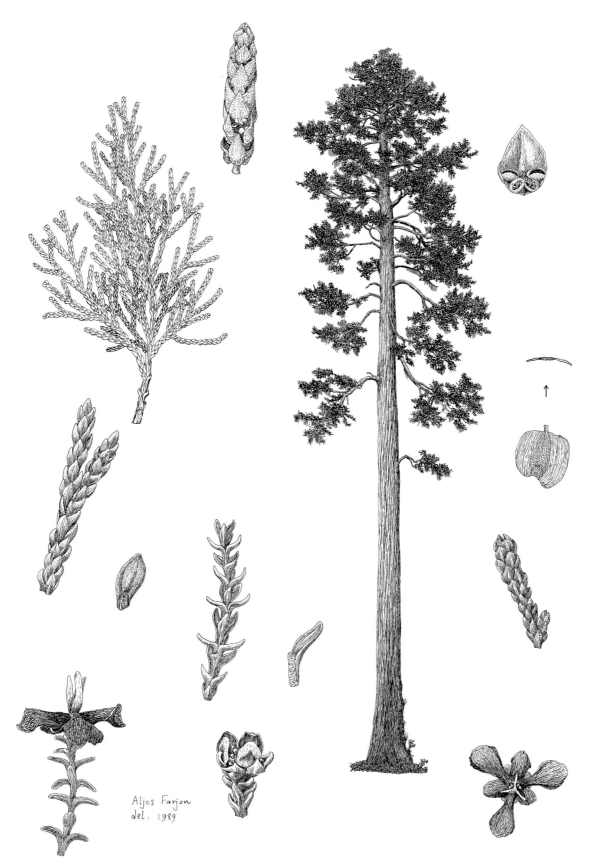

Fitzroya cupressoides, the alerce of southern Chile

est, growing up to 5 m (16 ft) in diameter and 50 m (165 ft) in height, although taller individuals may have existed. This species grows associated with other conifers, with *Pilgerodendron uviferum* (Cupressaceae), *Podocarpus nubigenus* (Podocarpaceae), and *Saxegothaea conspicua* (Podocarpaceae) being the most common of these. In swampy areas the trees retreat to the edges and a low, shrubby conifer appears, *Lepidothamnus fonkii* (Podocarpaceae). Among the angiosperms, *Nothofagus nitida* (Fagaceae) is usually the dominant tree, but other species of southern beech may occur at the higher altitudes. Also common at middle elevations is *Tepualia stipularis* (Myrtaceae), a tall shrub. Several of these trees and the coniferous shrub are endemic to the region and the only representative species in their genus. At lower elevations, *Fitzroya* is sparser and many other angiosperms are more numerous. These angiosperm forests are often punctuated with some tall conifers that emerge from the broad-leaved canopy. In this Valdivian rainforest *Amomyrtus luma* (Myrtaceae), *Drimys winteri* (Winteraceae), *Laureliopsis philippiana* (Monimiaceae), and *Weinmannia trichosperma* (Cunoniaceae) are the dominant trees.

The alerce does not seem to regenerate at all in many of these forest remnants. *Fitzroya cupressoides* individuals are often roughly of the same age in a particular area, often from 350 to 500 years old. This conifer is one of the slowest growing of all, with annual diameter increments often less than 1 mm (0.04 in). Trees have been found that are over 3000 years old—the record is 3622 years for a trunk of which a substantial part of the heartwood was missing. If ever a complete sequence of growth of a large tree was found, the alerce could dethrone the Great Basin bristlecone pine (*Pinus longaeva*) as the longest-living tree species. Regeneration of the two shade-tolerant podocarps, *Podocarpus nubigenus* and *Saxegothaea conspicua*, as well as that of angiosperms, is good in these forests. Usually, the canopy is not entirely closed, and small gaps are created from time to time by falling trees. Only very few seedlings of *F. cupressoides* appear to succeed to saplings in these openings. Many observers of these forests have interpreted these facts as evidence for the long-term demise of *F. cupressoides* even without human interference. Perhaps climate change, which began to have a drying influence in this part of the world some 2500 years ago, lies behind the decline of this big conifer.

What do the Waipoua Forest of North Island, the conifer forests of the Olympic Peninsula, and the alerce forests of southern Chile have in common? In all three, there are one or a few species of conifer that can attain both great size and great age. The very big trees are few and far between, looking like the sole survivors of a forest of giants that is on its last legs. When they die, only moderately large trees will be left. Their species may even be on the path to total extinction, as regeneration seems wholly inadequate to replace the trees that die. Angiosperms are apparently doing better in at least two of the above examples and, given time, could eventually replace the conifers. In the Pacific Northwest, the shade-tolerant western hemlock (*Tsuga heterophylla*) and the bigleaf maple (*Acer macrophyllum*) could be the only large trees to survive.

This was the impression foresters and forest ecologists had until some years ago, when careful studies were undertaken to unravel the dynamics of these ancient forests with giant conifers. The even-aged stands of the younger trees of the giant species are the key. For instance, in the Quinault area of the Olympic Rainforest, there is a small bit of forest known as the Miracle Acre. Trees, mostly Douglas fir (*Pseudotsuga menziesii*) in this spot, average 350 years in age and are 1.2–2.4 m (4–8 ft) in diameter and 85 m (280 ft) tall. There are so many trees in this grove of that size that it holds the record for biomass (weight of wood per hectare) in the entire Pacific Northwest. Older groves (stands of even-aged trees of one species) have fewer trees, but their age is in the range of 500–600 years, and they are larger (but not taller). Exactly the same age cohorts were found in the alerce forests of Chile. Eventually, few if any of the trees in these groves will survive to 1000 years or more and attain giant proportions. When they do, however, they become the trees that Bob Van Pelt has measured for his book *Forest Giants of the Pacific Coast* (2001). What is happening in these forests to allow the continued existence of these species? We have massive destructive events to thank for their persistence. It sounds paradoxical: Destroy the forest to save it? Well, that is too simplistic. The forest would of course persist without such large-scale disturbances, but it would eventually not contain the conifers we are discussing here. It is only they that need the episodes of destruction.

All the giant conifers mentioned here are light demanding. They cannot grow up in the shade of other trees in the forest, be it conifers or angiosperms. Small gaps that are continually created by one or two trees dying and falling are quickly filled in by the shade-tolerant species, which therefore are of uneven age and size in most parts of the forest. But at long intervals, a more catastrophic event occurs and creates large openings. Fire is the most common of these in the Olympic Rainforest and in the Coast Range of Chile. In the Andes, it is fire and ashfall from volcanic eruptions; here the two are usually working together. In the kauri forests of New Zealand, cyclones and fires may play equally important roles in natural large-scale forest disturbances. It may be a surprise to learn that fire plays such an important role in such a wet ecosystem as the Pacific temperate rainforest. But if you have been on the Olympic Peninsula in July or August, with some luck you may have experienced a few weeks with plenty of sunshine and no rain. Very rarely, this may extend to a substantial drought. Again, one of the Olympic groves of Douglas fir is 350 years old, another 500–600 years. Weather records have only been kept there for some 150 years. We know very little about long-term weather cycles from direct observation—it is the trees that tell us about the climate in the past. Fires have occurred recently, and back in 1977 I walked through one that had occurred in the Hoh Valley. If the fire is hot enough, it will kill all the smaller and average-sized trees. However, the bigger the tree is, the better its chance of survival. The bark of a giant Douglas fir can be 25 cm thick on the lower parts of the massive trunk and works as a fire shield. A giant kauri may survive both fire and cyclone, although its crown may be ravaged in the storm. In New Zealand, something similar to a cyclone happened with the massive logging of 100–150 years ago. In those areas of logged kauri forest where land use was not converted to grazing or forest plantations, a pioneer vegetation of *Leptospermum* (Myrtaceae) bushes was quickly invaded by *Agathis australis* seedlings, and a new cohort of kauri trees occupied the landscape.

All the species of giant conifers have light, winged seeds that can be carried far by high winds. Even the very old trees produce healthy crops of seeds. These crops typi-

Seed cones and foliage of western red cedar (*Thuja plicata*)

cally occur at irregular intervals of a few years, but frequently enough to take advantage of the newly created habitat. Some species grow fast in the early stages, such as the kauri and the Douglas fir. Other species are slow growers, such as Nootka cypress and alerce, although these two are also the longest lived, equalling or surpassing even the sequoias. Slow growth of seedlings and saplings is a risk. Other species that come to occupy the new space may be faster and overtop them. One disturbance event may not be enough to help the slow growers establish. But, once established and grown large, the giant conifers may survive repeated catastrophes that alter completely the composition of the surrounding forest.

In August 2005 Bob Van Pelt took me to the Quinault Lake Cedar, the largest specimen by volume of *Thuja plicata* on record. The surrounding forest is almost exclusively western hemlock (*Tsuga heterophylla*), which are tall but slender trees. The lone Quinault Lake Cedar looks dead until you walk round its massive, fluted, and barkless base and see a 50-cm-wide strip of bark going from the roots up to a living reiteration 21 m (70 ft) above the ground. Inside its hollow trunk, there would be room to camp with a party of 10, leaving everyone elbow space. The repeated forest fires, of which we now see no trace, nearly killed it. This time it may be dead before it can throw out seeds into the next fire clearing.

Eventually, the slow-growing conifers are under pressure to retreat to less fertile soils, wind-exposed ridge tops, and waterlogged flats or hollows, leaving the better sites to the faster growers. In particular, this seems to have happened to *Fitzroya cupressoides*, the alerce of Chile and Argentina. But even with these giant conifers, it is their capacity to outlive their neighbours and occupy their living space after rare events of forest destruction that enables them to survive among the more shade-tolerant conifers and angiosperms.

17 Imitating the Almighty Angiosperms

IN SEPTEMBER 1996 *a symposium was held at the University of Oxford in memory of Frank White, the former curator of the Oxford Herbaria and an authority on the flora and vegetation of Africa. One of the papers presented highlighted an aspect of conifer ecology and distribution that is seldom addressed. It compared distribution patterns of trees with those of fruit-eating birds across the continent (chorology in Frank White's terminology) and found very close matches for many species pairs. One of these pairs was the conifer species* Podocarpus milanjianus *(lumped with P.* latifolius *in the paper; White entertained a very broad species concept for the conifers of Africa) and the pigeon* Columba arquatrix. *The migratory habits of the bird explained the distribution of the conifer across sub-Saharan Africa. Here was a case of a conifer providing a bird with a reward to distribute its seeds far and wide. That is angiosperm behaviour, is it not? Conifers just drop their seeds or, if they have wings, the wind may help getting the seeds dispersed a little further. Mutualisms between plants and animals are too sophisticated for such primitive plants, you might think. Apparently, they are not. But if not, how common is this among conifers, and what forms does it take? And, what are its advantages, if any?*

▲ ▲ ▲

There are many mutually beneficial relationships (mutualisms) between animals and plants, almost all of which have developed with angiosperms on the plant's side of the deal. Pollination provides numerous examples, and it is the single reason why flowering plants evolved their nearly endless variation of flower designs. Although certain insects are now implicated in the dispersal of pollen of cycads and *Welwitschia mirabilis*, that weird plant of the Namib Desert, these remain the only examples among gymnosperms. Not a single conifer has any use of animals in this function, as they are all wind pollinated. Some angiosperms are wind pollinated, too. Think of birch trees (*Betula*) and alders (*Alnus*), both in the family Betulaceae, and grasses, but these are by and large exceptions. Wind pollination, especially for trees, is wasteful. In order to have any success at outcrossing, a tree must produce and disperse billions of microscopic pollen grains that float in the air as if they weigh nothing. Very few of these will meet and enter an ovule of the same species. In the spring, if you go to a small lake in the conifer forests of the north, you are likely to see a yellowish scum some centimetres thick that covers the surface in windless, still corners. It is the wasted pollen of the conifers on the shores. (When I say wasted, I am thinking from the conifers' point of view; the nutrients may be recycled and used by organisms in the lake.) It is obviously more efficient to let your pollen be carried by an insect from flower to flower. The use of a pollinator remained a trick conifers could not invent, or indeed inherit from an ancestor who had accomplished it. The great diversification of flowering plants and their pollinators—

The pollen cones of ponderosa pine (*Pinus ponderosa*) are magenta; it is unknown why they have this colour.

a job taken up by birds and mammals as well as insects—has often been attributed to the rise of this mutualism.

Once plant ovules have been pollinated and fertilized, they will develop into seeds. These have to be dispersed, especially for trees because seedlings will not develop in the canopy shade of the parent tree. In seed dispersal, another opportunity for mutualisms arises, and here several conifer species have been able to hop onto the bandwagon. If an animal eats the seeds, there should be enough transported but left uneaten to help the tree disperse and reproduce. Completely accidental dispersal by animals, as sometimes happens, is not a mutualism. To call it that, there must be evidence of special adaptation by the plant, the animal, or both. The animal must actively seek the seeds as food and transport them, and the plant must develop seeds with attractive value to the animal. In general, there are two mutualism scenarios with regard to seed dispersal. In one, the animal eats a fruit containing seeds, which pass through the animal undigested and are excreted some distance from the parent plant; and in the other, the seeds are transported and hidden to be eaten later, yet not all hidden seeds are eaten. Conifers have adapted to both scenarios, and the first one is more common than the second. Let us take a look at the details of the first scenario and how conifers have managed to adopt it.

As I have explained in the first chapter of this book, gymnosperms do not produce fruits like angiosperms. This may sound like a technical nicety that the birds could not care less about, and that is true. But to us it is important, because it allows us to appreciate that conifers had to imitate fruits in order to obtain the same result. That is much more unlikely to happen in evolution, as I shall explain. Flowers produce ovules encapsulated in ovaries formed by fused carpels, essentially flower parts homologous to leaves. The fertilized ovules ripen to seeds, and the ovaries become fruits. All that is needed for these to become attractive is to enlarge the ovary, add carbohydrates and sugar, and some attractive colour, and no fruit-eating animal can resist it. There are more complicated fruits, but these are the basics of it, almost an inevitable evolutionary consequence of the structure of the flower. To obtain similar results starting with a conifer cone is a different challenge. Yet, it has been accomplished by various means and with various rates of sophistication in five of the eight conifer families: Podocarpaceae, Taxaceae, Phyllocladaceae, Cephalotaxaceae, and Cupressaceae. In all cases the cone has been extremely reduced, in some cases it effectively disappeared. With few exceptions, the number of seeds has been reduced to one, for no bird will swallow a large woody cone. In many ways, the Podocarpaceae has been the most innovative as well as the most successful family of conifers to adopt this strategy of seed dispersal. Probably all extant species in the family have their seeds dispersed by animals, and this is the second largest family, with 186 species. Let me begin by explaining the structure

and growth of a seed cone of *Podocarpus nivalis*, from an early stage to maturity, when it is ripe to be picked off by a hungry bird.

The cone starts as a minute axis or shoot in the axil of a leaf. It bears two opposite bracts and an inverted ovule enveloped in the epimatium. The epimatium is usually interpreted as homologous to the seed scale in other conifers; it covers most of the ovule (later the entire seed) but leaves the micropyle, the opening for pollination, free. Its unequal growth inverts the ovule. A pollination drop excreted from the micropyle is sticky and catches the pollen that falls on it or even that has fallen within its reach. The pollen then floats upwards to the micropyle (Tomlin-

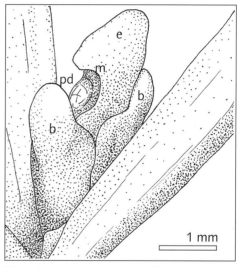

The early stage of development of the seed cone (at pollination) of *Podocarpus nivalis*, a New Zealand shrub common in cultivation (e, epimatium; m, micropyle; pd, pollination drop; b, bract). Drawn after Tomlinson and Takaso (2003)

A mature cone of *Podocarpus nivalis* with its bright red receptacle and single seed

Podocarpus macrophyllus, a species from China, with a full-grown cone of which the receptacle has not yet matured

Dacrycarpus dacrydioides (kahikatea) from New Zealand

The ripe purple-black seeds of Dacrycarpus dacrydioides on their orange and red receptacles

son and Takaso 2003), enters it, and grows a pollen tube towards the egg cell. Once the ovule has been fertilized, growth resumes rapidly and in a very specific way. The two bracts begin to swell at the base, fuse together, and expand enormously, forming a succulent, bright red receptacle (as in the *Podocarpus macrophyllus* photo in chapter 12). The epimatium expands, too, covering the seed integument and micropyle. The seed is pushed upwards by the faster growth of the axis with the receptacle, that is, the two fused bracts. The green tips of the bracts remain visible, peeking through the red. The end result is an imitation fruit with a seed on top. Its bright colour attracts birds, which swallow the structure whole, fly away, and digest the receptacle and the epimatium. In the process, the bird's gut causes scarification of the seed but leaves it otherwise intact and supplied with some fertilizer. If it drops in the right place, the seed will germinate almost at once.

The family Podocarpaceae has evolved diverse pathways by which imitation fruits are produced. Some end results are very similar to that of *Podocarpus nivalis*, whereas others are quite different in structure. *Dacrycarpus dacrydioides* (kahikatea), the tallest of New Zealand's trees at 60 m, starts its cone with spirally arranged scale leaves and bracts, one or two of which are fertile. Usually, the topmost bract produces the fertilized ovule, the others merge and form the receptacle, thereby producing a ripe "fruit" similar to that of *Podocarpus*. When the branches are laden with these they are a striking sight—like the tree itself, very different from what most people would associate with conifers.

A very different development produces the plum-like imitation fruits of the genera *Afrocarpus*, *Nageia*, *Prumnopitys*, and *Sundacarpus*. The taxonomy of these has been much confused because of the difficulty to correctly interpret the severely reduced seed cones. Understanding the biological functions of conifers has been crucial and no other researcher has contributed more to this than Barry Tomlinson of Harvard University, from whose publications my brief descriptions of early development are mostly taken. For the imitation plum in the conifers, I shall use the example of *Prumnopitys andina*, known as lleuque in southern Chile, where it is native. This medium-sized tree is moderately winter hardy and is planted in botanical collections like that of the Royal Botanic Gardens, Kew, where I had an opportunity to observe it at different times. In its initial stage, the cone is a dwarf shoot in the axil of a leaf with several whorls of fertile bracts and a few basal scales. Each fertile bract is associated with an ovule, so potentially many seeds may develop. The ovules are each placed in adaxial position on an epimatium that envelops it only partially. Presumably the first ovule that is fertilized causes the others to abort, because they do not develop and, along with their concomitant structures, wither away instead of forming a receptacle. The fertilized seed grows to about 8 × 7 mm (0.32 × 0.28 in) and is surrounded by the fleshy epimatium that reaches nearly 10 mm (0.4 in) in thickness. Development is slow and takes three years to ripeness, at which time the epimatium finally turns yellow, looking like a ripe plum. It does not taste like one, but birds don't mind and swallow the thing whole.

The epimatium develops in different ways in other genera of the Podocarpaceae and may cover the seed only partially or not at all and become brightly coloured (white or yellow, as in *Halocarpus* of New Zealand) or not. In *Dacrydium* sterile bracts that stand below the actual cone fuse and inflate, and the result is something similar to the receptacle of *Podocarpus*, but not as elegantly formed. Once again the birds don't mind, and it works for them and for the tree. These diverse morphological structures are all related to seed dispersal by birds, leading to parallelisms with superficially the same end product.

Yet another example of fruit imitation in the Podocarpaceae is presented by the New Caledonian conifer *Acmopyle pancheri*, one of only two species in a genus restricted to New Caledonia and Fiji. The development of this conifer was recently investigated by my colleague Robert Mill and his coworkers at the Royal Botanic Garden, Edinburgh (Mill et al. 2001). A single or sometimes two or three dwarf shoots with tiny scale leaves develop near the tip of a branch with normal, larger, and bilaterally flattened leaves. The scale leaves are helically arranged and among the topmost few, one or two bracts are fertile. They elongate first and bear an epimatium and normally one ovule each. There may be two seeds eventually, but usually one aborts and the other grows and ma-

Prumnopitys andina (lleuque), a podocarp from Chile, with plum-like imitation fruits

The fleshy seed cones of *Acmopyle pancheri*, an endemic podocarp of New Caledonia

The pollen cones of *Acmopyle pancheri*

Mature seeds with edible arils of the common yew (*Taxus baccata*)

tures. The ovule remains erect and is never inverted, as in *Podocarpus*. The uppermost scale leaves (bracts) swell strongly but irregularly, and the epimatium envelops the seed and swells strongly, too. The lowermost scale leaves remain small and cover the dwarf shoot, now the peduncle of the pendulous cone or imitation fruit, which is bluish purple with a waxy coating. Here is a cone that appears to combine the two modes of development described above for *Podocarpus nivalis* and *Prumnopitys andina*. We have no idea what kind of hungry bird savours this prodigious, lumpy "fruit" with its camouflaged seed. With only 76 indigenous bird species in New Caledonia, most of which can be eliminated out of hand as potential consumers, this must not be too difficult to find out. Among the consumers, we can rule out parrots because they crush seeds, which is not very helpful from the plant's point of view.

There is another option available to conifers leading to imitation fruits: Get rid of the seed cone altogether. This nihilist approach has been adopted by the family Taxaceae. In the axil of a foliage leaf of the common yew (*Taxus baccata*) grows a dwarf shoot with tiny scale leaves. This dwarf shoot branches again, and at the apex of this shoot is a single ovule. Sometimes there are two or three lateral dwarf shoots with ovules, and the primary dwarf shoot can branch in subsequent years to produce more ovules. There is no seed scale, only a few enlarged bracts at the base of the ovule. When this ovule grows to a seed in the following year, an aril develops at its base, green at first but swelling and growing over the seed, turning succulent and red. The aril leaves the apex of the seed free. The peculiar thing about edibility in the genus *Taxus* is that, except the aril of the seed, all parts of the plant and especially its leaves are lethally toxic due to taxine alkaloids. Because birds swallow the aril with the seed, it is best for them not to digest the latter. Unlike mammals, most birds don't chew their food, and the seeds come out as they went in, undamaged.

The final example of how conifers produce imitation fruits comes from the genus *Juniperus* in the Cupressaceae. Most people in Europe and North America are familiar with juniper berries, which are used to flavour gin. Botanically, berries are fruits, so these are technically not berries but conifer cones. This cone consists of several fertile bracts, which are homologous to the scale leaves as seen in several *Juniperus* species. Ovules are situated in the axils of these bracts. After fertilization, growth resumes and all the bracts swell and fuse together, enclosing the ovules. In many species it remains possible to trace the outline of the bract-scales on the mature berry-cone, and in most the bract tips remain visible. The consistency of the tissue around the seeds varies with the species from rather dry and pulpy to soft and succulent. The external colour varies, too, from reddish to black-blue to glaucous white, but in all cases there are birds and some small rodents that eat them. Some *Juniperus* species have gone minimalist and have reduced the number of seeds to one, usually large in proportion to the entire cone. The end product is once again a hard seed covered with an attractive, edible layer of food. This imitation of the fruit of angiosperms has proved very successful in dispersing the seeds of conifers with a minimal waste of resources.

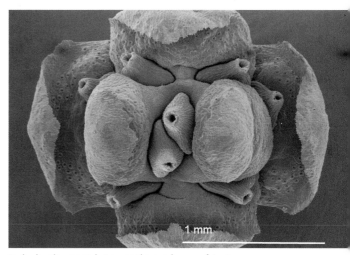

Early developmental stage in the seed cone of *Juniperus phoenicea*, showing ovules and bracts beginning to expand

The second strategy mentioned at the beginning of this chapter involves the ultimate consumption of the seeds of conifers by animals. Obviously, those seeds consumed are lost, so something must happen to ensure the survival of enough seeds so that some can germinate. The animal behaviour that guarantees this is the storage in caches of the seeds for later consumption. Squirrels do this with acorns and walnuts, and in the deserts of North America packrats store all kinds of seeds, including some of conifers, in their middens. For conifers, however, the really effective dispersal involving seed storage is accomplished by birds.

Mutualisms have evolved between nutcrackers (genus *Nucifraga*, family Corvidae) and several species of pine (*Pinus*

Juniperus pseudosabina, a species of juniper from Central Asia with berry-like seed cones containing a single seed

subgenus *Strobus*, Pinaceae). The best-studied cases are in Europe with the Eurasian nutcracker (*Nucifraga caryocatactes*) and Arolla pine (*Pinus cembra*) and in the United States with Clark's nutcracker (*Nucifraga columbiana*) and whitebark pine (*Pinus albicaulis*). The pines have evolved very similar cones and seeds, and the birds feed themselves and their young almost exclusively with these. The entire life cycle of the birds is adjusted to the seasonal growth of cones and seeds of the pines, which grow at subalpine elevations. Upon maturing, the cones open their scales only a little but enough so that the birds can pry the seeds out with their strong bills. This can begin in July or August in the Alps, a little later in the Rocky Mountains. As the season progresses the birds start hiding away more seeds and eating fewer as the seed coat hardens, now supplementing their diet with insects. The nutcrackers carry the seeds in specialized throat pouches that can contain several of the peanut-size wingless kernels. They tend to put them in all kinds of little cracks and hollows in the surrounding mountainside,

usually not far from the parent trees. The birds are busy caching seeds all through the late summer, and a single nutcracker may store between 25,000 and 35,000 seeds in this way. From both field and laboratory observations, it appears that nutcrackers remember all their caches; they can even find them under a thick cover of snow. Their orientation is mainly optical. It is still not clear how they detect caches under snow when optical clues have been

Arolla pine (*Pinus cembra*) is native to the Alps and some other high mountain ranges of Europe.

Seed cones of *Pinus cembra* do not open to release the seeds. Instead, they are removed by the strong bills of the Eurasian nutcracker (*Nucifraga caryocatactes*).

obliterated, but it may involve magnetic sense. Diagonal snow tunnels to caches of 130–300 cm (50–120 in) in length have been found; only when snow cover exceeds 150 cm (60 in) do the birds give up and leave their subalpine habitat. Nutcrackers feed themselves on the hidden seeds through the winter and spring. This means that the birds not only have to memorize the caches made, but also those already consumed. Who can maintain that only humans are intelligent?

How do the pines benefit from these remarkable birds and their feeding habits? First, no memory can be 100 per cent perfect, and, second, birds may store more seeds than they need in one year. As they repeat the cycle in the following year, it becomes advantageous from the birds' point of view to remember the fresh caches and forget the old ones that were not used. If some of those old ones were placed favourably for seed germination, new trees will have been planted. In populations of both pine species we often see two to five trees growing as if planted in the same hole. For *Pinus albicaulis*, the average number of seeds in a cache in one study was five, ranging from one to 10. Even if only a very small fraction of unrecovered seeds germinate, the sheer numbers of seeds stored by the nutcrackers would amount to successful dispersal. The cones do not release the seeds without the bird's effort because the seeds are firmly lodged in cupped cavities on the scales, which do not spread widely as in other pine cones. The cones of *P. albicaulis* and *P. cembra*, with or without good seeds, eventually fall and rot on the ground, and no seeds will germinate from them. The natural expansion upslope from old stands of *P. cembra* in the Alps, where the timberline has been artificially lowered for centuries by farmers for summer pasture, could only be possible with help from the nutcrackers. Such range expansion is happening in many places now that farming and pasturing in the mountains are in decline.

The Eurasian nutcracker (*Nucifraga caryocatactes*) is entirely responsible for the perpetuation of its main food source, the Arolla pine. Photograph by Jiri Bohdal

18 Facing the Enemy

WHILE VISITING AUSTRALIA IN 1997, *I went with a group of botanists from Perth to visit a nature reserve in the yarra forest (Eucalyptus marginata) to the southeast of the city famed for its rich plant diversity. Upon arriving we came to a signposted trailhead where there was a box containing plastic overshoes. A warning sign above it compelled every visitor to don the plastic outfit on penalty of prosecution should anyone be caught by a park ranger wearing uncovered boots. I had only encountered this kind of thing in palaces and country houses open to the public where they want to protect priceless carpets or floors. What is the purpose of this in a forest? The answer is* Phytophthora cinnamomi. *This obscure organism, commonly called a fungus but actually an oomycete belonging in a different kingdom Chromista, is the scourge of the forest. The genus name means plant destroyer, and the species epithet compares it with cinnamon, the powdery, aromatic spice from the bark of a tropical Asian tree.* Phytophthora cinnamomi *is transported from site to site in soil, and the smallest bit of it in the grooves of your boot soles may suffice to bring it here. In 19th-century Ireland, it was a species of* Phytophthora *that caused the infamous potato blight and with it the near depopulation of the country. In the yarra forest it is a newcomer, too, accidentally introduced from abroad. This species is a generalist pathogenic parasite invading about half of the Western Australian flora, with a particular liking of the family Proteaceae, which is such a highlight of the Australian flora. This pathogen has not affected the local conifers yet, and there is some reason to hope that it won't.*

▲ ▲ ▲

Plants are the living world's main primary producers of organic matter, sharing this function with some green algae and cyanobacteria, which mainly operate in the oceans. All other organisms do not produce organic matter but convert it to other organic matter—that of their own bodies. From a plant's point of view, they are almost all parasites, whether horse, human, fish, caterpillar, mistletoe, nematode, or pathogenic fungus. The only good organisms are those that help pollinate flowers and disperse seeds and the fungi that associate with roots as mycorrhizae. Also useful are a few ants that help fend off potential browsers and, of course, the saprophagous organisms that help decompose dead plant material in which plants would otherwise bury themselves alive. Plants could well exist without the rest of the menagerie of life. Perhaps there are planets in the universe where life is organized in this simple, happy vegetative manner, but I doubt it.

Life under Darwinian evolution is opportunistic and ultimately selfish. The rich and easy pickings provided by plants to sustain life cry out for the evolution of forms to take advantage of and have first call on these resources. We find consumers of living plants in all the major subdivisions of life, from higher plants themselves through animals down to the viroids, the simplest forms of life consisting of nothing but a bit of DNA. Against this onslaught, plants have to defend themselves. Their defences have led to more sophisticated attacks, resulting in the arms race through natural selection that is the major driving force behind biodiversity. In this chapter, I hope to show that the arms race in nature tends to lead to an armistice, not to a war of extermination. It is only when humans transport organisms to continents where they did not evolve together with the hosts they feed on that disasters threaten. Perhaps such accidental transports occurred occasionally before humans could play a role, but they must have been very rare. Unfortunately, such introductions are now becoming frequent.

What are the major threats to conifers, and how do they cope? Although humans are now the major threat, I shall reserve that discussion for later. Let us look at the natural biological threats to conifers and how they defend themselves against these organisms. First there is herbivory to consider. Herbivores are animals whose diet is mostly or entirely made up of plants. Commonly we have large animals in mind, from elephants to rabbits, but insects and their larvae that eat living plants are herbivores, too. I shall come to them in a moment, but first a few observations about the larger herbivores. Not many of the large herbivores eat conifers. In spring, rabbits and deer are apt to browse on the new foliage of young conifers, especially species in the family Pinaceae, but they will leave old foliage alone and don't bother with most of the species in Cupressaceae. It is generally thought that chemical compounds such as terpenes that develop in the leaves of conifers act as deterrents, for reasons of toxicity or because they tend to disrupt or hamper the digestive system of animals. Podocarpaceae are usually left alone, as are species of Taxaceae, some of which would kill the animal with their toxins. Araucariaceae species seem to be pretty safe from large herbivores, too. It is not monkeys that are puzzled by the monkey-puzzle tree (*Araucaria araucana*) but large native herbivores such as alpacas and llamas and, since Europeans took them to South America, cattle, horses, and goats. The biologically relevant question is not how to

The vicious foliage of monkey-puzzle tree (*Araucaria araucana*) is an effective deterrent to mammalian herbivores, but would it have discouraged dinosaurs?

climb the monkey-puzzle tree but how to eat it. Here a physical form of defence is added to the chemical one.

I mentioned goats, and these are indeed an exception to the "do not eat the conifers" rule, but only the domestic kind. Over many centuries in the Middle East and the Mediterranean, as human civilizations depleted forests and increased shrubby, thorny vegetation, goats were domesticated and selected to cope with the harshest of fodder, and this includes conifers. Goats can devastate a landscape that would without them be an open woodland with junipers, cypresses, oaks, and pistachios, as I have seen in Morocco and Turkey. Like *Phytophthora*, domesticated goats are therefore really a threat to conifers imposed by humans. The wild ancestor of goats, the ibex (*Capra hircus*), is not a threat to conifers.

Conifers have evolved strategies to resist large herbivores. Their evolutionary history goes back to before the Age of Dinosaurs: All extant conifer families had evolved

An ancient tree of *Juniperus thurifera* in the Atlas Mountains of Morocco is constantly clipped by climbing goats and may eventually succumb.

by the end of the Jurassic 150 million years ago. As is the case in nature today with mammals, herbivorous dinosaurs exceeded carnivorous dinosaurs in total biomass by a ratio of at least 10 to 1, because it takes on average 100 kg of plant food to produce 10 kg of herbivore biomass to produce 1 kg of carnivore biomass. Apart from ferns, conifers and other gymnosperms were the only substantial source of plant food, and there can be no doubt that dinosaurs had evolved to make good use of that resource. During millions of years of evolution, the arms race had caused plants to develop defences and dinosaurs to overcome them. Toxic ferns and conifers, hard and spiny leaves of cycads and conifers, tall conifers lifting their foliage beyond the reach of even the longest-necked sauropod dinosaurs were all "designed" to keep the browsers off. An armistice had been reached that allowed conifers and herbivores to coexist.

Then, at the beginning of the Cretaceous, the first angiosperms appeared, finding niches in the ecosystems on land and in swamps that were soon to be exploited to their full potential. A new food source presented itself and diverted attention away from the difficult, even obstinate conifers. Angiosperms, gymnosperms, and dinosaurs coexisted for another 60–70 million years, long enough for new modes of attack and defence to evolve. The pressure on conifers never disappeared, but angiosperms became so diverse that opportunities for food eventually outnumbered those presented by gymnosperms. When mammals started to take up the herbivorous and carnivorous niches left by the dinosaurs at the end of the Cretaceous, there were angiosperms almost everywhere. Conifers were no longer a necessary primary food source and were largely left alone. Admitting that this scenario is speculative, I think it is a plausible explanation why conifers today are not, under natural conditions, a major food source for large herbivores. How about the small ones?

The damage done by a large herbivore such as a deer seems to outweigh that done by an insect, but what insects lack in size and power they more than make up with their numbers. The impact of plant-eating insects on conifers is several orders of magnitude larger than that of mammals. Insects exploit all conifer components from the roots to the leaves and cones. The 37 native species of pine (*Pinus*) in Canada and the United States are host to more than 1100 species of insect, and some individual pine species are exploited by more than 200 different insects. More than half of these insect species consume the leaves of pines, as larvae or as imagos (adult phases). Large-scale damage is mostly done by the grazing of larvae of moths (Lepidoptera) on leaves. Seed-cone boring by the larvae of beetles (Coleoptera) and moths can destroy entire cone crops in a stand of pines, reducing the regeneration potential in some years. Although many species of beetle tunnel under bark and bore into wood, they do so mostly in weakened trees, and wood is dead matter anyway. However, the entrance of fungi via spores into the cambium layer and the underlying wood is often facilitated by boring insects. Weakness in a tree caused by drought or root rot fungi can increase the susceptibility to these attacks, and cyclic outbreaks of insect damage often coincide with periods of stress caused by climatic fluctuations.

Much of the research that has been done on insect damage to conifers has taken a forester's outlook. There the concern is centred on productivity of a stand of trees, but when we look at the natural history of conifers, it is survival of the species that counts.

Aleppo pine (*Pinus brutia*) is a species dependent on fire and death by insect attacks for long-term survival as a species.

In many cases, insect damage does not kill a tree but only slows it down or deforms it. And even if the tree dies, death is a natural and inevitable event in a forest ecosystem. Without dead trees numerous organisms would be absent, including many of those beneficial to living trees. Of any particular cohort of trees only a few contribute to the next generation, and in long-lived species this cycle takes many centuries. In some cases, there is an intricate relationship between insect-related death of pines, fire, and succession. For example, in the absence of fire in Turkish pine forests, species other than the Aleppo pine (*Pinus brutia*) would succeed. Insect outbreaks may cause the death of a proportion of the pine population, but these standing dead trees serve as fuel and increase the incidence and intensity of fire. Some trees survive both calamities and are able to seed themselves out into the cleared space. Eventually, a new outbreak of insect damage creates new fuel for fires. Nevertheless, there is a balance to be struck, and without the tree's defences several of the insects might get the upper hand and destroy their food resources.

All conifers have resinous leaves and most have resinous wood and seed cones. The resins of conifers are mostly terpenes, complex chemicals built by linkage of five-carbon (C_5H_8) isoprene structural elements (Langenheim 2003). These liquid to viscose substances are conducted through resin canals in the leaves and, if present, in the wood and cones. When bark beetles of the genus *Dendroctonus* (Scolytidae) invade the cambium of ponderosa pine (*Pinus ponderosa*), resin canals are severed and resin is excreted, trapping the insects. Unpalatable or toxic substances in the resin of leaves, which often differs chemically from that in the wood, deter defoliating insects. With their rapid cycle of generations, insects have mutated often and developed response mechanisms quite easily. Many conifer-eating insects can neutralize the toxic elements in resins; some species even turn them into repellents against their own predators. This again necessitated the conifers to evolve new chemicals, so that we have come to the situation where there are at present 30,000 different terpene structures produced by conifers, and new ones are continuously discovered. Trees with a novel or rare monoterpene pattern appear to be more resistant to a particular pest than neighbouring trees with a common pattern. As a first line of defence, resin flow has to be immediate and copious. In some conifers, such as species of kauri (*Agathis*), it is so copious that it has formed extensive layers on the forest floor, half buried under litter and soil. In many pines (*Pinus*), the resin is tapped from the trunk commercially for the production of turpentine. The seed cones of several species in the genus *Abies* (fir) excrete large amounts of resin even without being attacked by insect invaders. Climbing conifers to collect cones from the upper branches can be a sticky experience—if you don't wear a cap or helmet, you may be in for a rough haircut or a nasty wash with white spirit afterwards.

Decay fungi are largely responsible for the hollow trunks of old trees, including conifers. Fire may further hollow out the bole until only an outer layer, surprisingly strong, remains. As every engineer knows, a pipe is nearly as strong as a solid cylinder. Again, this is bad news for foresters, but trees hollowed like this can often survive for centuries. All the large individuals of giant sequoia (*Sequoiadendron giganteum*) are hollow at least in the lower part of their huge boles. Fungi decompose the heartwood, which then becomes brittle and can be entered by tunnelling organisms of many kinds, providing crucial habitat. The sapwood, which is vital for water and nutrient transport, and some of the heartwood must remain to ensure physical support of the tree crown. Large and long-lived conifers have evolved effective mechanisms to deter most decay fungi that would invade the outer layer of wood. Root rot fungi can be more destructive, however. Apart from the capacity to kill trees, their weakening effect on

The bark of ponderosa pine (*Pinus ponderosa*) forms large plates

A seed cone of Webb fir (*Abies spectabilis*) excreting resin to deter herbivores

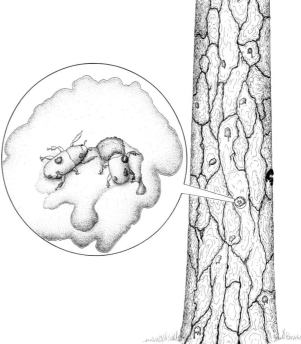

Bark beetles of the genus *Dendroctonus* bore into the bark of ponderosa pine to lay eggs. The beetles are initially repelled by a flow of resin. From Langenheim (2003); reprinted by permission of the author

tree health can cause uprooting even in moderate storms and make trees susceptible to attack by bark beetles. Fungal species of the genus *Armillaria* are particularly virulent and can cause circular infection centres of conifer mortality visible in forests from as high up as an over-flying jet liner. These fungi have a complicated role in the forest ecosystem because they are also important decomposers of dead tree roots, recycling nutrients into the soil. Through a heavy resin response, healthy trees can usually repel root rot fungi that may enter wounds with their spores.

Among the higher plants that parasitize conifers, the dwarf mistletoes (*Arceuthobium*, Viscaceae) are by far the most important and numerous. According to Hawksworth and Wiens (1996), there are 42 *Arceuthobium* species, 34 of which occur in North America from Canada and the western United States to Honduras and the Caribbean island of Hispaniola. The eight Old World species are mainly distributed from Morocco and Spain to southwestern China, with outliers in the Azores and eastern Africa. Centres of *Arceuthobium* diversity, with more than 10 species, are in Mexico and the western United States. Dwarf mistletoes only parasitize conifers in the families Pinaceae and Cupressaceae. In North America, the main host is the genus *Pinus* and no species of Cupressaceae are invaded. In the Old World, pines and other genera in Pinaceae are affected and several species of dwarf mistletoe parasitize species of *Juniperus*.

Dwarf mistletoes are flowering plants with decussate branching systems with extremely reduced leaves and are obligate parasites on the branches of conifers. They form a haustorium, a substitute for roots that penetrates a branch. The tree often reacts by forming witches' brooms, the shoots of which are sometimes also invaded by the parasite. After several years of growth, often when the parasitic plant is 10–15 cm (4–6 in) tall, flowering shoots appear (male and female on separate plants). The flowers are inconspicuous, but the berry-fruits that develop are relatively large and attached to curved stalks. Each fruit contains a single seed. The seed dispersal of dwarf mistletoes is very curious; it involves explosive discharge of the seed, which can be shot as far as 16 m (52 ft) at velocities around 27 m (89 ft) per second. The seed is coated with viscin,

a sticky substance that readily adheres to any surface. Within the crown of a pine tree, that is most likely to be a needle. With the first good soaking rain, the viscin is hydrated, whereupon the mistletoe seed begins to slide down the pine needle to its base, where the needle fascicle is attached to a branch. There, the viscin dries and the mistletoe seed will germinate. A haustorium derived from the seedling root then penetrates the host tree's bark and cambium, causing a swelling of the branch. Soon the first shoots of the dwarf mistletoe emerge from the swelling. The plant completes a life cycle in three to seven years.

The dwarf mistletoe *Arceuthobium tsugense* is parasitizing lodgepole pine (*Pinus contorta*). Photograph by Dan L. Nickrent

Conifer trees can be completely overwhelmed by dwarf mistletoes. The formation of witches' broom reiterations favours the parasite, because it causes the tree to produce more foliage. Although mistletoe seeds are ejected at high speeds, their mode of dispersal is slow and it will take a long time before a forest is infected from a single source. Many species of dwarf mistletoe are host specific, so in a mixed conifer forest where several conifer species remain immune, the spread of the mistletoes is slowed down

Pinus patula, a Mexican species of pine with drooping needles

The drooping needles of *Pinus patula* can rid themselves of the seeds of dwarf mistletoes, making this species of pine less vulnerable to the parasite.

further. In monospecific conifer stands this limitation does not apply. Several species of dwarf mistletoe are not host specific, and these parasitize different species of *Pinus* and invade mixed pine forests. As with some pathogenic parasites and insects, dwarf mistletoe has a similar relationship with fire and succession. An increased fuel load caused by the parasite intensifies fires, without which succession would often lead to dominance of conifers that are immune to dwarf mistletoes. Thus, the susceptible pines may well need the parasite in order to exist in the long term. Despite this, several species of pines have evolved a means to literally shake off the parasite. Pines with drooping needles are especially prevalent in Mexico. *Pinus patula* is an extreme example, with very long and thin, pendulous leaves. If a mistletoe seed is shot from a neighbouring pine and hits a needle of *P. patula*, it will stick. Come rain, it will slide down to the tip of the leaf, not to the base, where it may drop to the ground. In this way, pines with drooping needles have acquired a level of resistance to dwarf mistletoes, even though they are not immune.

The ultimate case of parasitism is that of a conifer parasitizing another conifer. In New Caledonia (where else?) occurs the only example of a parasitic conifer, *Parasitaxus usta*. It is parasitic on the root system of *Falcatifolium taxoides*, a small tree in the rainforest of the mountains on Grande Terre, the main island. Both are in the family Podocarpaceae. The parasitic conifer is a small shrub up to 1 m (40 in) tall, with numerous short, purplish red branches and leaves. The tiny seed cones are distinctly podocarplike, with a very small receptacle and a single, blue-white seed. *Parasitaxus usta* obviously always grows with its host, but its parasitic habit was for a long time unsuspected, because it seems to grow on the forest floor in the leaf litter. Nobody bothered to search for its roots. It was first described as a species of *Dacrydium* by Eugène Vieillard in 1861 and a few years later transferred to *Podocarpus* by other French botanists on account of the structure of its little seed cones, then to *Nageia* for less obvious reasons. It was David de Laubenfels who, in a short paper in the journal *Science* in 1959, announced its parasitic nature. In 1972 he erected the new genus *Parasitaxus* for it in the *Flora of New Caledonia*. Since then, this conifer's parasitism has been established beyond doubt, but exactly how its seeds germinate and the seedling becomes attached to the root of the host have yet to be determined. Attempts to germinate seeds in cultivation have so far failed, either with or without the roots of its host. There is no haustorium in *P. usta*, as in mistletoes, but the plant does not seem to have independent roots either. One line of investigation has suggested that a mycelian fungus may assist in establishing contact, meaning that initially the seed of *P. usta* would germinate in the soil and form a root. There is no direct observation to prove it. This is the only instance known among gymnosperms of a parasitic lifestyle, and it seems likely that its evolution was quite different from the various pathways by which angiosperms have found ways to exploit each other. The burden imposed on the host tree, *F. taxoides*, seems to be slight, as no ill effects are obvious.

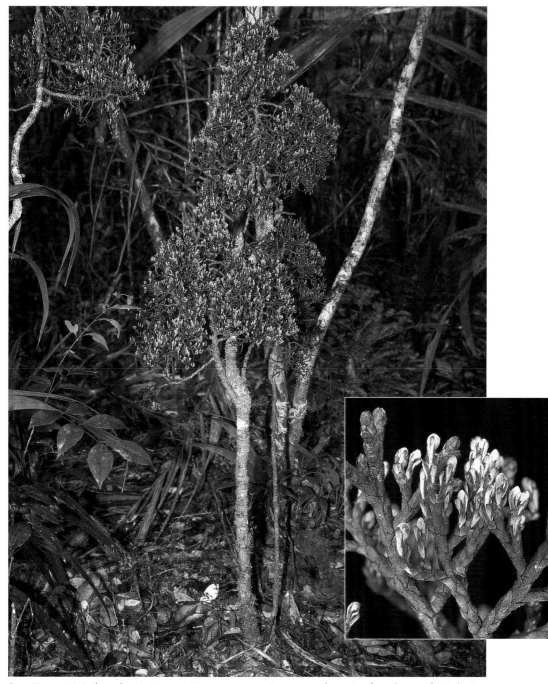

Parasitaxus usta is the only existing parasitic gymnosperm. It grows on the roots of another conifer, *Falcatifolium taxoides*, in New Caledonia. (Inset) Seed cones of *P. usta* with blue-white seeds. Photographs by William Baker, Royal Botanic Gardens, Kew

19 Climbing the Giants

THE GREAT PASSION *in the life and work of Bob Van Pelt is big trees. He is a researcher in forest ecology at the University of Washington in Seattle with a special interest in the role of giant trees in mature forest ecosystems. Giant trees have become tourist attractions, but Bob Van Pelt has a very special relationship with them. He has measured the giants in greater detail and with more scientific precision than anyone else. And he has climbed them. When I first met Bob, in August 2005 at his home in Seattle, I must admit I was somewhat bemused by this feat. I was greeted by a big, red-bearded man, who obviously enjoyed the excellent beer the many small breweries of the city produce. To climb giant trees, I thought, one needs to be small and agile, like a monkey. My assumption was utterly false, as would soon become apparent. In the course of the next two weeks, Bob took me to some of "his" trees, and I no longer had reason to doubt his fitness and stamina for climbing. Incidentally, he also introduced me to the best of Seattle's beers.*

▲ ▲ ▲

Tree measuring is a pastime taken up by many people across the world. Usually, it is merely a search for trees of different species, introduced or native, with the largest girth. If such trees are measured repeatedly, some data may be obtained about growth rates if the information is entered into a centrally managed database, such as one maintained by a dendrological society. But it usually does not go beyond this. Van Pelt's methods, as well as his purpose, are different. The principal instrument he uses is a Criterion 400 survey laser (Laser Technology, Inc.), a rather heavy, square box with lenses that shoots out a laser beam and calculates distances and angles and stores them in a computer. "These instruments were designed for survey work," Bob tells me, "but newer, GPS-linked models have made them obsolete for everything but measuring trees." The thought seems to amuse him. His other tools are a heavy tripod, clinometer, compass, graduated tapes and, of course, climbing gear including great lengths of rope. A sketchbook, notebook computer, and camera complete the outfit.

Van Pelt and I share a passion and talent for drawing trees, but his drawings have to be topographically accurate, while I can take the freedom to alter a branch as long as it remains a plausible branch. This is because he needs to calculate accurately the volume of wood and reconstruct the architecture and reiteration of an individual tree. Most estimates of tree size and volume ignore branches, but in the giant conifers some branches are larger than big trees. Much may be measured from the ground using the laser, but crowns can be very complicated, and neighbouring trees block the view from many angles. This often makes going up there necessary. Thin lines are shot over limbs with a compound bow, and climbing ropes are pulled up. On a huge coast redwood (*Sequoia*), several climbers are at work to rig the tree with arborist rope systems. Here,

First a line is shot with bow and arrow, which allows researchers to climb a tall Douglas fir (*Pseudotsuga menziesii*). Photographs by Robert Van Pelt

the ethics of rock climbing don't count: The ropes are used to climb up, with gripping tools called ascenders, the climber sitting in a harness. Once the tree is rigged, its crown becomes accessible. Photographs can be taken at a horizontal angle to avoid optical distortion. All branches and reiterations thicker than an arm are measured, noting their position on the stem, angle, length, curvature, and thickness. The tree crown is mapped out in three dimensions, which takes two weeks. Why is it done?

The most common architectural model of a conifer is a single, erect stem and pseudo-whorls of more or less equally long, horizontally spreading first-order branches, with second-order branches on either side similarly disposed. The picture resembles a Christmas tree, and the model is called Massart's model after the person who first formally described it. If the first-order branches are upturned towards the tips and there again form pseudo-whorls of branches, we have another common conifer model, that of Rauh. Most young trees conform well to either of these two models, and if the tree grows up protected from any damage it may retain it into maturity. But there are many hazards that may cause anything from light to heavy damage. As the tree gets bigger, it needs more foliage to maintain growth, so it must make repairs or perish. The tree will usually discard branches lower on the trunk if these are in deep shade of the forest, while it makes new ones in the crown that is exposed to sunlight. Many conifer species can activate so-called dormant buds, hidden in the bark below the place where a large

A giant coast redwood (*Sequoia sempervirens*)

branch has broken off. New branches are initiated in this manner that can eventually become as large as the lost ones. However, with this reiteration the original architectural model of the tree is disrupted, as branches can now grow from different points in various directions. In many cases, they assume a vertical position and start to grow branches in the manner of a young tree. In fact, it can be argued that new trees *are* growing upon the broken limbs of the old tree. A tree then becomes a "colony of trees," as the world expert on tree architecture, Francis Hallé, expressed it.

The coast redwood (*Sequoia sempervirens*) has a great potential for this type of architecture due to its rot-resistant wood and capacity to resprout both from lignotubers at the base and high above ground. The largest of the giant coast redwoods measured by Van Pelt, the Del Norte Titan, has 43 reiterated trunks. (Another tree has 62, the largest of which supports nine additional new trees.) The largest reiterated trunk on the Del Norte Titan has a diameter at the base of 1.6 m (5.2 ft) and is a tall tree in its own right, although it is dwarfed by the dimensions of its parent: 7.2 m (23.7 ft) diameter at breast height and 93.6 m (307 ft) tall. Sometimes these secondary trunks become fused somewhere to the main trunk or to each other by incorporating first-order branches. As this goes on for many centuries, the crowns of these giant conifers become very complex. A giant coast redwood known as Iluvatar in Prairie Creek Redwoods State Park, California, has 134 reiterated trunks arising from the main trunk, other trunks, or branches, including a sixth-class reiteration (that is, a trunk from a trunk from a trunk from a trunk from a trunk from a trunk from the main trunk). This individual is possibly the most complicated tree in the world (Sillett and Van Pelt 2000).

Because of this complex structure, in combination with the age of the trees, these reiterated crowns form special habitats. They are essentially small forests elevated 40–80 m (130–260 ft) off the ground. One of the crotches formed by three reiterated trunks in the Del Norte Titan holds a layer of canopy soil 2 m (6.5 ft) deep. This builds up from the bark strips and foliage litter falling constantly from above. This area of the crown is loaded with decaying wood, litter, humus, and epiphytes ranging from lichens, mosses, and liverworts to ferns and woody shrubs or even young trees, all germinated from spores or seed and with their own root systems.

After measuring and mapping the crown, the next project is to calculate the biomass accumulated in litter and epiphytes. Measured samples of litter and epiphytes are removed from branches and crotches of different size, sorted into their components, and dried before weighing. With the accurate measurements of the tree in hand, calculations of the total load of various materials can be made. It is truly amazing how much a single conifer tree crown can support. In a large Sitka spruce (*Picea sitchensis*) on Vancouver Island more than 1000 kg (2200 lb) of dried epiphytes can be present. Because it nearly always rains on the island, the extra weight the tree has to support is in fact three to four times more. Inventories of species of epiphytes on conifers are only now beginning to be made, and the harvest promises to be rich. Conifers have been neglected in the literature on vascular epiphytes and have received scant mention (Benzing 1990).

An accurate drawing by Robert Van Pelt of a giant coast redwood (*Sequoia sempervirens*) named the Terex Titan, showing a broken main top and many reiterated trunks.

Massive reiterations in a coast redwood (*Sequoia sempervirens*) known as El Viejo (The Old One). Photograph by Robert Van Pelt

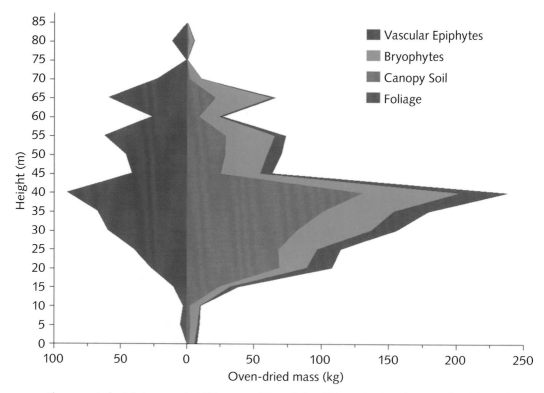

The amount of epiphytes on a giant Sitka spruce (*Picea sitchensis*) is greater than the mass of its foliage. This graph illustrates the oven-dried mass of foliage and epiphytes measured at various heights in the tree canopy. This tree, with an approximate age of 330 years, contained 571 kg of foliage compared to 1073 kg of epiphytes and canopy soil. Drawing and statistics by Robert Van Pelt

In the rainforest of the Pacific Northwest, epiphytic lichens are very prominent, followed by mosses, liverworts, and ferns. Of conifers, western hemlock (*Tsuga heterophylla*) not only grows on downed logs, it frequently germinates high upon living trees. These seedlings can grow to saplings or even trees when they are situated upon broken snags or in crotches with accumulated litter and canopy soil. Other woody plants, such as the various species of huckleberry (*Vaccinium*) can be growing there as well. The hemlock and most huckleberries are accidental epiphytes, and they normally grow in the soil on the ground. Facultative epiphytes are those that grow commonly in the trees but can also grow on the ground; the liquorice fern (*Polypodium scouleri*) is a good example in the northern redwood forest. Among vascular plants, obligate epiphytes are rare in the temperate rainforest of the Pacific Northwest, virtually restricted to some fern species and the lycopod *Selaginella oregana*. Families that have many epiphytic species in the Americas, such as Bromeliaceae and Orchidaceae, do not occur this far north or stay on the ground. Lichens, mosses, and ferns of the genus *Polypodium* therefore account for the bulk of the epiphytic biomass in this forest of conifer giants.

The coast redwood (*Sequoia sempervirens*) hosts an interesting canopy fauna. The invertebrates are mainly represented by arthropod species, of which around 8000 are known to occur in this forest type. How many of these are arboreal is unknown, but it can be assumed to be a high number given the abundance of canopy soil harbouring many species of mites. The few studies so far conducted reveal a highly diverse and distinct fauna, including such basic ecosystem modifiers as earthworms. The invertebrates living in moss mats on the big branches of the trees provide food for the California clouded salamander (*Aneides vagrans*). This amphibian lives in the redwoods, nesting and breeding in the canopy soil and in fern mats. Clouded salamanders do not have aquatic larvae, so they can complete their entire life cycle in the trees.

When kauri trees (*Agathis australis*) in New Zealand reach the forest canopy and begin to overtop it, the branching pattern changes drastically. The leading stem, which dominated the branches thus far, now gives way to several of the higher branches. These

The California clouded salamander (*Aneides vagrans*) lives in the lower canopy of coast redwoods (*Sequoia sempervirens*). Photograph by Gary Nafis

spread outwards and upwards, forming an ever-expanding, domed crown supported by a massive trunk that increases in girth but not in height. This growth pattern is typical for the genus *Agathis* and is particularly well developed in the New Zealand kauri. The giant trees of this species all have short but very massive trunks ending in several huge limbs that can form a crown twice the height of the trunk. The bark of *Agathis* is not welcoming to epiphytes because its outer layer continuously flakes off in a similar fashion as the bark of a plane tree (*Platanus*). But the crown shape of the big trees forms huge crotches, all at about the same height off the ground, in which litter accumulates. When decomposed to canopy soil, this provides habitat for epiphytes.

Several other conifer species in New Zealand that grow to giant size carry great

A large rimu (*Dacrydium cupressinum*) with epiphytes in Tongariro National Park, North Island, New Zealand

amounts of epiphytes. I shall only mention *Podocarpus totara* (totara), *Dacrycarpus dacrydioides* (kahikatea), and *Dacrydium cupressinum* (rimu) here, as I have some direct experience with these. As in the giant conifers of the Pacific Northwest, reiteration in the biggest and oldest trees (some are estimated to be 1500–1800 years old) has given them complicated crowns with massive branches and deep crotches filled with litter and humus. A conspicuous epiphyte on all these big conifers is *Astelia solandri* (Liliaceae), forming big tufts of linear leaves, both living and dead. The leaves collect water in their bases, and the dead leaves remain attached for a long time. These plants can form immense clusters perched in the forks and on the branches of trees and accumulate huge amounts of litter, forming substrate for yet other epiphytes. The orchids *Dendrobium cunninghamii* and *Earine autumnalis* are also common, and of course there are ferns, including the genera *Asplenium*, *Polypodium*, *Trichomanes*, and *Hymenophyllum*, and the lycopod *Lycopodium billardieri*. Often the huge liana *Freycinetia banksii* adds its grand tufts of sword-shaped leaves, but because it roots in the ground it is not a true epiphyte. The result of all this growth can be so burdensome that large branches break off, especially in times of heavy rain.

Research into the dimensions and canopy structure of giant conifers in parts of the world outside the Pacific Northwest has hardly begun. The study of New Zealand epiphytes by Walter Oliver published more than 75 years ago and consulted for this chapter (Oliver 1930) remains the most comprehensive treatment on this subject for that country. Of the fauna that occurs in these magnificent conifer-based epiphyte gardens we know even less. In New Zealand it was almost too late, because by the time Oliver published his account most of the forests had fallen to the axe and the destruction was still ongoing. Now the native forests are protected, but especially in the lowlands, few remain that preserve old growth trees. There are some other parts of the world where giant conifers have in their ancient crowns epiphytic life in abundance. In New Guinea, *Araucaria cunninghamii* and *A. hunsteinii* reach great size and in the humid, tropical climate epiphytes must be numerous. *Fitzroya cupressoides* (alerce) of Chile is another big, slow-growing conifer; although the true giants have unfortunately all been logged, some large trees rich in epiphytes do remain. I also must mention Taiwan, where a large stand of undisturbed old growth *Taiwania cryptomerioides* has been discovered recently. Some of these trees may have the proportions Ernest Wilson reported almost a century ago from the same island, but now logged. Some of the conifer forests in the eastern Himalayas are relatively untouched, as in Bhutan. Perhaps the tallest tree in Asia grows there, if the crude measurements of my friend Sabine Miehe are anywhere near their true size. This is *Cupressus cashmeriana*, reported to grow 95 m (312 ft) tall with a diameter above a buttressed base of 3.5 m (11.5 ft) in some secluded, deep mountain valleys. The long, drooping foliage of this beautiful conifer has long been known in horticulture, but it took until the second half of the 20th century before the species' native habitat became known to botanists. The giant trees seen by Miehe only became known to us a few years ago. For Bob Van Pelt and his colleagues, there is still a lot of exciting climbing and measuring to do.

The drooping foliage of Bhutan or weeping cypress (*Cupressus cashmeriana*)

Conifer
Geography

20 A Coniferous Island in the Tropics

IT HAS BEEN A LONG HAUL *by air from London via Singapore to Sydney and then an-other three hours across the Coral Sea, but we are finally approaching our destination. I always request a window seat because I want to see what passes outside, which I find a much better picture than the movies offered by the airlines. The first sign that we are approaching a substantial bit of land is a long line of clouds on the eastern horizon. Coming closer, I see mountains below them. The deep blue of the ocean suddenly turns turquoise, even blue-green, marked off by a tortuous white line of surf. As we descend towards the airport of Nouméa-la Tontouta in New Caledonia, below us are coral reefs and huge lagoons dotted with islands fringed with palm-lined white beaches. At the airport, a warm wind greets us and waving palms and red-flowering tropical trees sur-round the buildings. It seems to be the unlikeliest place on Earth to come to and look for conifers. That impression is wrong. New Caledonia is something like Mecca for conifer enthusiasts, and we all would like to make at least one pilgrimage to it.*

▲ ▲ ▲

New Caledonia is situated in the southwestern Pacific Ocean, approximately 1500 km (940 mi) east of Australia and roughly halfway between New Guinea and New Zealand, between 19° and 23°S and between 164° and 167°E. The main island, Grande Terre, is about 450 × 50 km (280 × 30 mi); several satellite islands are much smaller, of which the Loyalty Islands to the east are low volcanic islands. All the islands are surrounded by a great coral reef, the Grande Récif, second in size only to the Great Barrier Reef along the eastern coast of Australia. Grande Terre is very mountainous, with the highest peaks rising to 1628 m (5340 ft) on Mont Panié and 1618 m (5307 ft) on Mont Hum-boldt. The steepest and rainiest side is on the eastern coast, where Mont Panié receives more than 8 m (26 ft) of rain per year and it rains almost every day in the year. The western coast, in the rain shadow of the mountains, receives less than one-eighth of this amount of moisture. Yearly temperatures are nearly constant, ranging between 22° and 24°C (72° and 75°F), although at times it can be much cooler in the mountains. The coral reefs form wide and shallow lagoons and protect the coast from ocean waves, so that trees grow right up to beaches and mangroves are widespread near the mouths of rivers. There are four seasons, with two periods of increased rainfall: December to March with cyclones and June to August with cool rains. Often the rain clouds coming from the southeast are caught by the mountains and lose much of their water there, leaving the western coast sunny and dry.

The geology of Grande Terre is complex, and I shall only give a few general facts about it to help explain the rich flora, among which the conifers are so prominent. Underlying younger formations of largely volcanic origin over much of the island is an ancient Palaeozoic core of metamorphic rocks. These rocks are acidic; they come to the surface largely in the northern part of Grande Terre, where the volcanic deposits may be absent. The volcanic rocks were formed during the Mesozoic and again during the early Tertiary, when mountain building elevated the central chain and magma out-pourings forming oceanic crust were pushed up and over the old core of the island, forming in places a 2000 m (6300 ft) thick crust of peridotite. This has eroded away in many places, especially in the northern half of the island, exposing the older rocks. The peridotite is a dark igneous rock low in silicates, which are bound to iron and magnesium. It is rich in many other metals as well, especially nickel and cobalt, which have been liberated from bonds with the rock by the weathering action of a moist tropical climate. These ultrabasic eroded rocks still cover about a third of the main island and are also found on the Île des Pins, a satellite island to the southeast of Grande Terre. Apart from the southeast, these rocks are concentrated in the mountain massifs that run the length of the island, mostly nearer the western coast. In many places a meta-morphic type of rock, serpentine, replaces the peridotite. Iron oxides are usually closest to the surface and have formed a reddish or brown laterite crust, and cobalt and man-ganese have oxidized to form a yellowish laterite crust. Nickel is concentrated near the unaltered bedrock, which may lay deeper or near the surface, and this metal is associ-ated with magnesium silicate. This highly metalliferous rock, also known as ultramafic rock, is poor in nutrients for plants, especially nitrogen, and is in fact toxic. As a result, many plants cannot survive on ultramafic rock, and those that do are usually highly adapted to these disadvantageous conditions. Again, such conditions often suit coni-fers, which can cope with the reduced resources for plant growth better than many angiosperms.

There are 44 species of conifers in New Caledonia, all of which are endemic, which means they do not occur anywhere else. This is by far the highest concentration of conifer species in the world, given that it is such a small area. The family Araucariaceae has nearly half of its 41 species represented in New Caledonia, with five species in *Agathis* and 13 species in *Araucaria*. The family Podocarpaceae is represented by 19 species, eight in *Podocarpus*, four in *Dacrydium*, two in *Retrophyllum*, and one each in *Acmopyle, Dacrycarpus, Falcatifolium, Prumnopitys,* and *Parasitaxus,* the last being monotypic and the only parasitic conifer (see chapter 18). Then there are six species in Cupressaceae, two in *Callitris,* three in *Libocedrus* and another monotypic genus, *Neo-callitropsis.* Finally, in Taxaceae, there is the monotypic genus *Austrotaxus,* the only member of the family in the Southern Hemisphere. For a territory the size of Wales or Massachusetts, this is an amazing diversity of conifers. There is only one other gymno-sperm native to New Caledonia, the cycad *Cycas seemannii,* and unlike the islands' conifers, that species is widespread in the SW Pacific. Something truly remarkable has happened here with conifer diversity.

In this part of the book, we are primarily looking at the biogeographical aspects, that is, how conifers are distributed in the world and what the possible causes are of the distribution patterns that we find. While we shall look more closely at the bigger pic-ture in the next chapters, the conifers of New Caledonia are excellent examples to in-troduce some of the issues. In general, we can divide the conifers between those of the Northern Hemisphere and those of the Southern Hemisphere. The New Caledonian

conifers belong to families and genera of the Southern Hemisphere, perhaps with one exception, *Austrotaxus spicata*. Although the Taxaceae are nearly restricted to the Northern Hemisphere, this singular member extends the family well south of the equator. The New Caledonian member of the family can grow to a sizable tree and with its large leaves resembles *Podocarpus* more than *Taxus*. To be sure of its identity, one needs to see the seed and its orange aril that nearly encloses it. In Grande Terre, it is mysteriously absent from the south, even though in other parts of the island it grows on the serpentine in habitat that is abundantly present in the south as well.

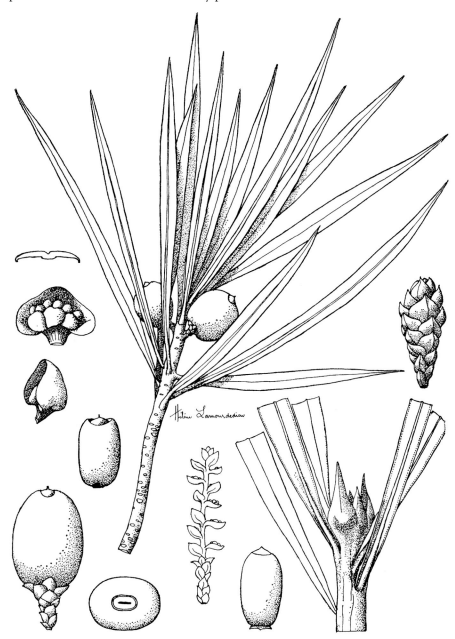

Austrotaxus spicata, from New Caledonia, is the only member of the Taxaceae in the Southern Hemisphere. Drawing by Hélène Lamourdedieu, from de Laubenfels (1972, pl. 2), reprinted by permission of Muséum National d'Histoire Naturelle, Paris

Opposite: Conifers in New Caledonia, with *Araucaria muelleri* and *Dacrydium araucarioides* growing together on the Rivière des Lacs

So how did a member of the Northern Hemisphere Taxaceae come to grow in New Caledonia? In principle, there are two explanations for geographical distributions of organisms: dispersal and vicariance. Dispersal involves active movement, whereas vicariance implies passivity. This needs some explanation, because you could rightly argue that all plants belong to the passive category, unlike mobile animals. However, for plants we may consider dispersal of spores or seeds (propagules) by wind, water, or animals as active movement. Plants do migrate in this way across barriers, provided that these are not insurmountable, and in this respect they are not different from animals. The seeds of *Austrotaxus spicata* are dispersed by birds, as in other members of the family, and so the species or its ancestor could have migrated from island to island and arrived in New Caledonia. Is that a likely scenario? The problem is that we know this genus and species from nowhere else. Where did it come from? *Austrotaxus spicata* is sufficiently distinct to make it likely that it has had a long evolutionary history, but no fossils have been found that can be assigned to this genus. Given that it looks like *Podocarpus* without the fertile organs, this species could be difficult to recognize in the fossil record.

The other explanation has an arcane name, vicariance, from the Latin *vicarius* ("substitute"). In biogeography, vicariance refers to a kind of allopatric speciation whereby a geographic barrier develops that divides a formerly continuous population; the separated populations then diverge into separate species. In common terms, the distribution of the areas explains the distribution of the species. One could, with a bit of licence, say that the areas moved and the organisms stayed put. The populations became separated by the movement of those areas. New Caledonia was once connected with Australia and New Zealand as part of the supercontinent Gondwana. During the Mesozoic it was much closer to Australia than it is now, and the southern Coral Sea and Tasman Sea areas were above sea level much of the time. The distance to what is now Southeast Asia was much greater and the Tethys Ocean lay in between, so that route of migration is not likely if it occurred very long ago. Perhaps, then, *Austrotaxus spicata* had one or more relatives in Australia and/or New Zealand, now extinct. The areas drifted farther and farther apart and in the end only the species *A. spicata* survived in New Caledonia. This implies that Taxaceae were formerly present in Gondwana, that is, in the Southern Hemisphere. No fossils have been found there of this family, or its possible early relatives, like the fossil *Palaeotaxus*. *Austrotaxus spicata* is not the only enigma of conifer distribution posed by the New Caledonian conifers.

The solution to this problem is not easy, because both dispersal and vicariance are plausible explanations. To decide whether the presence of *Austrotaxus spicata* in New Caledonia came about via a dispersal or migration event from Malesia or as a vicariance event separating it from congeners in Australia requires additional data, such as from the fossil record. The circumstance that many other unrelated taxa occur in New Caledonia as well as in Australia and New Zealand, coupled with the geological history, makes vicariance probable. If a plant has the capacity to be dispersed across a distance of ocean, such statistical probabilities cannot disprove dispersal. We are still only talking about probability, not certainty. Both vicariance and dispersal can explain the distribution of species across the globe, and we need more evidence than mere statistics to demonstrate a case for either.

With the 13 species of *Araucaria* now present in New Caledonia, the story is different and we can fortunately say more about this genus with reasonable certainty. In the Mesozoic, the genus had a more or less worldwide distribution and occurred both in the Northern and Southern Hemispheres. By the Upper Cretaceous, however, araucarias had become rare and eventually extinct in the Northern Hemisphere; they also disappeared from southern Africa and from India. Since then, *Araucaria* has been an exclusively Southern Hemisphere group of conifers, but its origin predates the drifting apart of the continents. Still existing in the early Tertiary in South America, Antarctica, and Australasia, the ranges of the species continued to contract further when Antarctica cooled and eventually refrigerated and Australia turned largely into desert. Only one species, *Araucaria araucana* (monkey-puzzle tree), has adapted to a cool climate with winter snow and frost; the others remained dependent on subtropical to tropical climates.

We can analyze the phylogenetic relationships of the current 19 *Araucaria* species and compare the results with their geographic distribution (the vicariance method), which offers some interesting results. The two South American species *Araucaria araucana* and *A. angustifolia* are closely related, their sister group is *A. bidwillii* (bunya pine) from Queensland with *A. hunsteinii* from New Guinea. The next clade is formed by *A. cunninghamii* from New Guinea and Queensland, and finally there is *A. heterophylla* from Norfolk Island. The 13 New Caledonian species have so far eluded attempts to resolve their relationships, but they are as a group most closely related to the Norfolk Island pine, *A. heterophylla*. In other words, the DNA sequences that resolve relationships for the other species have hardly evolved in the New Caledonian species. Perhaps we must search for DNA sections that evolve (that is, produce mutations) faster. Yet the species on the islands are highly diverse morphologically and perfectly good species. The Norfolk Island pine is their nearest relative. Norfolk Island is a tiny remnant of the landmass that once connected Australia, New Zealand, and New Caledonia. Araucarias disappeared from New Zealand, but a few clung onto the Australian eastern coast. One of these, *A. cunninghamii*, belongs to the same section *Eutacta* as the Norfolk Island pine and all the New Caledonian species. It now becomes clearer: The New Caledonian araucarias probably have a single ancestor, and this ancestor diversified into 13 species on the islands.

The five species of *Agathis* in New Caledonia account for one-quarter of the total of 20 or 21 species. This is one of the most tropical of all conifer genera, with only one species, *Agathis australis*, in the subtropics of the northern tip of New Zealand. The genus occurs throughout Malesia, but is absent from Java and the Lesser Sunda Islands, and extends into the southwestern Pacific (not in the Solomon Islands) and the coast of northern Queensland, Australia. This range seems to indicate a palaeotropical origin in Asia, but its presence on the southwestern Pacific islands would then require a dispersal event across wide expanses of ocean that once separated the two regions. That is not easy to imagine with winged seeds that will only travel a few kilometres before falling into the sea. Alternatively, the genus originated in Gondwana, got to New Caledonia in the same way as *Araucaria* (and to Fiji and New Zealand) and only spread to New Guinea and the rest of Malesia after Australia established contact with this archipelago. The fossil record, while not as old or as abundant as that of *Araucaria*, seems to give some support to this idea. *Agathis* is restricted to the Southern Hemisphere, with unambiguous *Agathis* fossils in Australia going back to the Eocene. Again, we could then postulate a single ancestor for the five New Caledonian species.

The taxonomy of this genus is notoriously difficult. Unlike other conifers, in *Agathis* there are more informative morphological characters in the pollen cones than in other parts of the plant. Attempts at phylogenetic reconstruction using DNA sequence data have yielded even more limited results than those with *Araucaria*. Like elsewhere, most *Agathis* species in New Caledonia are large emergent trees in tropical rainforest dominated by angiosperms. Only one species, *Agathis ovata*, has adapted to the ultramafic soils and open scrub (*maquis minier*) in the south of Grande Terre. There it grows to a robust, low tree with a spreading, candelabra-shaped crown and, like its congeners, usually occurs in groves of a few score to more than a hundred trees. While most species occupy lower to middle elevations, *A. montana* is restricted to the higher parts of Mont Panié from about 1000 m (3280 ft) to the summit. These trees look like large versions of *A. ovata*, with enormous spreading crowns and branches contorted into fantastic shapes, all made even more impressive as they loom into view through an almost perpetual mist and rain that surrounds the mountain.

The family Podocarpaceae is the most diverse group of conifers in New Caledonia.

Araucaria montana, a species distributed on mountains throughout the main island in New Caledonia

The genus *Podocarpus* is pan-tropical, extending to subtropical latitudes in the Northern Hemisphere and to temperate latitudes in the Southern Hemisphere. The eight species in New Caledonia cover much of Grande Terre and the Île des Pins and range from low shrubs to tall trees on all major rock or soil types. The genus is presumably of Gond-

wanan origin, and its successful seed dispersal mechanism (see chapter 17) has caused it to be carried far and wide by birds. Dispersal and vicariance have become mixed up and are probably impossible to disentangle for *Podocarpus*.

Dacrydium, with nearly one-fifth of the 21 species in New Caledonia, has a similar but wider range than *Agathis*, extending from southern China to South Island in New Zealand. We have already met *Dacrydium araucarioides*, which is common in the *maquis minier* of the south (see photos in chapters 2 and 15); some of the other species are medium size to large trees. *Dacrydium guillauminii* has an extremely restricted distribution and is in fact one of the rarest coni-

Foliage and pollen cone of *Agathis ovata*

Agathis ovata on the Col de Yaté in the south of Grande Terre, New Caledonia

Dacrydium guillauminii on the Rivière des Lacs, New Caledonia, is one of the rarest conifers in the world. Photograph by Alexander Schmidt

fers in the world. This is a dwarf tree 1–2 m (3–7 ft) tall restricted to the water edge along the Rivière des Lacs in two or three small populations. It appears to germinate in wet soil that lines the river between the water and exposed rocks of ironstone and serpentine. The foliage of *D. guillauminii* seems to retain a perpetual juvenile stage, with thin needle-like leaves.

Dacrydium guillauminii is accompanied by another rarity, *Retrophyllum minus*, which is one of the oddest of the podocarps and a true rheophyte (a plant that grows in streams). It is also a dwarf tree and has a very thick, spongy bark. The genus *Retrophyllum*, with two of five species in New Caledonia, is one of those Gondwanan relicts with at present a highly disjunct distribution. One species is widespread from the Moluccas to Fiji, two are endemic to New Caledonia, and two occur in northeastern South America. Because *Retrophyllum* is restricted to the tropics, one can see how two events, the drifting apart of the southern continents and the cooling and desertification of large parts of these, have pushed the species of this genus to the mountainous tropical regions where they now occur. When Australia contacted with Malesia, one species could expand into that region, colonizing New Guinea and reaching the Moluccas.

We met *Acmopyle pancheri* in chapter 17, and the other species in the genus, *A. sahniana*, is endemic to Fiji. Recent discovery of fossil foliage from the Palaeocene to early Eocene of Argentina that is very similar to that of *Acmopyle* seems to indicate that this genus is a relict in New Caledonia and Fiji. The fossils have to be studied in more detail to be sure of their identity. Similar fossil foliage attributed to *Acmopyle* has been found on the Antarctic Peninsula, Tasmania, and mainland Australia. This is not an uncommon distribution at all. *Prumnopitys* is another genus in Podocarpaceae discussed in chapter 17, with *P. ferruginoides* in New Caledonia and eight other species: one in Queensland, two in New Zealand, and the other five in Central and South

Retrophyllum minus in the Plaine des Lacs, New Caledonia Photograph by Stephan Schneckenburger

America from Costa Rica to southern Chile. If we were to look at angiosperms, we would find many other examples in the New Caledonian flora showing this link with South America. *Dacrycarpus* and *Falcatifolium*, each with one species in New Caledonia, show the other common pattern: a Malesian distribution extending to New Caledonia (*Falcatifolium*) and beyond to Fiji and New Zealand. Yet fossils of *Dacrycarpus* are also known from South America, Tasmania, and Australia. The parasite *Parasitax-*

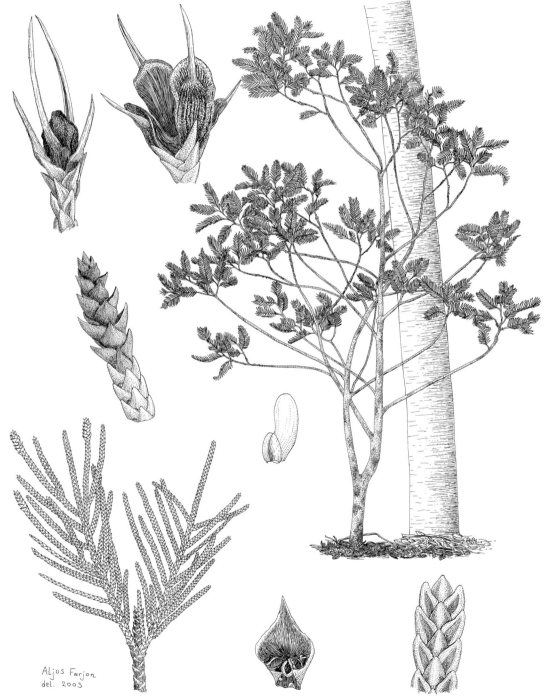

Aljos Farjon
del. 2003

Libocedrus austrocaledonica (small tree) and *Libocedrus chevalieri* (botanical details) from New Caledonia

us usta (see photos in chapter 18), is dependent on its host *Falcatifolium taxoides* and both are endemic to New Caledonia. None of the other five species of *Falcatifolium* are known to have this or another coniferous parasite, which makes it likely that *Parasitaxus* evolved in New Caledonia with this particular host species. It is possible that the extremely nutrient-poor ultramafics played a part in the evolution of the parasitic habit of this little conifer.

The family Cupressaceae is the only cosmopolitan conifer family. However, the six species of this family in New Caledonia belong to genera that are of a southern origin. *Callitris* is widespread in Australia, including Tasmania, and its only outlying station is New Caledonia, with two species. *Callitris neocaledonica* and *C. sulcata* are probably closely related (Farjon 2005b, p. 497), but we do not yet firmly know their relationship to the Australian species. A dispersal event seems unlikely, so the genus could date back to the time when there still was a land connection before about 80 million years ago. *Callitris* is very rare in the fossil record, and no remains older than Oligocene (35 million years ago) are known, so these two types of evidence are in disagreement with each other. Both species are restricted to serpentine and its derivatives in the southern half of Grande Terre and are quite rare. Five species comprise the genus *Libocedrus*; three of these are endemic to New Caledonia, and the other two are found in New Zealand. The New Caledonian species are all shrubs or small trees and the genus occurs across the main island. All three grow where there is very abundant rain and/or along perennial streams. Fossil remains of *Libocedrus* are known from Australia and Tasmania. Finally, there is the species *Neocallitropsis pancheri* (see photo in chapter 2), which is related to *Callitris* and the only species in its genus, endemic to New Caledonia. This species is highly specialized in its adaptation to the most extreme ultramafic soils, heavy with poisonous metals, and is most abundant in the far south of Grande Terre, where these soils prevail.

This array of conifers demonstrates not only the extraordinary biodiversity of New Caledonia, which has a flora of more than 3000 indigenous vascular plant species in 156 families, with about 80 per cent endemism. It is also a showcase of conifer biogeography in a nutshell. As we have seen, the biogeography of the New Caledonian conifers and their closest relatives show two major patterns. One is the so-called Australasian distribution. Here New Caledonia is a link between roughly Vietnam and New Zealand (both countries have a highly diverse conifer flora). Within this distribution pattern of genera, New Caledonia has an exceptional high species diversity; more species evolved here than in any other area of this region. Factors such as the islands' long and extreme isolation and the geological peculiarities have played a role in this formation of species. The other pattern, showing the links with Australia, New Zealand, and ultimately South America, tells the story of the separation of continents. The same factors as mentioned before, such as isolation and topography, caused speciation, as seen in *Araucaria*. This second pattern relates to a bigger picture of conifer distribution, especially apparent in the Southern Hemisphere and it is the story I wish to tell next.

21 Riding the Continents

THE 630 SPECIES OF CONIFERS *cover a large proportion of the land surface of the Earth. In the world map below, the greatest area of distribution is clearly to be seen in the Northern Hemisphere, which is due to the extensive conifer forest of the boreal zone in Eurasia and North America. Few species occur there, however, and the diversity increases dramatically further south, while the areas covered decrease. There are large gaps at around 30°N, which continue across the equator into the Southern Hemisphere. In the far south there is much less land, although, with the exception of Antarctica, the land is quite well covered with conifers, with few large gaps. What does this map tell us about the world distribution of conifers?*

▲ ▲ ▲

Conifers occur in almost all the major vegetation types of the world (see Table 3 in chapter 3). They are absent in only a few, but very rare in some others. In the north, a few conifers occur in tundra vegetation, mostly in the transition zone from boreal forest to tundra. In the High Arctic (a cold desert) they are left behind, which explains the white areas on the map in northern Canada and Siberia, while the Greenland icecap prevents any form of vegetation. The steppes can have some conifers here and there, but are also largely without them—hence the white areas in North America (the three small ones are the Great Lakes), central Asia, Tibet and Mongolia, large parts of sub-Saharan Africa, and Patagonia in South America. Although a few conifers occur in deserts,

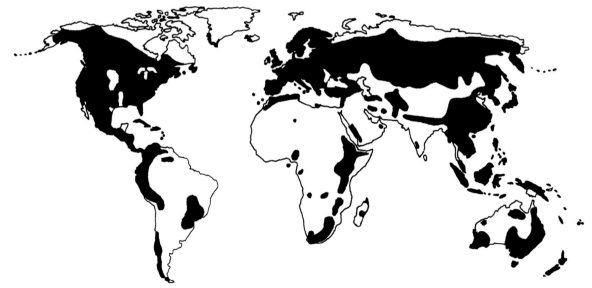

The global distribution of conifers shown on a world map with approximate equal area projection. The black areas on the map are not uniformly covered with conifers; they occur together with angiosperms or in patches too small to separate on this scale.

most of the regions of the world covered by deserts are devoid of conifers. This explains the great white areas on the map representing the deserts of central and western Asia, Arabia, the Sahara, and Australia. In chapter 3, we also observed that lowland tropical rainforest does not have conifers, and I gave a possible explanation for this remarkable fact, namely that here angiosperms outcompeted conifers due to universally good conditions for plant growth. In the present geographical context, it explains the great white areas of the Amazon Basin and the Congo Basin and also smaller areas such as the Yucatán Peninsula in Mexico, Bangladesh, the middle part of the Malay Peninsula, and the southern lowlands of New Guinea. Some lowland areas with deciduous angiosperm forest had no conifers and are now given over to agriculture and urbanization, especially in western Europe and northern China.

Have we now explained all the white areas on the map? Not quite, and those that remain cannot be resolved with an ecological explanation. Large parts of South America, even larger parts of Africa, and the Indian subcontinent are the major gaps in conifer distribution that have no explanation in terms of unsuitable climate or soils. Smaller areas are western Madagascar and Sri Lanka. We are left, then, with some intriguing white areas, the largest situated in South America, Africa, Madagascar, and India, for which there seems to be no ready explanation. Did they ever have conifers, and if so, why did they lose them?

Perhaps the Indian subcontinent is the best example with which to approach this question. In India today, there are conifers in the Himalayas and some adjacent highlands in the northeast. From a biogeographic point of view, these are not really Indian—they are all northern genera, such as *Pinus, Abies, Picea, Juniperus, Cedrus, Cupressus, Larix*, and *Taxus*. One other conifer, *Nageia wallichiana*, occurs naturally in the Western Ghats in the southwest of the subcontinent; this conifer is widespread in Southeast Asia and Malesia, and this disjunct population may be the result of a dispersal event, as its seeds are carried by birds. India, as you may know, only became a part of Asia after it collided with that continent at the end of the Cretaceous and in the Palaeocene, in the process pushing up the highest chain of mountains in the world. India was part of Gondwana, the ancient southern supercontinent, and it drifted through the eastern Tethys Ocean (now the Indian Ocean) in a northeasterly direction from southern latitudes right through the tropics to where it is now. The northern conifers entered the territory after that connection was made but stayed in the northern mountains. On page 168 are four maps showing the position and configuration of landmasses in the Middle Triassic (225 million years ago [Ma]), Lower Cretaceous (130 Ma), Palaeocene (60 Ma), and Miocene (15 Ma). These maps are rough sketches of continents as they may have appeared at these times, but they have merit because they attempt to reconstruct land and sea as it was and not merely the present continents in different positions.

The position of the Indian subcontinent in the Triassic is in fact uncertain. Some researchers have placed it wedged between southern Africa and Antarctica, much further away from Asia than in this map. The Indian subcontinent was certainly connected with Antarctica in still earlier times. Its connection with Africa is not disputed, nor its independent journey through the ocean, crossing the equator. In the fossil record of India there are several conifers dating from the Permian (such as *Buriadia* and

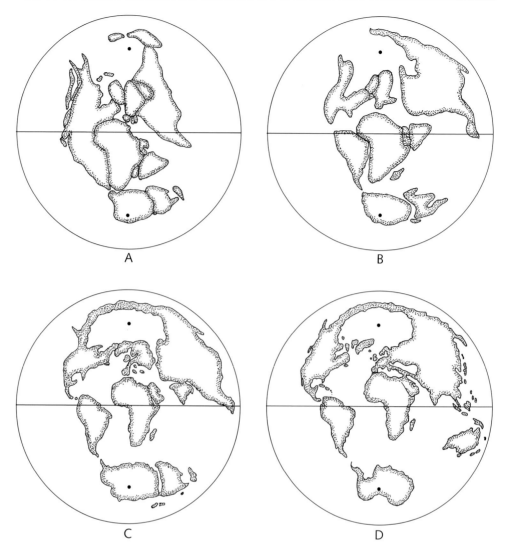

Positions of landmasses on the globe in four periods: (A) Middle Triassic (225 Ma); (B) Lower Cretaceous (130 Ma); (C) Palaeocene (60 Ma); and (D) Miocene (15 Ma). The two poles (dots) are on one side of the map and the equator is indicated. Drawn after Briggs (1995)

Walkomiella), Triassic (*Araucaria*), Jurassic (*Araucaria*, Podocarpaceae such as *Elatocladus jabalpurensis*, *Nipaniostrobus*, and *Retinosporites*), to the Lower Cretaceous (Podocarpaceae). None of these extend beyond collision time: by the end of the Cretaceous they had all become extinct. Later fossil conifers all have northern affinities. There are two possible explanations for the demise of the southern conifers. One is that they were already rare and were outcompeted by the angiosperms after these evolved in the Lower Cretaceous. Without major mountain building going on while the subcontinent had a tropical, hot and moist climate, it must have been much like the Amazon Basin, where no conifers occur today either. The other possibility is that conifers survived in some areas until the catastrophic flood basalts at the end of the Cretaceous, known as the Deccan Traps, covered nearly a third of the subcontinent and wiped out all vegetation. No conifers with pioneer recolonization capacity were available to compete with the returning angiosperms after things had cooled down. Possibly these two factors worked together. The conifers of India were riding a continent towards their doom.

Africa is the poorest continent for conifers today. Because Africa was also part of ancient Gondwana, we should exclude for this discussion the conifers along the Mediterranean Sea in North Africa, as they are really European in origin. One species of juniper, *Juniperus procera*, extends from Arabia and Yemen across the Red Sea and follows the highlands of Ethiopia and along the Rift Valley south to Zimbabwe across the equator. This species is closely related to *J. excelsa* of western Asia, and it dispersed from the north, making use of the Afromontane pathway. The few other African conifers are of southern origin: *Widdringtonia* (Cupressaceae), with four species, is restricted to southern Africa; *Afrocarpus* (Podocarpaceae), with six species, is fairly widespread but virtually limited to the Afromontane forests from Ethiopia to the Cape; and *Podocarpus*, with four species, scattered from Cameroon and Kenya to the Cape. Vast areas of sub-Saharan Africa have no conifers at all.

The genus *Widdringtonia* is closely related to the Australian genus *Callitris*, demonstrating the distant link from the time of Gondwana. The distribution of the angiosperm family Proteaceae is another well-known example of this link. But whereas *Callitris* has done well in Australia, where it is the most widespread conifer genus with 15 species, *Widdringtonia* has only one widespread species (*W. nodiflora*) while the other three are on the brink of extinction. Both genera occupy similar habitats, where rainfall is highly seasonal and fire is a recurrent disturber of the vegetation. In the case of *Widdringtonia*, however, only *W. nodiflora* is well adapted to frequent fires, as it will resprout from its base (coppice). The adaptation of *Callitris* to fire varies with the species from well adapted to low tolerance, and they occupy various habitats accordingly. Fires severely limit the three rare species of *Widdringtonia* and it seems that this has been the case for a very long time.

Clanwilliam cedar (*Widdringtonia cedarbergensis*) is restricted to the Cedarberg Mountains of South Africa

Afrocarpus and *Podocarpus* are conifers restricted to rainforest or wet montane habitats where there is no prolonged dry season. Australia moved away from Antarctica in a northerly direction and passed from cool, moist latitudes to hot, dry latitudes. *Podocarpus* only survived in a few still wet localities in Tasmania and on the eastern coast and a little corner of southwestern Australia, where it became an understorey scrub in the yarra forest (*Eucalyptus marginata*). In Africa, climatic changes have been severe, too, but the topography is more complex than that of Australia, with more high mountains and more montane rainforest as a result. It is unclear why more podocarps have not survived in these extensive mountain systems. The formation of savannas in the Miocene and Pliocene came at a time when conifers were perhaps already on the decline, and no suitable species were there to adapt to this new environment. In Madagascar, there are today only five or six species of *Podocarpus*, all with very limited distributions. Madagascar separated from Africa as early as the Jurassic. The genus does not appear to date that far back, so it is likely that the species in Madagascar derive from a common ancestor that was dispersed from Africa to the island, perhaps when it was still closer to Africa. No conifers that could adapt to the more arid conditions of the western half of the island have made the jump.

In South America the uplifting of the Andes, which continues today, blocked the rains from the Pacific and created the steppes and semi-deserts of Paraguay and Argentina. Among the extant conifers, adaptation to aridity is a specialization of some genera in Cupressaceae and a few pines. South America has three species in this family, *Austrocedrus chilensis*, *Pilgerodendron uviferum*, and *Fitzroya cupressoides*. All three occur on the wetter, Pacific side of the Andes and only *A. chilensis* is moderately adapted to a dry environment, as it occurs partly in the climatic zone with summer drought and winter rains. Many more conifers, including Cupressaceae, are known from fossils in South America, but all are very likely of the moisture-loving kind. They became extinct due to climate change caused by the moving of the continents and its effects upon the topography.

Thus, it appears that isolation, caused by the break-up of Gondwana and the increasing separation of its constituent landmasses, is a major factor behind the white gaps in the conifer map of the Southern Hemisphere. Connections remained much longer in place with the break-up of Laurasia, the northern supercontinent, and it became less fragmented. The only wide gap is the North Atlantic Ocean, which opened late in the history of conifer evolution. Through much of the time, the Bering land bridge connected Asia and North America, and its climate was much milder, allowing trees to migrate in both directions and fill the gaps left by extinctions.

Both dispersal and vicariance played a part in the history of conifer distribution leading to the present situation. However, due to the size, proximity, and orientation of continents in the Northern Hemisphere, dispersal accounts for much of the distribution of genera and species. Many genera had or still have closely related sister species in Eurasia and North America. During the Palaeogene the species were often identical on both continents, as there were land connections at both ends. Examples are found in *Sequoia*, *Taxodium*, *Metasequoia*, *Glyptostrobus*, and *Pseudolarix*, all of which are now restricted to a single or at most two species with limited distributions. In other genera, separation of populations by widening or emerging barriers did cause divergence into several distinct species. The epicontinental sea of the Cretaceous dividing North America almost in two halves could account for many different species of conifers on that continent. But often, emerging barriers such as mountain ranges that block migration for lowland species are at the same time connecting corridors for upland species. The genus *Cedrus* may once have occurred more or less continuously in mountains along the shores of the western Tethys Sea from northwestern Africa and southern Europe to western Asia and the emerging Himalayas. The formation of deserts and extinction in Europe during the Pleistocene ice ages isolated the western, central, and eastern populations. Only the Himalayan species *Cedrus deodara* is morphologically distinct; the central (*C. libani, C. brevifolia*) and western (*C. atlantica*) remnant populations show overlapping characters. In one area of the Taurus Mountains in southern Turkey, I have seen trees that could be assigned to all three species based on their morphological characters. Perhaps there are genetic differences, but to find out a large and laborious sampling of DNA sequence data from all regions would be necessary, and no one has taken up that challenge. This seems to indicate that there was one species of *Cedrus* in the Palaeogene and that only the Himalayan population has been separated long enough to become a distinct species.

The fossil age of the genus *Cedrus* and its phylogenetic position in the family Pinaceae are in conflict. Cladistic analyses using DNA sequence data have resulted in a basal position for this genus, meaning it shares a nearest common ancestor with all the other genera in Pinaceae. The fossil record does not extend further back than the early part of the Tertiary and not beyond the shores of the Thetys Sea, indicating a late evolution. Fossils are indistinguishable from extant species, which themselves show little var-

Lebanon cedar (*Cedrus libani*) in the Taurus Mountains of southern Turkey

Himalayan cedar or deodar (*Cedrus deodara*) is distinct morphologically from the western cedars, which may be one species or three.

iation. These findings all point to a young instead of an old genus. We must find more fossils, but we must also try hard to understand more about DNA sequence data. The question to be answered is this: Are molecular data trees equivalent to taxon trees?

The long history of the assemblage and subsequent fragmentation of the two supercontinents, Laurasia in the north and Gondwana in the south, is apparently still reflected in the distribution patterns of conifers across the globe. If we look at the different taxa, this is even more clearly demonstrated. At the family level, Cephalotaxaceae, Pinaceae, Sciadopityaceae, and Taxaceae are Laurasian and Araucariaceae, Phylloccladaceae, and Podocarpaceae are Gondwanan, although *Araucaria* (Araucariaceae) once extended into Laurasia. Cupressaceae as a family is cosmopolitan, but the 30 genera that make up this family today are divided in Northern and Southern Hemisphere groups, with a few trespassers, some only known from the fossil record. Some of these exceptions are intriguing enough, though. The South African genus *Widdringtonia* has been found in the Upper Cretaceous of North America, and *Austrosequoia wintonensis* from the Cretaceous of Australia is very similar to *Sequoia* and *Sequoiadendron* of Laurasian origin. Such widely distant occurrences of taxa in the Cupressaceae seem to throw into doubt the separation of extant conifers into northern and southern origins. *Araucaria* may have originated before the separation of Pangea into two supercontinents, but as far as we know, the Cupressaceae evolved after that event. It is clear that we do not know everything there is to know about the distribution and evolution of conifers.

When the supercontinent of Gondwana broke up and its constituent landmasses drifted apart, many species of land-based organisms became fragmented into disjunct populations. Over time, these separated populations often evolved to become separate species. Separation and speciation by vicariance have been common with conifers in the Southern Hemisphere. In some instances new centres of diversity were created, and dispersal from these centres, creating founder populations for new species, may have played a part. Examples are *Araucaria* in New Caledonia and *Callitris* in Australia, and in the past others may have existed. Losses were also common, and in some cases we find conifers once distributed on several Gondwanan fragments now reduced to one or two. Table 5 lists 18 genera of conifers that have been found, as fossils or living plants, in eight southern lands that were once parts of Gondwana. I have not included Africa, Madagascar, and India because two of these parts of former Gondwana only shared *Podocarpus*, a pan-tropical genus, while India shared none. These areas have already been discussed above. Genera are only listed if they have been found in at least two separate areas.

Table 5. The distribution of 18 conifer genera across eight dispersed fragments of the ancient supercontinent Gondwana

GENUS	SA	ANT	TAS	NZ	AUS	NC	FI	NG
Acmopyle	✖	✖	✖		✖	▲	▲	
Agathis			✖		▲	▲	▲	▲
Araucaria	▲		✖	✖	▲	▲		▲
Athrotaxis	✖		▲	✖				
Austrocedrus	▲		✖					
Austrosequoia			✖		✖			
Coronelia	✖		✖					
Dacrycarpus	✖		✖	▲	✖	▲	▲	▲
Dacrydium			✖	▲	✖	▲	▲	▲
Falcatifolium					✖	▲		▲
Fitzroya	▲		✖					
Lepidothamnus	▲			▲				
Libocedrus			✖	▲	✖	▲		
Papuacedrus		✖	✖					▲
Pherosphaera			▲		▲			
Phyllocladus			▲	▲	✖			▲
Podocarpus	▲		▲	▲	▲	▲	▲	▲
Retrophyllum	▲			✖	✖	▲	▲	▲
Totals	**10**	**2**	**15**	**9**	**12**	**9**	**6**	**9**

Note: SA, South America; ANT, Antarctica; TAS, Tasmania; NZ, New Zealand; AUS, Australia; NC, New Caledonia; FI, Fiji; NG, New Guinea; ✖, extinct; ▲, extant
Source: Data from Hill and Brodribb (1999); Farjon (2001), amended

The high number of genera in Tasmania, all but four only known from there as fossils, is in part a product of the research of Bob Hill and his collaborators. The poverty of Antarctica is due to the inaccessibility of the fossil record, which is mostly covered by an icecap. In many cases these two Gondwanan fragments, one a moderately sized island, the other a continent, are keys to the link between South America and Australasia and the southwest Pacific. Fossils of these genera have not been recorded from New Caledonia, Fiji, and New Guinea. Due to the geology of the first two islands, fossils, especially older ones, are unlikely to exist or they are very rare. That is not true for New Guinea, which has excellent geological conditions for fossils. Here it is the research that has been lacking. From the information in Table 5, we can nevertheless make some observations that shed light on the past and present distribution of these genera belonging to four families: Araucariaceae, Cupressaceae, Podocarpaceae, and Phyllocladaceae. New Guinea shares as many conifer genera with Tasmania (seven) as does New Zealand (seven), and it shares four genera with South America. New Zealand separated from Antarctica and Australia in the Lower Cretaceous and drifted further and further away from these continents. Tasmania remained connected with Antarctica to the end of the Eocene and then drifted north with Australia (see four maps on page 168). Australia reconnected with New Guinea in the Miocene and Pliocene. New Zealand has therefore been isolated for a much longer time, even longer than New Caledonia. Extinctions in Tasmania and Australia have been severe, so that many of the conifers linking these parts with South America, New Zealand, New Caledonia, Fiji, and New Guinea have disappeared there. An example that still exists in South America, New Caledonia, Fiji, and New Guinea but has been found as fossils in Australia and New Zealand is the genus *Retrophyllum* (Podocarpaceae). This genus is easily recognized by its peculiar attachment and positioning (phyllotaxis) of its leaves. Although spirally inserted, each successive leaf alternately twists left and right and also in such a way that it turns the same side up, with the stomatal bands below and the glossy green surface above.

Other genera are now extinct in South America as well as in Australia and Tasmania, but live on in New Caledonia and Fiji, such as *Acmopyle* and *Dacrycarpus*, the latter

Juvenile foliage of *Retrophyllum minus*. Plant grown at the Royal Botanic Garden, Edinburgh

also in New Zealand, New Guinea, and through Malesia to Southeast Asia. *Dacrydium* has disappeared from Australia and Tasmania, and there is as yet no evidence that it occurred in South America. The genus is widespread from Southeast Asia to New Zealand, but its presence in New Zealand, New Caledonia, and Fiji and a fossil record in Tasmania and Australia going back to the Eocene make it clear this conifer genus originated in Gondwana. By riding the continents, an ancestral species eventually made contact with Asia, whereupon new terrain was colonized by dispersal. Of a total of 21 species, 11 now occur in lands that were once far distant from Gondwana and its remnants. In the next chapter, we shall see what dispersal has done for conifer distribution across the world.

22 The Success of Dispersal

WHEN CRO-MAGNON PEOPLE *painted wild animals and hunting scenes deep in the limestone caves of Lascaux and Altamira about 15,000 years ago, the landscape outside was arctic tundra. It was the last and one of the coldest phases of the most recent ice age, and almost all of Europe was a treeless expanse, bordered in the southeast, south, and southwest by high mountains that were covered in huge glaciers. The northern icecap, expanding from Scandinavia, terminated along a line from northern England across the dry North Sea Basin to northern Germany and Poland. Reindeer were the main source of subsistence for these Ice Age Europeans, who would follow the twice-yearly migration of the herds. In summer they moved northward to near the ice front, and in winter down to southwestern Europe, where the cave entrances in steep-sided valleys gave protection against the worst of the winter snows. We know from the great art in these caves which large animals were hunted and which, such as cave bears, were feared and revered at the same time. The fauna was one of tundra and steppe, not of forest. Trees were sparse in the realm of the reindeer hunters, although they probably knew some aspen, birches, and willows, for without firewood they would not have survived the long winters. Conifers and most other trees had retreated beyond the mountains into the Iberian, Italian, and Balkan Peninsulas and into refugia around the Black Sea and Mediterranean. Europe resembled Greenland and the Canadian Arctic of today.*

▲ ▲ ▲

Beginning some 12,000 years ago, the climate became rapidly milder and the icecaps shrank and retreated, to disappear completely about 9000 years ago. Trees returned in rapid succession. Palynologists, who find pollen grains in datable peat and clay deposits and can identify them to different genera or species of trees and other plants, have reconstructed the vegetation of Europe as it changed with time. Because many records of the last warming episode have been preserved, we know more about it than about the earlier interglacial periods. Conifers again play a part in the recolonization of Europe by trees after the latest ice age, as they did in previous warmer interglacial periods. After successive glacial periods fewer species returned, however, and during the present warm period, only a handful have made it back to Europe north of the Alps and the Pyrenees. In central and western Europe the first conifers to return were *Pinus sylvestris* and *Juniperus communis*, together with *Betula* forming open pine-birch forests. These alternated a few times with a return of the tundra, leaving only local stands of trees on south-facing slopes. Eventually, the forest prevailed in central Europe about 9000 years ago, but then *Quercus pubescens* and other oaks and angiosperms began to replace the pines and birches, at least in the lowlands. In the uplands other conifers, especially *Picea, Abies*, and *Larix*, returned and held sway against angiosperms or in

Norway spruce (*Picea abies*) near the Rhône Glacier in the Swiss Alps

Seed cones of *Picea abies* Photograph by Peter A. Schmidt

mixture with them, especially *Fagus sylvatica* (European beech). In the north, pines retreated in Britain to the Scottish Highlands and gave the most widespread species of pine, *Pinus sylvestris*, its English name, Scots pine. These pines are common around the Baltic Sea and in Scandinavia, and in Russia all the way to the Amur River. With the oaks, *Taxus baccata* followed; yews do well on chalk in more open terrain but are capable of germinating and growing in the shade of most trees except beeches. All this returning of trees in Europe happened through dispersal.

Let us follow one conifer, *Picea abies* (Norway spruce), on its journey back into Europe in more detail. The following is largely based on information in volume 1 of the book *Die Fichte*, a two-volume monograph on the Norway spruce by Helmut Schmidt-Vogt (1987), the unsurpassed scholar on this tree. The refugia in southern and eastern Europe were usually small, but sometimes larger, forests in a landscape dominated by steppe or mountain scrub. For *P. abies* during the latest glacial period, these refugia were all in the eastern half of Europe, from central Russia, the southern Carpathians in

Romania, the northern and central Balkans reaching to the eastern margin of the Alps. While the south-facing valleys of the Pyrenees and other parts of northern Spain may have offered suitable habitat for spruce refugia, no evidence can be found that they were there during this time or later. Unlike during earlier interglacial periods of the Pleistocene, *Picea* would not return to the westernmost parts of Europe, where it had once stood on the Atlantic coast of Ireland. The routes of dispersal after the last glacial period across Europe run from east to west and, secondarily, from south to north. The spruces in Scandinavia and along the Baltic Sea all derive from small refugia in central Russia. They moved through Finland between 5000 and 3500 years ago and then crossed the Gulf of Bothnia, finally reaching southern Sweden about 2000 years ago. Their spread through Sweden was made easier as there was open birch-pine woodland into which the spruces invaded. Crossing the Scandinavian mountains was much slower, and Norway spruce did not reach some valleys in central Norway until 1000 years ago or even later. Various ecological conditions prevented spruces from reaching Norway's west coast; the only naturally occurring conifer there is Scots pine (*Pinus sylvestris*). Most of central Europe's natural spruce forests derive from refugia in the Carpathian Mountains, and the spruces here followed the numerous old mountain ranges rather than the valleys and lowlands. Around 6000 years ago they reached a westernmost point in Germany in the Harz Mountains; it took them another 4000 years to reach the Vosges Mountains across the Rhine. The Harz population was isolated from the main distribution further south by an as-yet-unexplained gap of 70 km (44 mi). Dominance of spruces in the forest often followed long after their first arrival and is sometimes correlated with a cooling and wetting of the climate. Such a climate change allowed Norway spruce even to spread out onto the North German Plain around 2500 years ago, only to retreat again later when the climate warmed up.

The Alps were colonized from refugia in the Carpathians, with spruces travelling from east to west, and possibly from locations in or near the southeastern Alps. Here small pockets of forest in a steppe-like vegetation consisted of the conifers *Pinus cembra, P. sylvestris, Picea abies*, and *Larix decidua* and the angiosperms *Alnus* (alder) and *Betula* (birch). Conifer pollen is usually not distinct at the level of species, so we do often not know for certain which species were there. However, the present distributions of species tell us what is most likely, and sometimes macrofossils provide evidence. In previous interglacial periods, *Picea omorika* returned to central Europe, as macrofossils testify, but now it stayed behind in its only refugium on the Drina River in Serbia, where it still is. Another spruce for which there is some evidence of wider distribution before the more recent ice ages but now confined to the Caucasus and northeastern Turkey is *Picea orientalis* (oriental spruce).

Norway spruce reached the Vosges Mountains 2000 years ago and the Dauphiné Alps in France 2500 years ago. These were the westernmost natural sites for spruces in Europe before foresters transplanted them to suitable and unsuitable areas further west. One of these areas is the Hautes Fagnes in the Belgian Ardennes, a high plateau of Palaeozoic gneiss and schist reaching 600 m (1970 feet) above sea level. Winters are colder and snowier and summers cooler and wetter here than in the rest of Belgium. For centuries the Hautes Fagnes were exactly that: high moors covered in heathers

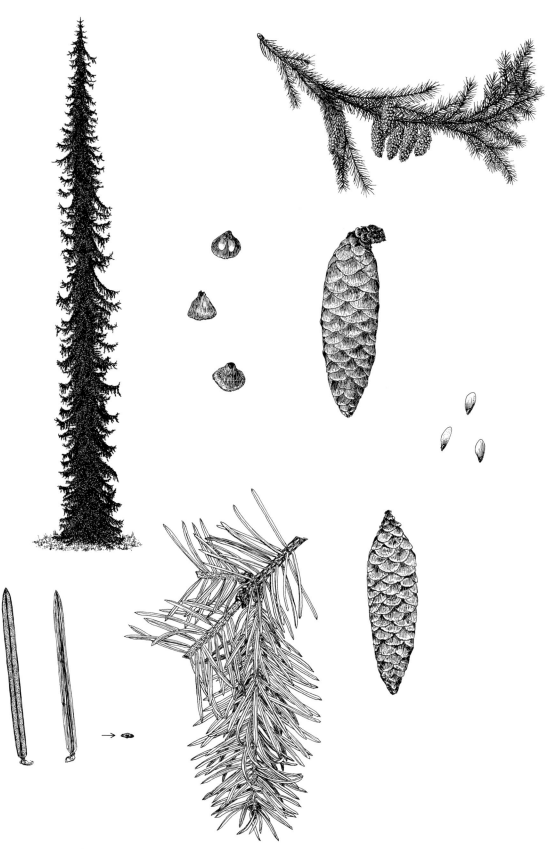

Serbian spruce, *Picea omorika*

The young pollen cones of *Picea orientalis* (oriental spruce) are bright red

(*Calluna vulgaris* and *Erica tetralix*) and purple moor-grass (*Molinia caerulea*), drained by acidic streams running through peat bogs. Because the region is unfit for agriculture, foresters in the 19th century finally found that Norway spruce does very well here, if one can tolerate some wind throw by autumnal storms. Vast areas of the moors were afforested, until during the middle of the 20th century it was realized that nature conservation and tourism demanded the preservation of what was left of the moors. The greatest threat to the moors is now the invasion of Norway spruce from the surrounding plantations. Attempts at cutting it back amount to mopping up water from the kitchen floor with the tap still running and do not solve the problem. This example demonstrates well that the natural absence of Norway spruce west of the Vosges Mountains and the Rhine is not due to unsuitable habitats but is connected with a slowing down of migration rates after deciduous broad-leaved trees became dominant.

The long separation in refugia and the separate pathways of migration sometimes resulted in the segregation of different forms of Norway spruce. One of the most interesting examples is the segregation of two types of branching, called in German *Kammfichte* and *Plattenfichte*. The first, in which branches form a comb, have pendulous foliage branches; the second form has flat sprays spreading more or less horizontally. We find the *Kammfichte* in the western Alps, Black Forest, and Jura Mountains and the *Plattenfichte* in the eastern Alps, the Carpathians, and in Scandinavia. They are adaptations to different kinds of snow: wet and heavy in the western Alps and Jura Mountains and dry and powdery in Scandinavia. The wet snow falls through the pendulous branches, but on horizontal branches it would remain and cause breakage. Spreading foliage horizontally is more advantageous for the interception of sunlight in relatively dense stands of trees; in the cold and dry east and north this is not a problem. Perhaps not surprisingly, Scandinavian spruces used in forestry in Germany proved to be a disaster and were soon given up.

Siberia, while even colder than it is now, was only partly glaciated during the ice ages. For glaciers and icecaps to form there must be snow that does not melt away in summer, and there probably was not enough of it in most areas. Despite this, trees retreated to refugia, leaving most of Siberia to tundra. Three species of pines have been studied in some detail in relation to postglacial return: *Pinus sylvestris*, *P. sibirica*, and *P. pumila*. Both *P. sylvestris* and *P. sibirica* had refuges in the upper (that is, southernmost) drainages of western Siberian rivers, such as the Irtysh and Yennisy, where they were present 15,000 years ago. With the onset of a warming climate, *P. sylvestris* migrated north and east on a broad front, reaching a point well north of its present limit on the Yennisy River at least 8000 years ago. The return of lower temperatures later pushed it back south again. Around 4000 years ago *P. sylvestris* had reached Lake Baikal, and it then marched further east to the Amur River, its present easternmost limit. The Scots pine likes it relatively dry and warm in summer and is a pioneer of open forest types. Unless these open areas are perpetuated by fires, succession would replace it with other conifers, among which is *P. sibirica*. The two species occupy much the same range in Siberia today, but exclude each other ecologically. The seeds of Siberian pine are dispersed by birds (see the story of *Pinus cembra*, a close relative, and the Eurasian nutcracker in chapter 17), so it travelled more slowly than the Scots pine, which lets its seed be carried by the wind.

The shrubby Siberian dwarf pine (*Pinus pumila*; see drawing in chapter 14) is extremely tolerant of cold. Its present range is northeastern Siberia, including the Kamchatka Peninsula, with southern extensions to Lake Baikal on the continent and Sakhalin and northern Japan in the Pacific. The shrub may be covered in snow in winter, which will protect it from severe frost, although this pine will resprout from roots, thereby spreading over hills and slopes. Apparently, this species was present in the area

Scots pine (*Pinus sylvestris*) growing in the Cairngorm Mountains of Scotland, which may serve as a present-day refuge.

even during the latest ice age, although less abundant and frequent. Therefore *P. pumila* had less far to travel to reoccupy lost ground. The Japanese populations, now restricted to alpine zones in the mountains, are relicts of ice age refugia.

North America had two huge icecaps during the latest glacial period, separated by an ice-free corridor that ran from central Alaska southwards along the eastern margins of the Rocky Mountains. In the west was the Cordilleran Ice Sheet and in the east the Laurentian Ice Sheet; the latter reached south to cover the Great Lakes. Tree refugia, depending on species, could be far to the south as no mountain barriers blocked the trees' retreat. The migration of conifers northward following the retreat of the Laurentian Ice Sheet has been well studied. *Pinus banksiana* (jack pine) has a present distribution that coincides with the extent of the Laurentian Ice Sheet. This species had refugia both east and west of the northern Appalachian Mountains and possibly on a stretch of ice-free Atlantic coast in Canada. Recent research in DNA variation across the present range could trace the provenances related to these refugia. Because glacial periods last three to four times longer than interglacials, separation in disjunct refugia can produce lasting genetic differences, and it may even produce species.

I will now take up the story of *Pinus strobus* (eastern white pine), for which I think the latter applies. During the latest ice age, called Wisconsin glaciation in North America, *P. strobus* had refugia on the Atlantic Coastal Plain, which due to a substantial drop in sea level was much wider than it is now. From there it moved northward and westward, replacing *Pinus banksiana* in many places. By 5000 years

Foliage and seed cones of *Pinus sylvestris*

The seed cones of jack pine (*Pinus banksiana*) remain closed on the branches

ago, eastern white pine had reached north beyond its present range, only to retreat when the climate cooled again. Its westward movement was slower and it reached Minnesota only 1000 years ago. During the Wisconsin, and indeed earlier during other glacial periods, a natural pathway of southward migration of *P. strobus* would have been along the Appalachian Mountains. Fossils of spruces (*Picea*) as far south as Mississippi and Louisiana dating from the Late Pleistocene indicate a cool climate and conifer forest type well suitable for *P. strobus*, although we do not know if this species reached this far during the Wisconsin glaciation. Other northern trees did, however, and at some stages of the Pleistocene reached Mexico. Today, the mountains of Veracruz and even Chiapas in the south of Mexico share several tree species with the Appalachian Mountains in the eastern United States. These mountain systems are separated by the subtropical lowlands around the Gulf of Mexico, into which the southern pines (*Pinus* subsection *Australes*) returned from their refugia. In these Mexican mountains we find an uncharacteristic pine for the region, first described by the Mexican conifer specialist Maximino Martínez as *Pinus strobus* var. *chiapensis*, but later raised to species rank as *P. chiapensis*. When I studied Mexican pines for a monograph published in *Flora Neotropica* (Farjon and Styles 1997) I visited these pines in Chiapas. The cones are quite variable in size, but otherwise only slightly and not consistently different from *P. strobus*; other morphological characters are very similar. It was decided to maintain its varietal status, but it can be postulated that here is an ice-age refugium relict that could eventually evolve to a distinct species by vicariance (and after dispersal). Many botanists have argued that similar limited distinction of uncertain consistency exists between eastern white pine and western white pine (*P. monticola*), separated by the Great Plains of North America. How old is that separation, and were they once a single population? The success of dispersal observed in the postglacial history of the distribution of the northern conifers shows that this is possible. Because we cannot distinguish the fossil pollen left by such closely related conifers, we need to follow other lines of evidence. As seen with the jack pine, DNA seems to be promising as it provides markers that trace the origin of widely dispersed populations of conifers.

23 Relicts to Be Discovered

ACCORDING TO THE OXFORD DICTIONARY, *a* relict *is an animal or plant known to have existed in the same form in previous geological ages. Webster's dictionary gives a similar explanation, but mentions extinction: a relict is a remnant of an otherwise extinct species known from the past. This is the meaning I want to use here because in the Oxford version almost all conifers can be called relicts, as few species can be assumed to have evolved very recently.*

▲ ▲ ▲

A relict must have some evidence of decline from the geological past to the present. *Extinction* is perhaps too strong a word, as it would imply oblivion altogether. In chapter 13 we saw that many conifers now restricted to small ranges were once widespread, even across continents. Examples include *Sequoia sempervirens* (coast redwood) and *Metasequoia glyptostroboides* (dawn redwood), and many other conifers could be added. Decline is a common trend in the history of conifer distribution, and for many species it started millions of years ago. In addition, much of the recent decline has been caused by people. Since Europeans arrived in California, the coast redwood has been driven back to only remnants of its historical area of occupancy, even though its extent of occurrence remains much the same. I shall return to the human factor later when we will discuss conservation, as well as to these terms. Here I wish to ignore the human factor and only consider those conifers that are probably relicts from natural causes. To shorten the list as well as to concentrate on the most interesting cases, I shall restrict it to species (that is, excluding lower ranks) and to those conifers known only from a single locality.

Next, we need to consider what evidence there is for the limited occurrence. How do we know that a species does not also occur somewhere else? Commonly a newly described species is at first known from a single location and additional localities may be found later. As a first rule of thumb, the longer a species remains known from only a single locality, the more probable it is that it is really restricted to that place. It also depends on the efforts being made to find more of it, and such efforts may vary with regions as well as species. When *Wollemia nobilis* was discovered in September 1994, the search for more was on almost immediately. Even helicopters were being used to scan the many canyons of the Wollemi National Park, but so far only three tiny subpopulations, very close to each other, have been found. In contrast, several species of *Podocarpus* have been described recently from one or a few herbarium specimens gathered at a single location, and as far as I know little or no fieldwork has been done to search for these species in their areas. Usually such fieldwork yields further herbarium specimens, from the same locality or from additional places. If no fieldwork has been done, we must question whether the species is in fact a relict. It is likely, but of course not certain, that it will be found in other localities if searches are made, as experience shows. To define a locality is also somewhat tricky. In extreme cases, such as with *Abies beshanzuensis* and *Pinus squamata*, only a few trees are known to exist; in other cases there are hundreds or thousands of individuals but occurring in a single, small area of a few square kilometres. Sometimes there are two or more very small subpopulations separated by short distances, and these have also been taken as occurring in one locality. Based on these rather broad criteria, in Table 6 I present the conifer species considered to be relicts.

Table 6. Relict conifer species known only from a single locality, based on broad criteria

FAMILY AND SPECIES	COUNTRY (LOCALITY)	YEAR DESCRIBED
Araucariaceae		
Agathis kinabaluensis	Borneo (Sabah, Mount Kinabalu)	1979
Agathis montana	New Caledonia (Mont Panié)	1969
Araucaria heterophylla	Australia (Norfolk Island)	1807
Araucaria nemorosa	New Caledonia (Port Boisé)	1969
Araucaria schmidii	New Caledonia (Mont Panié)	1969
Wollemia nobilis	Australia (New South Wales, Wollemi National Park)	1995
Cupressaceae		
Cupressus dupreziana	Algeria (Tassili n'Ajjer)	1926
Juniperus bermudiana	Bermuda Islands	1753
Thuja sutchuenensis	China (Chongqing, Dabashan)	1899
Widdringtonia cedarbergensis	South Africa (Cedarberg)	1966
Widdringtonia whytei	Malawi (Mount Mulanje)	1894
Xanthocyparis vietnamensis	Vietnam (Bat Dai Son Mountains)	2002
Pinaceae		
Abies beshanzuensis	China (Zhejiang, Baishan-zu)	1976
Abies fanjingshanensis	China (Guizhou, Fanjingshan)	1984
Abies nebrodensis	Italy (Sicily)	1904
Abies yuanbaoshanensis	China (Guangxi, Yuanbaoshan)	1980
Cedrus brevifolia	Cyprus (Troodos Mountains)	1880
Picea koyamae	Japan (Yatsugadake Mountains)	1913
Picea omorika	Serbia (Tara Mountains)	1876
Pinus maximartinezii	Mexico (Zacatecas, Sierra de Morones)	1964
Pinus rzedowskii	Mexico (Michoacan)	1969
Pinus squamata	China (Yunnan, Qiaojia Xian)	1992
Podocarpaceae		
Acmopyle sahniana	Fiji (Viti Levu)	1947
Dacrycarpus kinabaluensis	Borneo (Sabah, Mount Kinabalu)	1941
Dacrydium gibbsiae	Borneo (Sabah, Mount Kinabalu)	1914
Dacrydium guillauminii	New Caledonia (Rivière des Lacs)	1949

Table 6. (continued)

FAMILY AND SPECIES	COUNTRY (LOCALITY)	YEAR DESCRIBED
Podocarpaceae (continued)		
Dacrydium leptophyllum	New Guinea (Mount Goliath)	1941
Pherosphaera fitzgeraldii	Australia (New South Wales, Blue Mountains)	1880
Podocarpus beecherae	New Caledonia (Col de Yaté)	2003
Podocarpus brevifolius	Borneo (Sabah, Mount Kinabalu)	1894
Podocarpus capuronii	Madagascar (Mount Ambatomenaloha)	1972
Podocarpus lophatus	Philippines (Luzon, Mount Tapulao)	1978
Podocarpus monteverdeensis	Costa Rica (Monteverde Reserve)	1991
Podocarpus palawanensis	Philippines (Palawan)	1988
Podocarpus pallidus	Tonga (East Tongan Island)	1959
Podocarpus purdieanus	Jamaica (Mount Diablo)	1844
Podocarpus smithii	Australia (Queensland, Mount Lewis)	1985
Prumnopitys ladei	Australia (Queensland, Mount Spurgeon)	1905
Taxaceae		
Taxus floridana	United States (Florida, Apalachicola River)	1860

How can we know whether these species are relicts? The alternative hypothesis is that they originated at the locality where we find them now and that they never spread to other areas. Because they are separated from other species, it is likely that these disjunct populations have evolved to become distinct species. Did they have a wider range in the past? Direct evidence in the form of a fossil record would confirm this, provided we have confidence in the identification. Fossils cannot easily be identified to species equivalent to living species because we nearly always only have fragments, not whole plants. Despite this, we can confirm a few species in Table 6 as relicts based on fossil evidence. But in most cases we have no fossils that can be assigned to the extant species. Another approach is to consider the phylogenetic relationships of species. If a species now represents a distinct clade, it is likely to be a remnant of a group of similar species, all of which became extinct except the one still living in a single location. When compared to other related living species, these remnant species also often appear to have very distinct characters. Because evolution progresses by small steps, not by leaps, this is further evidence for relict status. Other species differ but little from their congeners and could have evolved as a small, isolated population to become distinct enough to be considered a species. To judge whether they are still relict, ecological considerations may help. If they occur in an environment that has itself been reduced in extent from a distant past when it was more widespread, we may infer that the species has declined, too. If none of these criteria apply, we cannot assume a relict status and have to remove the species from the list. In doing this, Table 7 lists the conifer species that I believe are truly relicts and confined to a single locality.

Table 7. Relict conifer species known only from a single locality, based on more restrictive criteria

FAMILY AND SPECIES	COUNTRY (LOCALITY)	YEAR DESCRIBED
Araucariaceae		
Araucaria heterophylla	Australia (Norfolk Island)	1807
Wollemia nobilis	Australia (New South Wales, Wollemi National Park)	1995
Cupressaceae		
Cupressus dupreziana	Algeria (Tassili n'Ajjer)	1926
Thuja sutchuenensis	China (Chongqing, Dabashan)	1899
Widdringtonia cedarbergensis	South Africa (Cedarberg)	1966
Widdringtonia whytei	Malawi (Mount Mulanje)	1894
Xanthocyparis vietnamensis	Vietnam (Bat Dai Son Mountains)	2002
Pinaceae		
Abies beshanzuensis	China (Zhejiang, Baishan-zu)	1976
Abies nebrodensis	Italy (Sicily)	1904
Picea koyamae	Japan (Yatsugadake Mountains)	1913
Picea omorika	Serbia (Tara Mountains)	1876
Pinus maximartinezii	Mexico (Zacatecas, Sierra de Morones)	1964
Pinus rzedowskii	Mexico (Michoacan)	1969
Pinus squamata	China (Yunnan, Qiaojia Xian)	1992
Podocarpaceae		
Acmopyle sahniana	Fiji (Viti Levu)	1947
Pherosphaera fitzgeraldii	Australia (New South Wales, Blue Mountains)	1880
Prumnopitys ladei	Australia (Queensland, Mount Spurgeon)	1905
Taxaceae		
Taxus floridana	United States (Florida, Apalachicola River)	1860

You will note from Table 7 that Araucariaceae and especially Podocarpaceae have few single-locality species that can be assumed to be true relicts. None of the species in the genus *Podocarpus* fit the criteria; they are too similar and do not occur in habitats that are now much less extensive than at times in the geological past. Most are tropical montane species that may have become isolated a long time ago due to climatic changes in the Pleistocene. It is most probable that these *Podocarpus* species evolved where they are now. Expansions and contractions will have occurred with climate change, but on a limited scale. This leaves us with the unambiguously relict conifers known from single localities. What conclusions may we draw from this collection of rare species? They seem to be randomly distributed among the families and genera, but with rather few in the ancient family Podocarpaceae. The relicts are almost equally distributed between the Northern and the Southern Hemispheres. They have been discovered and described over a period of nearly 200 years, on average once every 11.5 years, but none in the years between 1807 and 1860.

The three pine species listed in Table 7 belong to a section of the genus that has itself long been considered to represent a relict group, the section *Parrya*. Most of these relict species occupy marginal habitats and do not compete well even with other pines, many of which evolved in more recent times and are good invaders of new territory. Nowhere else did I find this better illustrated than during my visit to one of the three subpopulations of *Pinus rzedowskii* in 1994. I was on an extensive tour to see the pines in Mexico, where they are most abundant and diverse, travelling with two Honduran assistants in a Land Rover. We had followed unpaved, narrow roads through the Sierra Madre del Sur for several hours and I was beginning to doubt that we would reach the village of Dos Aguas. It was often a guess which of two alternatives continued as the main road, and signposting left much to be desired. My Spanish-speaking companions hailed an on-coming truck full of pine logs and got directions sketched on a piece of paper. We arrived and found ourselves a local guide to direct us to the rare pines. We needed this help very much, because we had seen little else but pine forest all the way to here but none of these were *P. rzedowskii*. Most abundant were *P. oocarpa*, *P. pseudostrobus*, and the small-coned *P. herrerae*. The locality we visited where *P. rzedowskii* grows is geologically very distinct from the surrounding mountains, which are mostly of volcanic origin. Large karst limestone blocks and boulders made the going difficult and, due to the sharp edges of the rock, hazardous. The vegetation abruptly changed as well, with much smaller trees than in the surrounding forest. Among shrubby oaks (*Quercus*) and *Clusia salvinii* (Guttiferae) we saw

Pinus rzedowskii, a relict pine known from three very small subpopulations in the mountains of Michoacan

The seed cones of *Pinus rzedowskii* are very different from those of other pinyon pines, which have specialized scales holding the wingless, large seeds.

large agaves (*Agave*) and tall herbs. At Cerro Chiquerita, which has a fire-lookout near-by, the only pine among the limestone rocks we could see was *P. rzedowskii*. Its soft needles, in bundles of five, are bright green, its thick bark reddish brown. This remarkable pine, although classified in subgenus *Strobus* section *Parrya*, shares certain morphological traits with species in subgenus *Pinus*. The thick bark is unlike any in subgenus *Strobus* and much resembles that of *P. devoniana*, another Mexican pine. Its seed cone scales are similar to those of *P. merkusii* from Southeast Asia. The small seeds are fully winged, unlike those in the pinyon pines to which it is presumably closely related. This means *P. rzedowskii* has retained a primitive state, while the other species evolved large seeds without wings to be dispersed by birds. This unique pine could only survive where competition from larger and faster-growing pines is absent. These limestone outcrops appear to provide a suitable habitat; only one *P. rzedowskii* subpopulation has been found partly outside these, mixed with some other pines.

Thuja sutchuenensis was the only species of conifer listed as extinct in the wild in the global red list of conifers (Farjon and Page 1999). We only knew it from a few herbarium specimens collected by the Jesuit missionary P. G. Farges in the vicinity of the city of Chengkou, now in Chongking Municipality, China, between 1892 and 1900. Unfortunately, his locality notations were extremely vague, and despite later searches in the area by European and Chinese botanists, it could not be found again. The genus *Thuja* is otherwise almost absent from China. (*Thuja orientalis* L., sometimes still treated as Linnaeus did in 1753, is not in *Thuja* but in a distinct genus *Platycladus*; the correct name is *P. orientalis* [L.] Franco.) Aside from *T. sutchuenensis*, the only other species known from China is *T. koraiensis*, just within the country's borders far to the north. The genus has a relict distribution, with two species, east and west, in North America and three in eastern Asia, mainly in Korea and Japan. *Thuja* disappeared from Europe and high latitudes during the ice ages of the Pleistocene.

When I visited Beijing in the autumn of 2000 I was in for a pleasant surprise. I knew that Farges had not left specimens in China when he returned to France, but the Paris Herbarium might have provided some later, so I asked my colleagues in the Institute of Botany of the Chinese Academy of Sciences if there was something of this rarity in their collections. They had nothing from Farges, but I was told that they had just recently received several herbarium specimens. Upon seeing them I was able to confirm that the specimens were from *T. sutchuenensis*, after comparing them with the Farges specimens. This species is quite easily distinguished from other species of *Thuja* by its tiny leaves and cones. The species had been rediscovered when botanists the year before surveyed the Dabashan Mountains just north of Chengkou. *Thuja sutchuenensis* also grows on limestone rocks. Thus, it seems that many relict species of conifers occupy this kind of habitat. Father Farges must have found it on the same steep rocks, and perhaps later botanists thought that is an unlikely place for this genus. Delighted that a presumed extinct conifer was resurrected, my Chinese colleagues and I published a paper about its rediscovery and current status in the wild (Xiang et al. 2002). The Chinese are now keeping their new herbarium specimens in China and it is difficult to criticize them for that.

Are there more single-locality relicts to be discovered among the conifers? The ter-

Thuja sutchuenensis, a rediscovered relict conifer from China, drawn from specimens first collected by the Jesuit missionary P. G. Farges more than a century ago

restrial world seems pretty well explored, and it would be difficult to tread where no one has gone before. Yet one relict conifer species was discovered in 2002, three altogether since 1992. They tend to be in remote places, but two are growing near large cities. Not surprisingly, it needs a specialist to recognize them for what they are—thousands of people may have seen them just thinking they are a common conifer. Consider the story of the botanical discovery of *Pinus maximartinezii* by the botanist Jerzy Rzedowski in Mexico in 1964. His attention was drawn to the huge pine seeds the size of brazil nuts offered for sale on the market of the little town of Juchipila in Zacatecas. They were at least four times larger than the common *piñones* (pinyon nuts), usually from *Pinus cembroides* and its close relatives *P. edulis* or *P. monophylla*, which occur from the southwestern United States to southern Mexico. Where could a pine with such remarkable seeds grow, Rzedowski asked. The people pointed to a range of low mountains along the western horizon, and villagers riding donkeys led him to the trees. The massive cones that produce the seeds are among the largest and heaviest in the genus *Pinus*, bending the branches on which they grow down. Rzedowski named it after the doy-

The heavy cones of *Pinus maximartinezii* pull the branches down.

en of Mexican botanists, Maximino Martínez, using his name to denote the extraordinary size of the cones and seeds in the species epithet. Martínez had studied Mexican conifers for most of his long career as a botany professor in Mexico City, but he never knew of this species, or of *Pinus rzedowskii*, the other Mexican relict pine. When specialists go out on expedition, they may recognize something to be special and collect it for closer study. But many of the relict species have been spotted among specimens gathered on general collecting expeditions. Such forays are becoming less frequent with the increasing restrictions imposed on collecting by many countries. I believe that there must be several very interesting relict conifers still to be discovered. Karst limestone formations and hidden canyons or isolated mountain summits in the subtropics and tropics are the places to look out for them.

Opposite: *Pinus maximartinezii*, a pinyon pine with giant cones and seeds, was discovered on a mountainside in Mexico in 1964.

24 Encircling the Great Eternal Ocean

ASTRONAUTS CAN APPROACH THE EARTH *at a certain angle and a distance of 40,000 km (25,000 mi) and see almost nothing but water. They would be over the Pacific Ocean, 166 million km2 (104 million mi2) of sea, with Tahiti in the centre of this watery world. It covers almost a third of the surface of the planet, with an average depth of 4300 m (14,000 ft). The Pacific is in some regions dotted with thousands of islands, elsewhere there is only water. The islands are usually vegetated, but except on some situated along the fringes of the ocean basin, there are no conifers. Salt water and conifers are an unhappy mixture for the latter, and unless seeds have been transported by air (often inside a bird) conifers have not reached the true oceanic islands. These true oceanic islands, unlike fragments of continental plates, arose from the bottom of the sea as volcanic sea mounds. The few marginal oceanic islands in the Pacific with some conifers are the Ryukyu Islands and the Bonin Islands (Ogasawara Gunto) south of Japan, with* Juniperus taxifolia *and* Pinus luchuensis, *and Guadalupe Island off Baja California, with* Cupressus guadalupensis *and* Pinus radiata *var.* binata. *All the other Pacific Rim islands with conifers are of continental origin, and together with coastal mountain systems on continents, they provide refugia to a very large proportion of the present diversity in conifers.*

▲ ▲ ▲

Moving in a clockwise direction, these diversity centres for conifers are Japan, the Pacific Northwest, California, southern Mexico and Guatemala, southern Chile, New Zealand, Tasmania, New Caledonia, Fiji, the coast of New South Wales and Queensland, New Guinea, Borneo, the Philippines, and Taiwan. In total, the Pacific Rim is home to 335 species in 58 genera in eight families. In contrast, the coastal areas of the Atlantic and Indian Oceans do not have such diversity of conifers, with the exception of Morocco, which has a moderate diversity of 12 species, and perhaps Florida, with 10 species. Before I move into some informed speculations about the possible causes of the diversity of conifers around the Pacific, it would be helpful to give a brief review of the conifers in the different centres mentioned above. I shall first present some statistics (Table 8).

Of the total of 630 conifer species, 324 (51 per cent) occur in these 14 centres of diversity along the Pacific Rim. All families and 83 per cent of the 70 genera are represented. There are 94 of the 228 species of Pinaceae, 125 of the 186 species of Podocarpaceae, 65 of the 133 species of Cupressaceae, and 35 of the 41 species of Araucariaceae. Much of the conifer diversity in the world is concentrated around the Pacific Ocean. The first botanist to note this was Adolf Engler (1926). Li (1953) sought a general explanation for this phenomenon, and his ideas, published well before plate tectonics became understood and the drift of continents was generally accepted, are here corroborated.

Table 8. Diversity centres for conifers situated in parts of the Pacific Rim, with numbers of families, genera, and species in each

DIVERSITY CENTRE	FAMILIES	GENERA	SPECIES
Japan	6	18	45
Pacific Northwest	3	13	29
California	3	14	48
Southern Mexico and Guatemala	4	7	39
Southern Chile	3	8	9
New Zealand	4	10	19
Tasmania	3	8	12
New Caledonia	4	14	44
Fiji	1	5	8
New South Wales and Queensland coast	3	8	23
New Guinea	4	10	36
Borneo	3	8	35
Philippines	5	8	22
Taiwan	5	17	26

Japan

The conifers of Japan are remarkably diverse, with six families, 18 genera, and 45 species. The genera *Pinus* and *Picea* in Pinaceae have nine and seven species, respectively, on these islands. One, *Picea koyamae*, is a single-locality relict. Japan is also the only area in the world where Sciadopityaceae is still represented by its only species, *Sciadopitys verticillata*, sometimes known by the misnomer umbrella pine. The largely southern family Podocarpaceae is represented by one species in *Nageia* and three species in

Cryptomeria japonica is monotypic and endemic to Japan. This conifer was introduced to China long before it came to Europe.

Podocarpus; these are among the most northerly representatives of that family. In Cupressaceae, well represented with six genera and 16 species, *Cryptomeria japonica* is monotypic and endemic to Japan, where it is the nation's foremost forest tree. Despite the few species of Podocarpaceae, Japan's conifer flora is markedly northern (Laurasian) in its origins and relationships, with some links to the Pacific Northwest of the United States. Endemism at species level is high, but most of Japan's conifer genera are widely distributed on both sides of the Pacific.

The Pacific Northwest

This region includes coastal British Columbia and the Alaskan panhandle, but these northerly parts have no conifer species of their own. The states of Washington and Oregon represent the Pacific Northwest; in fact, by just calculating the diversity of Oregon we will include all species of this region. With 29 species, the Pacific Northwest is quite diverse given its northerly position between 42° and 49°N. *Pinus* has 10 species and *Abies* six, but *Picea* only two. In Cupressaceae there are six genera, but some in fact spill over from California, which is a more diverse region. *Picea sitchensis* is a sister species to *P. jezoensis* in the Russian Far East south to Japan, indicating a continuous distribution that once connected the two across the Bering land bridge. Species diversity of several genera increases going south in this region, but few are endemic.

California

By counting species, California is one of the most conifer-rich areas in the world. With 48 species, it tops the list of conifer centres around the Pacific Ocean. Yet its diversity at higher taxonomic ranks is moderate in comparison to Japan, directly opposite at the same latitudes. The Californian Floristic Province is recognized on the basis of flowering plant diversity and distribution, and the conifers, many endemic to it, confirm its

The seeds of *Torreya californica*, the only species of Taxaceae native to California

unique status in biogeography. Going eastward from the California coast continentality and aridity increase, and some conifers in the eastern mountains should perhaps not be listed as Pacific Rim species. To draw the line is difficult, however, so I have included them in this count. Here we have 22 species of *Pinus*, eight of *Abies*, and 11 of *Cupressus*; for this last genus California is the centre of diversity. Pinaceae and Cupressaceae make up the bulk of species, the only other family Taxaceae has a single species, *Torreya californica*. Unlike Japan, California has no representatives of southern (Gondwanan) conifer families or genera.

Southern Mexico and Guatemala

Within this region, 22 of the 39 species are pines (*Pinus*). In Cupressaceae, *Juniperus* is represented by seven species. Here *Podocarpus*, with two species, appears farthest north on this side of the Pacific. Southern Mexico and Guatemala are far to the south (around 20°N) of where the genus reaches in Japan (around 35°N). The cold California Current finally peters out here, which may be a climatic factor limiting the spread northward of this largely tropical genus. Further south, the pines and all other northern (Laurasian) conifers disappear well before the equator is reached. The presence of *Taxus globosa* in this region and further south along the mountains of Central America is peculiar, as the genus is missing in the region between Oregon and southern Mexico. A similar disjunction in this genus occurs on the other side of the Pacific, but further to the south and on islands, which makes its absence less curious.

Southern Chile

Conifers are rare along a very great distance of the Andes of South America, until a sudden but modest diversity reappears in southern Chile. Modest in the number of species, this region (including a bit of Andean Argentina) is diverse in genera, with all but one of its eight genera represented by a single species. We are with the southern (Gondwanan) conifers here and clearly looking at relict species (see chapter 21); all are endemic. The family Araucariaceae appears for the first time on this side of the Pacific, with one species, *Araucaria araucana*, the familiar monkey-puzzle tree. The other conifers belong to Cupressaceae and Podocarpaceae, of which *Podocarpus* has two species. This southwestern part of South America has biogeographical links with Australasia, not with North America or Africa; This indicates that evolution of present-day conifers in South America and Australia began well after the Triassic, when links with North America and southern Africa had been broken (in chapter 21, see map of the land-masses during the Lower Cretaceous [B]). The conifers of Chile are a good example of this southern connection.

New Zealand

This region has a modest but highly distinct conifer flora with 19 species, all endemic, in 10 genera and four families. The family Podocarpaceae is clearly the most diverse, with seven genera and 13 species. The related Phyllocladaceae, with its only genus *Phyllocladus*, has three species in New Zealand, making it a modest centre of diversity for this genus. Cupressaceae is represented by *Libocedrus* with two species and Araucariaceae with just one, *Agathis australis*, the famous kauri. These are all southern (Gondwanan) conifers with links to Australasia and some even to South America, as we have seen in chapter 21, but New Zealand's long isolation has allowed the evolution of distinct species and even some genera. The limited number of species compared to genera points at relict status, without much radiation of new species on the islands, but it is less extreme than in southern Chile.

Tasmania

The present diversity of conifers in Tasmania is modest and mostly consists of relicts. The two species of *Callitris* (Cupressaceae) also occur in mainland Australia, and the other 10 species are endemic to the island. *Athrotaxis*, with three species, once also oc-

Athrotaxis cupressoides in Tasmania, a basal member of Cupressaceae

curred in New Zealand and South America. In the fossil record there are many more genera, now extinct in Tasmania, showing links with South America and Australasia (see Table 5 in chapter 21). The western half of the island is mountainous, cool, and wet and it is here, almost exclusively, that all of the relict species of conifers occur.

New Caledonia

The extraordinary diversity of the conifers of New Caledonia has been mentioned in this book several times already and was discussed in some detail in chapter 20. The diversity rivals that of Japan and California on a much smaller island. For one family, Araucariaceae, New Caledonia is the world centre of diversity, with 13 species in *Araucaria* and five in *Agathis*. Another species, *Araucaria heterophylla*, is endemic to Norfolk Island, a tiny speck of land between New Caledonia and New Zealand. All 44 species on the islands of New Caledonia are endemic and clearly members of the southern (Gondwanan) conifers except perhaps the genus *Austrotaxus*, which belongs to the northern (Laurasian) family Taxaceae.

Fiji

The island group of Fiji is the farthest outlying remnant of a segment of continental plate (terrane) that once belonged to Gondwana. Its conifer diversity is much less than that of New Caledonia, with which its genera and species have the closest affinity. Seven of the eight conifer species belong to the family Podocarpaceae, in five genera; the only exception is *Agathis vitiensis* in Araucariaceae. With New Caledonia, Fiji uniquely shares *Acmopyle*, a relict genus that once also occurred in Australia, Antarctica, and South America.

The New South Wales and Queensland Coast

This long section of the Pacific Rim is separated from the dry interior of Australia by the Great Dividing Range. It harbours the last remnants of a lush rainforest that was much more extensive in the Palaeogene, as well as cool temperate alpine and subalpine vegetation types in the south. Quite a few species of conifers, 23 in total, occur along the New South Wales and Queensland coast. Among them are six species in all three genera in Araucariaceae, including *Wollemia nobilis*. Eight species of *Callitris*, most of them in montane habitats but one a rainforest tree, represent the Australian element. Outside the continent, this genus only has two species, in New Caledonia. I have excluded species that occur only west of the divide as these do not seem to belong to the Pacific Rim. The remainder are in Podocarpaceae, among which are five species of *Podocarpus*. Despite the proximity of Malesia, nearly all species are southern (Gondwanan) in affinity and origin.

New Guinea

This enormous island, another accreted terrane of Gondwana, has a very diverse conifer flora and one that is probably not yet completely known. The 36 species known at present belong to 10 genera and four families, of which Podocarpaceae clearly dominates with 30 species. Fourteen species of *Podocarpus*, seven of *Dacrydium*, and five of *Dacrycarpus* make up the bulk of these; there are three other genera in the family that account for the remainder. Araucariaceae is represented by two species in *Araucaria* (*A. cunninghamii* shared with Queensland) and two in *Agathis*. Endemism is high in New Guinea, but some species have wide ranges in Malesia. *Papuacedrus papuana*, the only member of Cupressaceae, is nearly restricted to New Guinea, with a few outliers in the Moluccas. There are fossil records from the Tertiary of this genus in Tasmania and Antarctica.

Borneo

Conifer diversity is largely restricted to the northern part of this large island, although the totals in Table 8 are for the entire island. Again, Podocarpaceae dominates with 29 of the 35 species; 12 of these are in *Podocarpus* and seven in *Dacrydium*, much as in New Guinea. Indeed, some of these species are shared. *Agathis* is quite well represented with five species, the same number as in much smaller New Caledonia. Borneo is part of the Asian landmass and lies west of Wallace's Line, a sea divide that is traditionally considered to separate Asian from Australasian biota. The conifers do not seem to have taken any notion of this divide; their affinities are either Australasian or more or less pan-tropical.

The Philippines

This group of islands links Borneo and Taiwan along the Pacific Rim and has 22 species of conifers in eight genera. The family Podocarpaceae still makes up the bulk of species, with 17. But here two species of *Pinus* announce that we are returning to the northern (Laurasian) conifers as we circle toward Taiwan, the last centre of conifer diversity in our journey around the Pacific Rim.

Cephalotaxus harringtonii foliage and seeds. As in Taxaceae, only a single seed develops but the structure of the cone is more evident.

Taiwan

The island of Taiwan is much more diverse in conifers than neighbouring areas on mainland China, especially if its moderate size is taken into consideration. Taiwan also has a number of endemics among its 26 species. Its 17 genera and five families further indicate a separate position from the mainland in floristic terms, as indeed is borne out in its rich angiosperm flora. Geologically, Taiwan stands apart as well; much of southeastern China was an epicontinental sea during the Mesozoic, while Taiwan was a continental fragment of Laurasia. Although there are four species in Podocarpaceae, we are clearly back among the northern (Laurasian) conifers. The dominant families are Cupressaceae and Pinaceae, each with nine species in six genera; all genera in Cupressaceae are northern. Cephalotaxaceae and Taxaceae make up the remainder with a few species.

Explaining Conifer Biogeography

Upon completing this tour around the Pacific Ocean inspecting the impressive diversity of conifers, a few generalizations impress themselves upon us. The first is a division between northern (Laurasian) and southern (Gondwanan) conifers, lying between Central America and South America on the eastern side and between the Philippines and Taiwan on the western side of the Pacific. This division is true for the Earth as a whole, with a few exceptions past and present, and relates to the division of Pangea into Laurasia in the north and Gondwana in the south by the end of the Triassic, when the first modern conifer families arose. Within these two divisions, we find close taxonomic relationships mostly with regions outside the Pacific Rim and much less often between its fragments. What is also apparent is an increased diversity at species and sometimes higher levels in most of these regions bordering the Pacific Rim compared to their hinterlands. Ecological factors to account for this are mountain topography and oceanic climate, in most cases persisting over very long periods in geological history. Biogeographical factors are separation and isolation, both regionally and locally, promoting independent evolution.

The Pacific Ocean is at least as old as the Triassic. The hypothesis invoking a vanished continent "Pacifica" is not only untenable on geological grounds, the distribution of conifers refutes this as well. In the Northern Hemisphere, the similarities between Japan, the Pacific Northwest, and California suggest they are part of a Laurasian distribution of conifers across Eurasia and Europe, using the Bering land bridge and connections via Greenland and northern Europe. Dispersal and vicariance explain the distributions in these three regions. These affinities peter out further south in Taiwan and Mexico, which share no sister species and few genera. In the Southern Hemisphere, connections are demonstrably via Gondwana, now broken up. Vicariance biogeography explains much of the relationships and these Gondwanan connections have been discussed in chapter 21. The southern conifers only seemingly crossed the Pacific Ocean, for instance, between Chile and New Zealand. Such a connection never existed; those who still follow Léon Croizat in believing so understand little about the Earth's mechanics and history. At least as long as the modern conifers have existed, the Pacific Ocean was and is eternal.

Conifers and People

25 The Woods of the World and Their Uses

ABOUT 4600 YEARS AGO *40 ships sailed up the Nile to Memphis, laden with cedar wood from the port of Byblos in Lebanon. The wood was delivered to King Snefru of the Fourth Dynasty of ancient Egypt, who ordered the building of the pyramids of Dahsjur and Meidum. It is the first recorded import of timber, but it is certain that the Egyptians, short of big trees as the Nile valley was, had gone to Lebanon before to obtain this vital resource. This particular shipload of timber was used for shipbuilding and for the heavy doors of the king's palace. The conifer* Cedrus libani *(Lebanon cedar) has supplied building material for many civilizations in the Mediterranean and the Middle East, perhaps for as long as 5000 years. These civilizations, including the Egyptians, Sumerians, Assyrians, Hittites, Minoans, and Babylonians, all had to import timber from beyond their borders. Together, they virtually depleted the resource, and many wars were fought over what remained. They exploited a natural and renewable resource unsustainably. After five millennia, the wood of conifers is as important today as it was for these early civilizations. It is now used on a global scale by almost everyone, and conifer wood is put to uses both known to the ancient Egyptians and utterly unknown to them. Conifers provide about 60 per cent of all wood used for industrial purposes. Depletion of the resource is not unfamiliar to us either, but we have learned a few lessons and now have at least the knowledge to make conifer wood a sustainable resource.*

▲ ▲ ▲

Traditionally, the wood of conifers is known as softwood and that of angiosperms as hardwood. Perhaps that is a reflection of reality if you were in Europe and compared the wood of pine with that of oak. But from what I have explained about conifers already, you will appreciate that conifer wood must be much more diverse than that. Indeed, if you had a piece of the wood of the Great Basin bristlecone pine (*Pinus longaeva*), you would have difficulty driving a nail into it because of its density and hardness. In reality, different genera and species of conifers can have quite different properties of their wood, which can and have been put to very different uses.

Density and weight are usually a function of growth: fast-growing conifer trees produce larger tracheids and softer wood compared to slow-growing trees. The strength of conifer wood, important for construction timber, also varies widely and is linked with wood anatomy and growth. Durability (resistance to rot and decay) is markedly different among conifers as well. Generally, members of the family Cupressaceae are resistant to extremely resistant to decay, while Pinaceae and Podocarpaceae are much less durable. The coarseness or fineness of grain, the amount or lack of resin in the wood, knots from branches on the stem, and many other factors determine its properties for use.

A section of the wood of Great Basin bristlecone pine (*Pinus longaeva*). Due to this species' extremely slow growth, it has some of the densest and hardest of all woods.

Today the world trade in coniferous wood is huge. Conifers dominate industrial wood supply because of both technical and economic advantages over wood from angiosperms. The vast reserves of natural conifer forest in the boreal zone of the Northern Hemisphere play an important part in this supply, but plantations, especially in the Southern Hemisphere and particularly of pines, make up an increasing proportion of this. Nearly all this mass production goes into pulpwood for the paper industry, although about two-thirds of conifers in the world's plantations are destined for timber. This reflects growing concerns about exploitation of natural conifer forests by way of clear cutting, which damages all sorts of environmental values, some of which may be more valuable than the timber that is harvested. The more specialized, high-quality woods used for all the versatile applications mentioned in this chapter come from forests that can be allowed to grow older. Selective cutting of chosen trees allows the forest and its ecosystem to remain intact, if done under good management. The wood will be more expensive, but its high-grade uses and a growing market for such products would justify that. Paying the right prices for such wood—or even better, finished products—to countries in the tropics would be a major step towards safeguarding conifers and their valuable wood there, too.

In this chapter I shall give examples of most of the conifer families and some major genera and the properties and uses of their woods. This will range from purely industrial uses, such as chipboard and paper, to specialized, small-scale uses such as furniture and art work. I shall start with the Pinaceae and *Pinus*, as the economically most important family and genus, and finish this short excursion to the conifer woods and their uses with a few rarities and their special uses.

Pinaceae

Pinus

The properties of the wood of this genus are as varied as its uses. Fast-growing species in managed forests or plantations produce wide annual increments to the stem and soft wood with a variable but substantial content of resin. Pine wood has industrial uses such as pulpwood for paper manufacturing and chips or fibre for boards used in the internal construction of buildings. The fastest-growing pines are those in managed plantations, especially *Pinus radiata* (radiata pine) in New Zealand, where record growth in height of 2.5 m (8.2 ft) per year has been attained.

A very different use is made of the wood of the pinyon pines in the southwestern United States and northern Mexico, with species such as *Pinus cembroides* and *P. edulis*. These short, crooked-growing pines are widely used for firewood in rural communities. The wood has a high heat value comparable to oaks and burns with a pleasant and distinctive aroma. Its physical properties are similar to the most important timber tree in the United States, *P. ponderosa* (ponderosa pine). Contrary to pinyon pines, this species grows a tall, straight bole, which can attain great size on the mountain slopes facing the Pacific coast. The wood of ponderosa pine is not pulped nor burnt but sawn to specification for many uses, mainly in construction and furniture. Even better properties, such as high dimensional stability, straight grain, softness, and workability are provided by the large stems of old growth *P. lambertiana* (sugar pine). The finished milled wood of this "king of pines," as the great American naturalist John Muir called it, makes sugar pine ideal for high-standard windows and doors and even musical instruments, such as organ pipes and piano keys. There is, of course, a sustainability issue with the harvesting of old growth trees, as these take centuries to attain great size.

A closely related but more widespread species in the American and Canadian West is *Pinus monticola* (western white pine), with similar nonresinous wood. Its sister species in eastern North America is *P. strobus* (eastern white pine). In the

The lower trunk of a large sugar pine (*Pinus lambertiana*) in the Sierra Nevada of California

early years of European colonization of North America, eastern white pine played a crucial role in the exploitation of the forests and was an important factor in European expansion into Native American territories. The British Navy claimed all larger trees within the American colonies for its ship masts and had them marked by its surveyors with a broad arrow symbol. Any person who cut such a tree without being authorized to do so could face a penalty of £100, a huge sum in those days. This injunction, not surprisingly, became one of the grievances giving rise to the American Revolution. Consequently, these restrictions were scarcely heeded before and certainly not after independence of the United States. As a result, by the late 19th century most of the old growth stands of eastern white pine had been logged, and large trees are now a rarity both in the United States and Canada. Ship's masts, where still required, are now mostly of metal alloys, but the wood of eastern white pine is still highly prized for furniture and other specialized uses.

There are other uses of pine wood that were important in the past but have been largely replaced by nonwood materials. Railway sleepers and fence posts consumed vast numbers of pine trees with European expansion across North America. The famous Great Plains tribes such as the Cheyenne, Blackfeet, and Dakota used *Pinus contorta* (lodgepole pine) for their movable homes (tepees) and transport (*travois* poles), but only after they had acquired the horse from Europeans. They have now acquired pick-up trucks. In Europe, the coal mine shafts and tunnels were propped with "pine," but this may have been spruce (*Picea*) as well. Such mixed naming is still common. When I buy "pine" furniture in England in one of the many retail shops specializing in this nice commodity, no salesperson is able to tell me if the wood really came from pines, let alone from what species.

Abies

Unlike *Pinus*, the genus *Abies* grows consistently into tall, straight trees if conditions are right. Sizes differ with species. Some, such as *Abies koreana* (Korean fir), remain

(387)

Anno Nono

Annæ Reginæ.

An Act for the Preservation of White and other Pine-Trees growing in Her Majesties Colonies of *New-Hampshire*, the *Massachusets-Bay*, and Province of *Main*, *Rhode-Island*, and *Providence-Plantation*, the *Narraganset* Country, or *Kings-Province*, and *Connecticut* in *New-England*, and *New-York*, and *New-Jersey*, in *America*, for the Masting Her Majesties Navy.

Whereas there are great Numbers of White or other Sort of Pine-Trees, fit for Masts, growing in Her Majesties Colonies of New-Hampshire the Massachusets Bay, and Province of Main, Rhode-Island, and Providence-Plantation, the Narraganset Country, or Kings-Province, and Connecticut in New-England, and New-York, and New-Jersey, fit for the Masting Her Majesties Royal Navy: And whereas the same growing near the Sea, and on Navigable Rivers, may commodiously be brought into this Kingdom for the Service aforesaid: Wherefore, for the better Preservation thereof, Be it Enacted by the Queens most Excellent Majesty, by and with the Advice and Consent of the Lords Spiritual and Temporal, and Commons, in this present Parliament Assembled, and by the Authority of the same, That from and after the Twenty fourth Day of September, which shall be in the Year of our Lord, One thousand seven hundred and eleven, no Person or Persons within the said Colonies of New-Hampshire, the Massachusets-Bay, and Province of Main, Rhode Island, and Providence-Plantation, the Narraganset Countrey, or Kings-Province, Connecticut in New-England, and New-York, and New-Jersey, or any of them, do or shall presume to Cut, Fell, or Destroy any White or other sort of Pine-Tree
Eeee 2   fit

A page from the "Act for the Preservation of White and Other Pine Trees," which prohibited, from 24 September 1711 onwards, the cutting of those trees fit for Her Majesty Queen Anne's fleet in the American colonies.

rather small, and other uses than wood have been found for them, such as horticulture. The wood of firs is creamy white to pale brown and very similar in structure among the species. It is lightweight and relatively soft. Fir wood is used industrially for chipboard and pulpwood, but high-grade timber is sawn for framing material and for plywood and veneer. In the United States, *A. procera* (noble fir) wood is valued higher than that of the other fir species for construction wood because of its greater strength. In the past, loggers called it "larch" to avoid the prejudice timber merchants had against fir. The two Larch Mountains on opposite sides of the Columbia River near Portland, Oregon, were named for the noble fir that grows on their summits (J. F. Franklin in Burns and Honkala 1990). The wood of *A. procera* has been used for special purposes such as the propellers of aircraft. In Europe only one fir species, *A. alba*, is abundant enough to be of commercial interest. Here its wood is not chipped or pulped, and trees are carefully selected before felling to be taken to mills and sawn to the requirements of the prospective users of the wood. Its most famous use in the past was for the masts of 17th-century ships. The purist master ship builder Willem Vos used this tree in 1985–1995 for the reconstruction of the Dutch indiaman *Batavia*, the original of which suffered one of the most haunting wrecks recorded in history off the Australian western coast in 1629.

Picea

Spruces, like firs, are mostly tall, straight trees, but their wood properties are quite different. Spruce wood retains more knots than that of fir. The wood of most species is yellowish to orange-brown, has long fibres, and is often resinous. *Picea* was formerly used for mine timbers, both in North America and Europe, but industrial use has now shifted to pulpwood as well as timber products. In the northern boreal forests, it was and is the principal tree for the construction of log houses, with *Picea glauca* and *P.*

How many oars could be made from the giant trunk of this Sitka spruce (*Picea sitchensis*)?

Opposite: The ancient wooden *stave* church of Borgund in Sogn og Fjordane, western Norway

engelmannii used in Alaska and Canada, *P. abies* in Scandinavia, and *P. obovata* in Siberia. In Norway, the ancient village churches were entirely made of wood, in which Norway spruce (*P. abies*) and Scots pine (*Pinus sylvestris*) provided most of the construction timber. They date from the time of the introduction of the Christian religion nearly 1000 years ago. Spruce wood is the preferred material for the sounding boards of pianos, organ pipes, guitar faces, and violins. The famous antique violins made by Antonio Stradivari of Cremona in Italy have bodies of Norway spruce from the Alps. The great Sitka spruce (*Picea sitchensis*) of the Pacific Northwest yields wood with a high strength-to-weight ratio, which makes it an excellent wood for masts and spars for sailing boats as well as oars. In this age of metal and polyester, beautiful wooden ships are still being custom built, and the wood of conifers such as Sitka spruce is indispensable for these.

Larix

Larches are common in the boreal forests and in the great mountain ranges to the south, such as the Alps, Himalayas, and Rocky Mountains. The wood is resistant to weather and rot to a greater extent than that of other members of the Pinaceae. In the Alps, many of the traditional wooden houses and storage sheds, with their characteristic stone disks above pedestals to keep vermin out, are built with logs from *Larix decidua* (European larch). Railroad sleepers were another use until concrete and steel replaced them. As with other genera in the Pinaceae, pulpwood of larch is a major industrial use for the paper industry, and the transparent windows in envelopes are a paper made from larch wood. High-quality veneer is produced from larch wood, which is hard and strong and has an attractive brick-red colour in the heartwood, especially from the species that attain large sizes in the Alps (*L. decidua*), Himalayas (*L. griffithii*), and Rocky Mountains (*L. occidentalis*).

Pseudotsuga

Although this genus occurs both in western North America and in eastern Asia, there is only one species of sufficient size and abundance for its wood to be of export value, *Pseudotsuga menziesii* (Douglas fir). In fact, this value is so great, that Douglas fir is the most important timber tree in North America, with roughly equal distribution in western Canada and the United States. This species has been introduced by foresters in many temperate regions around the world. *Pseudotsuga menziesii* was once perhaps the tallest species of tree in the world, as Bob Van Pelt has found after careful study of loggers' reports in the archives of Seattle and Vancouver. Those super giants have all been logged, but several existing giant trees of this species are still impressive enough (see the photo in chapter 16). The wood, erroneously known as Oregon pine or British Columbia pine, is fairly light and strong, from yellowish to light reddish brown. The reason why Douglas fir is such an important timber tree derives largely from its rapid growth and sheer bulk, providing large quantities of timber without knots from branches. Its wood is used for plywood and construction, both exterior and interior, and its reasonable good durability makes it useful for telephone poles and railway sleepers. The more continental variety, *P. menziesii* var. *glauca*, grows much more slowly and to a more moderate size; this tree yields denser, heavier wood, which is excellent for cooperage for vats and tanks for breweries and distilleries.

Cupressaceae

The wood of Cupressaceae is very different in its properties from that of Pinaceae. It is more fibrous and contains less resin. In many species resin only occurs in the leaves and cones or is produced in the wood only after injury. Nearly all genera, including those formerly classified in Taxodiaceae, have decay-resistant wood, some extremely so. For instance, stumps and trunks of *Fitzroya* have been found along the Chilean coast at exceptionally low tide that are several thousand years old. The fibrous long grain in the wood of several species allows big planks to be split without the use of saws. Some extremely slow-growing species of Cupressaceae have the densest and hardest wood of all conifers. Others are fragrant with volatile terpene compounds, and many are beautifully grained and coloured.

Chamaecyparis

The wood of *Chamaecyparis* is strong and durable, even-grained, and highly valued, especially in Japan. *Chamaecyparis obtusa* (hinoki) was heavily exploited in Japan for centuries, so that few large old growth trees remain. The Japanese now import similar wood of related species from the United States and Taiwan. This wood has been used in the construction of temples and other ceremonial buildings. At the Royal Botanic Gar-

The Japanese Gateway, a feature of ceremonial architecture donated by Japan to the Royal Botanic Gardens, Kew, was built with the wood of *Chamaecyparis obtusa*.

Chamaecyparis obtusa, hinoki cypress

Aljos Farjon
del. 1990

dens, Kew, the Japanese Gateway was built with the wood of *C. obtusa*. Other uses are flooring, boat decks, boxes, Venetian blind slats, and telephone poles. The fragrance of freshly cut wood of *Chamaecyparis* is especially valued in eastern Asia.

Xanthocyparis

This newly described genus has two species: *Xanthocyparis vietnamensis*, a new discovery from Vietnam, and *X. nootkatensis* (Alaska cedar), in most conifer literature known either as *Chamaecyparis nootkatensis* or *Cupressus nootkatensis*. Such name changes, resulting from new systematic research, take a while to filter through to the users of plant names, such as foresters and horticulturists. The new genus name refers to the yellow or golden heartwood of both species, and the Alaska cedar is also known among lumbermen as yellow cedar. Although not a true cedar (*Cedrus* in Pinaceae), we do not require vernacular name changes when the taxonomy shifts.

The Vietnamese species is only a small tree on steep limestone ridges, yet its wood is much desired and local people climb to hazardous places to get it. The North American species is much more widespread and abundant, ranging from Alaska to California. Its slow-growing wood is moderately hard, extremely durable, and suitable for special purposes such as boat building, outdoor flooring, cladding and shingles, sash windows and doors, panelling, canoe paddles, cabinets, musical instruments, and wood carving. Due to its slow growth, some large Alaska cedar trees are extremely old, with a possible record of 3500 years.

Thuja

The reddish brown wood of *Thuja* splits easily into shingles and planks and is weather resistant as well as nearly immune to fungal attacks. These properties made *Thuja plicata* (western red cedar), of which great trees grow on North America's western coast, the ideal tree for native seafaring tribes to build their great houses with. A large tree was chosen and a scaffold erected to reach high enough above the fluted or buttressed base. Because the people had no tools to fell these giant trees, wooden wedges were driven in from above, splitting off long, thick planks. The tree need not be killed by this practice if it was done carefully and sparingly. Roofing with shingles is still a common use of the wood of *T. plicata*, but commercially even more important is its use for greenhouses, sheds, and saunas. Unfortunately, much of this timber still comes from old growth forest and is unsustainable. Bringing western red cedar used for greenhouses under a certificate scheme that guarantees a de facto renewable source, such as plantations, is very much needed.

Juniperus

Not all species of this genus grow to trees and yield good sizes of wood. Those species that do produce sizable trunks have dense, durable heartwood but often with many twists, warps, and branch traces or knots. The wood often overgrows strips of bark, which become embedded deep inside. Juniper wood is fragrant with volatile terpene compounds (cedrol), which makes it pleasurable for firewood. I have fond memories of campfires in the canyon lands of Utah and Arizona, where dead wood of *Juniperus*

Juniperus osteosperma (Utah juniper) in the San Rafael Reef near Wild Horse Butte, Utah. It makes excellent, slow-burning, fragrant campfires, but only dead wood should be used, as this tree grows very slowly.

osteosperma is abundant on the sandstone plateaus and among the mesas. In North America in the past, but in western and central Asia still today, the durability of juniper wood makes it excellent for fence posts. Small-scale uses for furniture, wood inlays, and wood turning take advantage of the difference in colour between sapwood (light) and heartwood (darker, reddish), often with brown or white streaks. Pencils are still mostly made from the wood of juniper trees, in the United States mostly from *Juniperus virginiana*.

Sequoia

The great redwood forests of coastal California have been heavily logged since Europeans settled in large numbers after the discovery of gold in 1849. The durability of the wood as well as the sheer quantities obtained from a single giant tree made it excellent for outdoor use, and many 19th- and early-20th-century houses in the San Francisco Bay area were built almost entirely of it. Secondary growth, with much smaller and younger trees, yields less resistant wood than old growth trees. Fortunately, those old growth trees that remain are now virtually all under protection and cannot be logged. *Sequoia sempervirens* has red-brown heartwood and often produces large burls on the trunks; the contorted wood of these, known as *vavona* burl, is highly prized for wood turning and table tops.

Taiwania

Taiwania cryptomerioides has very light, smooth, and straight-grained durable wood, as resistant to fungi and insect attacks as many other woods of the Cupressaceae. These properties and the large size of old growth trees have made it a highly sought after wood in China. This species was called "coffin tree" because wealthy people wanted to be buried in it and paid high prizes for coffins made from its wood. Although naturally restricted to three very disjunct locations, the Chinese have planted *T. cryptomerioides* in the past in some other areas, where it survives. Its wood can be turned into finer work as well. I own an attractive pen and case made of it, given to me by the director of the Taiwanese Forestry Research Institute.

Cryptomeria

Cryptomeria japonica wood has properties very similar to that of *Sequoia* and is Japan's most important forestry tree. Old growth forests have been exploited nearly to oblivion, but this species is now widely planted and this afforestation has been very successful. Its wood is mainly used in construction and building, but *C. japonica* does not have the high qualities of *Chamaecyparis*, so it is not carved into ornamental pieces.

Cunninghamia

Cunninghamia lanceolata is one of the few conifers that will coppice readily. Its wood is soft and easily worked. Coppiced poles are used in rural China for stakes, tool handles, and fence posts. Larger wood is used for nearly every purpose imaginable, including firewood. Millions of hectares of this species, known as *shan mu* or Chinese fir, have been planted in southern and eastern China.

Tetraclinis

The Romans were very fond of the ancient coppice stools (that is, the cut stumps) of a North African conifer, *Tetraclinis articulata*. Few conifers coppice, but this species in Cupressaceae does it well. In addition, due to the dry summers in North Africa, the shoots regrow rather slowly. The burning or cutting of stems just above the ground causes new shoots to arise in many different spots. When these are cut the process renews itself, almost indefinitely. Some of these stools could be very old indeed. By sawing them through in a plane, table tops are obtained which, when smoothed and polished, display an amazingly intricate figure and different hues of reddish brown to black. This type of the tree's wood is known as lupia or burl, but it is not strictly speaking from burls. It makes excellent material for wood turning, too. Of course, grubbing up such ancient coppice stools is not sustainable. This wood was expensive in Roman times, and it is so now. In fact, in many areas it is illegal to remove coppice stools.

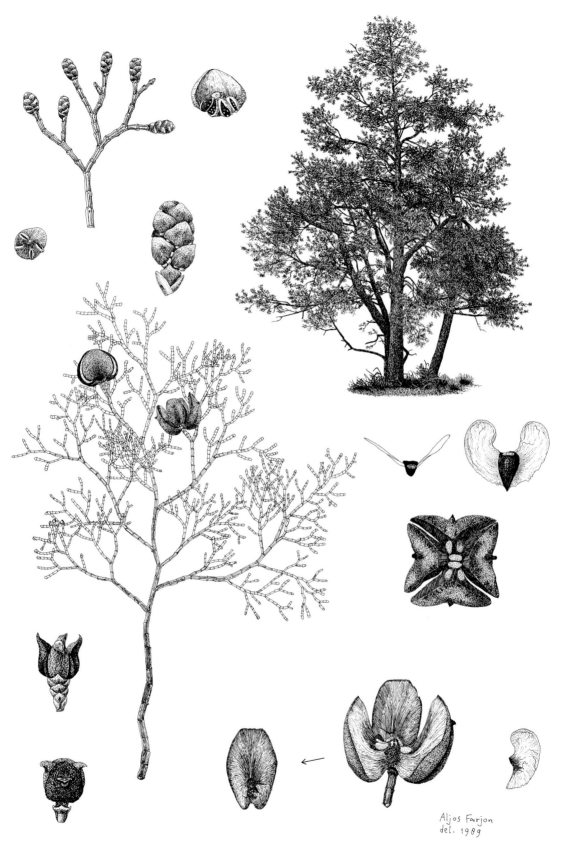

Tetraclinis articulata, known as araâr in Morocco, is one of the few conifers that can be coppiced. Its large coppice stools are prized for wood turning.

Taxaceae

Taxus

The wood of *Taxus* is hard, dense, heavy, and resistant to decay. The numerous burls, reiterations of branches, irregular growth patterns, and short, many-branched trunks make the wood unfit for timber, but it has many special uses. Perhaps most famous were the English longbows made of yew whose powerful arrows could penetrate a knight's armour. Wood carving and turning are today's most common and more peaceful uses of yew wood. Its many patterns and colours, especially in wood from old, burly trees, make it one of the best for this purpose. Other applications are furniture parts, such as for the traditional Windsor chair, and joinery. The wood of *Taxus* comes closest to the stool wood of *Tetraclinis* if taken from old trunks of trees, such as those growing in English churchyards. When the famous Selborne yew blew over in a storm raging over southern England in 1990, a large slab was cut, polished, and displayed in the entrance porch of the village church. Its wonderfully complex patterns of irregular grain and different colours are like a piece of decorative art.

Araucariaceae

Araucaria

By far the most heavily exploited species in this genus is *Araucaria angustifolia* (known in the trade as Paraná pine) from southeastern Brazil and a small area in Argentina. This species was almost exploited to oblivion. Other species are much more locally distributed, so exploitation, if it occurs, is more limited. The wood is light or heavy and dense, with pale brown heartwood and light honey-coloured sapwood, with a straight grain and even texture without visible annual rings. It is easily worked and does not require special treatment to take paint or varnish. The wood is not durable, however, so without treatment it is not suitable for outdoor applications. Veneer and plywood are the most appropriate uses, but all kinds of indoor light construction can be performed with its wood as well. *Araucaria angustifolia* still is Brazil's major export timber, but much of it now has to come from plantations.

Agathis

This most tropical of the conifer genera is one of the most valued timber trees in Australasia, from Malaysia to Fiji and New Zealand. The wood, known by its Maori name of kauri in the timber trade, is light and soft, pale yellow or straw-coloured, often with darker heartwood ranging from pink to dark red-brown. It has a straight grain and fine texture, and the sapwood is not resinous. Large trees are free of knots from branches, and their wood is easy to saw and plane. Kauri wood has many uses, from indoor construction, panelling, boat masts, joinery, furniture, and wood turning to pencils, matches, matchboxes, rulers, and piano parts. It is excellent for plywood and veneer, while more industrial uses of lower-grade wood are pulp for paper manufacturing and burning to produce high-grade charcoal. In Indonesia and Malaysia *Agathis* is exploited heavily for export of raw timber (round logs); in the Philippines this has already led to a total ban on further cutting, while export is banned from Papua New Guinea.

Podocarpaceae

In tropical countries the wood of this family is usually highly valued, and trees are often selectively logged for timber. Most podocarps occur scattered in mixed forests, and as a result these species do not yield large quantities of timber for export. Some countries prohibit export to ensure processing the logs in local sawmills for local or regional use. The genus *Podocarpus* is the most important because it is the most widespread, with over a hundred species. *Dacrydium* and *Dacrycarpus* are of importance in Australasia, *Nageia* in Southeast Asia, and *Afrocarpus* in Africa. All yield light to medium-weight, pale-coloured wood, known as podo in the trade, with a straight grain and even texture that is easy to saw and plane but is often brittle. Podocarp wood is not durable when exposed to the weather, so its building applications are for indoor construction only. High-grade wood can be put to the manufacture of door and window frames, panelling, veneer, cupboards, furniture, cabinet work, joinery, household utensils, and engineering instruments such as drawing boards and rulers. The New Zealand species *Podocarpus totara* provides the only softwood that is resistant to attack by marine borers, so it is used for ship and boat building as well as wharf building and harbour construction. The Maori built their famously long war canoes with the wood of this large indigenous tree.

26 Clothing My Estate

"I REJOICE TO TELL YOU *of a new species of* Pinus, *the most princely of the genus, perhaps even the grandest specimen of vegetation," David Douglas wrote from Oregon to Sir William Hooker in 1826. Douglas had just come back from the wilds of the Cascade Range, where he found this tree, barely escaping with his life, but not forgetting the specimens, of course. On 26 October, he left his guide at camp to attend his horse and dry their clothes from the previous day's bad weather, and Douglas set out on foot. After a while he met a native, whom he persuaded with sketches of the tree and its cones and sign language to take him to the great pines, some 20 km (15 mi) distant. Arrived there, Douglas stood in awe under huge trees of a species he named and later described as* Pinus lambertiana *(sugar pine). Douglas wanted the cones that were suspended high up at the ends of long branches. "Being unable to climb or hew down any," he wrote in his diary, "I took my gun and was busy clipping them from the branches with ball when eight Indians came at the report of my gun." The eight were armed with bows and arrows and in war paint and looked anything but friendly. When they appeared to make ready for attack, Douglas backed himself against a tree and cocked his gun. For ten minutes Douglas and the men stared at each other, and then he signalled to them that he could give tobacco for more pine cones. They went off, Douglas grabbed three cones from the ones he had brought down, and made back for his camp as fast as he could. He had no tobacco to give them.*

▲ ▲ ▲

Such were the conditions and risks that plant hunters had to endure to satisfy a passion for growing exotic trees that had befallen the landed gentry of Europe and especially the United Kingdom. Douglas was sent out on behalf of the new Horticultural Society of London. Plant-hunting trips were usually subscribed by landowners who desired novelties for their estates, parks, and pleasure grounds and wanted the plants from their wild sources. Above all else, what was needed were the seeds, but David Douglas was a good botanist and took cones and some foliage as well. Not much survives of this collection today, but at Kew there is a herbarium sheet with three small branches (no cone) and a little piece of resin annotated "Gum from a Larch tree, eaten by the natives, Douglas." I designated the two pieces collected by him on this sheet as the lectotype of the species in Volume 75 of *Flora Neotropica*, which treats the pines (Farjon and Styles 1997). The resin of *Pinus lambertiana* has high sugar content and was probably not eaten but enjoyed as a form of chewing gum. Douglas would never learn that his magnificent pine, gathered at such risk to his life, was not a horticultural success in Europe. He met an untimely death in Hawaii, gored by a feral bull, in 1834 when on another collecting expedition. Yet Douglas had succeeded to introduce into England from the American West an impressive list of magnificent conifers. He could have been even

217

The type specimen of *Pinus lambertiana* at the Herbarium of Kew is perhaps all that is left of the collection from David Douglas's famous pine, which he nearly paid for with his life.

more successful if he had recognized the rather subtle differences between some species that have ranges in either eastern or western North America. Douglas held them for the eastern species, which he had already collected on earlier trips, and therefore did not gather the western material. Other collectors, such as John Jeffrey on behalf of the Oregon Association, a Scottish club of landowner-subscribers, and Karl Theodor Hartweg, again for the Horticultural Society of London, went after Douglas to the American western coast and Mexico and collected many more conifers and other trees.

When North America seemed explored and exhausted of novelties, attention turned to China and Japan, countries that had become more accessible in the latter part of the 19th century. The French had played an important role in plant collecting in China through their network of Jesuit missionaries, who each stayed in one location but made plant collecting forays into the surrounding countryside. Pères Armand, David, Delavay, Franchet, and others each made introductions into Europe of conifers, many of which are named after them. Among the secular plant hunters in China, Ernest Wilson (known as "Chinese Wilson") was the most famous and perhaps the most successful. First sent out to China by James Veitch & Sons of the Royal Exotic Nursery in Chelsea, London, in 1899, Wilson made several subsequent expeditions to China, Japan, and Korea for Veitch and the Arnold Arboretum of Harvard University. Augustine Henry had gone before him to China and others followed; many are household names in the introduction of plants and trees to Europe. Of these, George Forrest, Francis Kingdon-Ward, and Heinrich von Handel-Mazzetti collected many new conifers from China and the eastern Himalayan region between the 1880s and 1920s. Most of them tried to make a living from these long and dangerous expeditions by the payments they received from potential growers of their seeds. They would never be rich. For the first year Wilson got £100 for a trip into the virtually unknown, based on what had been paid a century earlier for a similar journey to collect plants in South Africa. John Jeffrey was in continuous trouble over payments for his specimens, and it seemed as if his sponsors would dispute every shilling. The landed gentry who wanted the trees appeared to be a parsimonious class of people.

Where did this 19th-century craze for trees come from? For an answer, we have to look at the changes in society, cultural perceptions, views of nature, and fashions that took place in industrializing Europe, and particularly in the United Kingdom, during that century. Although the Industrial Revolution caused disruption of traditional rural life and held millions in poverty in the cities, it much increased the number of people with wealth. In addition, the rationality of the Enlightenment was followed by a Romantic reaction, with idyllic views of nature, while retaining an interest in natural history and science among the elite and well-to-do classes. The newly wealthy therefore acquired land—on the one hand imitating the nobility who had always possessed it, and on the other renewing ideas about how to manage it: less to gain an income, more for pleasure.

In the 18th century, the great landowners had already created parks with lakes and vistas and romanticized them with follies such as ruins, Greek temples, and unnecessary bridges over imaginary rivers. In such landscapes trees had a decorative function, and various kinds were needed for this. But Europe, and particularly Britain, is naturally poor in tree species. The British Isles have only three native conifers: juniper (*Juniperus communis*), Scots pine (*Pinus sylvestris*), and yew (*Taxus baccata*). Landscape effects could often be better realized with exotics, which first came from other countries in Europe. With the expansion of European colonial empires, geographical exploration greatly increased. Ships were sent out to chart the oceans and survey the coasts of all the continents, and the ships' surgeons and naturalists brought back great numbers of new plants and animals. Botanists described trees never known to Europeans before. Then the collector's bug bit and those infected transferred the contagion to their fellow landowners. Rivalry to have a tree no one else had must have been a stimulant, but so was generosity, as many new species were often quickly distributed to neighbouring estates. In fact, some would-be discoverers tried to capitalize on this. There was a fellow named Benedict Roezl who based himself in Mexico and who described in his 1857 seed catalogue 82 new species of *Pinus*. He took care to name many of them after the landed gentry of England, so that each earl and duke could have his own pine species. Roezl then simply waited for the orders to come in. Needless to say, all his names are synonyms save one, an accidental hit. Furthermore, many Mexican pines do not grow very well in cool Britain, so their lordships were in for a double disappointment if they bought Roezl's seeds.

More than any other country, the United Kingdom "offers hospitality to exotic vegetation," as W. T. Thiselton-Dyer, a former director of the Royal Botanic Gardens, Kew, wrote in the preface to *The Trees of Great Britain and Ireland* (Elwes and Henry 1906). The reasons for this hospitality are the climate, private ownership of land, and this national passion for tree growing. The rather mild climate allows more trees to grow more successfully in the United Kingdom than almost anywhere else but in New Zealand, which has become in many respects an imitation of Britain. Private land ownership was and still is widespread, even though the National Trust is now the custodian of many a country house and estate. And, looking at the membership list of the Inter-

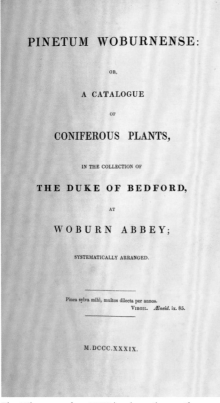

PINETUM WOBURNENSE:

OR,

A CATALOGUE

OF

CONIFEROUS PLANTS,

IN THE COLLECTION OF

THE DUKE OF BEDFORD,

AT

WOBURN ABBEY;

SYSTEMATICALLY ARRANGED.

Pinea sylva mihi, multos dilecta per annos.
VIRGIL. Æneid. ix. 85.

M.DCCC.XXXIX.

The title page of an 1839 book on the conifers planted on the estate of Woburn Abbey, seat of the Duke of Bedford in Bedfordshire, England

national Dendrology Society, those with residence in the United Kingdom are in the majority by a wide margin, followed by the United States (a much larger country), and New Zealand. Going on an excursion with that society, you may easily find yourself sitting in the tour bus with an earl or marchioness, several viscounts, and less illustriously titled owners of estates and parks planted with many exotic trees. I always hope they will not ask where I plant my trees: if I were to plant two, my garden would be full.

A pinetum (pl. pineta) is a garden or park planted with specimen conifers, species as well as cultivars, maintained as a living collection. The first pinetum in England was established in 1816, but it has long since disappeared. During the following 25 years many others followed—the Duke of Devonshire at Chatsworth in Derbyshire, the Duke of Bedford at Woburn Abbey in Bedfordshire, Lady Rolle at Bicton in Devon, and Lord Grenville at Dropmore in Bucking-

hamshire—to name just a few famous ones of the period. During the late 19th and 20th centuries some botanic gardens established pineta. William Dallimore planted one at Kew and then went on in the 1920s to create a larger one in the sandy hills of Kent at Bedgebury near the village of Goudhurst. When Kew obtained a lease on Wakehurst Place in Sussex from the National Trust in 1961, they decided to concentrate their efforts on that estate and withdrew from Bedgebury Pinetum. It is now solely under the jurisdiction of the Forestry Commission, a governmental body, and has grown to be the most important pinetum in Britain. A famous one in the United States was created within the Arnold Arboretum, for which Ernest Wilson collected many of the earliest plantings.

Conifers became very fashionable in the second half of the 19th century, and almost everyone planted them. Many of these plantings from the Victorian era have come to full maturity after 150 years and magnificently adorn the designed landscapes around country houses and stately homes all over the British Isles. A fashion of the time that still characterizes some of these landscapes was to plant avenues of conifers. The monkey-puzzle tree (*Araucaria araucana*) is an outstanding species, and the famous avenue of them at Bicton, Devon, still exists, despite some gaps now being replanted. Bicton once housed a collection of conifers unrivalled in England. Another example of an avenue of monkey-puzzles is at Castle Kennedy in Scotland. An avenue of mixed *Arau-*

caria and *Sequoiadendron* was planted at Coombe Wood, Veitch's nursery in Surrey, although this has sadly disappeared under the steamroller of London's urban sprawl.

Avenues of giant sequoias (*Sequoiadendron giganteum*) were also popular, with a fine example at Benmore in western Scotland. That tradition is now continued with recent plantings of avenues at Biddulph Grange in Staffordshire and Pampisford Hall in Cambridgeshire. The English still call this tree Wellingtonia, the botanical genus name given to this giant conifer by John Lindley when he first described it in the *Gardener's Chronicle* of 1853. A big row over naming immediately ensued, as Americans rejected the name of an English duke and military hero for their champion tree. It should be *Washingtonia* instead, as everything big and grandiose in America should be associated with their hero. The irony is that both names already had been used for another plant, and the rule of priority in botanical nomenclature outlaws using them again for a different plant. It took a long time before the situation was solved by J. T. Buchholz in 1939 with the neutral name *Sequoiadendron*. I think the English should demonstrate their gallantry and adopt the vernacular names big tree or giant sequoia instead.

The passion for conifers in 19th-century Britain commissioned some great books as well. Foremost of these and one of the most remarkable books ever published in botany

The avenue of *Araucaria araucana* at Bicton, Devon, England. Photograph by Derek Spicer

An illustration of *Pinus strobus* (eastern white pine) from Aylmer Bourke Lambert's *A Description of the Genus Pinus* (1803–1824). Reproduced by permission of the Lindley Library of the Royal Horticultural Society, London

is Aylmer Bourke Lambert's *A Description of the Genus Pinus*. This elephant folio tome was issued in instalments of plates with descriptive text, to which one could subscribe. When a volume was complete, buyers would take care of binding themselves. The first edition appeared between 1803 and 1824 in two volumes, and two more editions followed. The illustrations, from copper plate engravings, could be hand coloured depending on prices paid. Those of the first edition are almost all based on drawings by Ferdinand Bauer, considered by many the most gifted botanical artist of all times. It must have been a delight for the owners of parks and estates to receive these pages and then to try to obtain the conifers described and illustrated therein.

Just as massive, if not as masterly in its illustrations, is Edward Ravenscroft's three-volume *The Pinetum Brittanicum*, similarly released in instalments begun in 1863 and completed in 1884. The plates were chromolithographs and the text was written by John Lindley, Andrew Murray, and finally Maxwell Masters (although Lindley issued a disclaimer having anything to do with the first instalments of the book and criticized the quality of the drawing). Much smaller and more useful books appeared in abundance, dealing with conifers or with trees in general. John Loudon's *Arboretum et Fruticetum Brittanicum*, with a Latin title but written in English and dedicated to Hugh Percy, third Duke of Northumberland, appeared in 1838. It remained long the *vademecum* for every owner of park and pleasure ground in the British Isles. According to Loudon, "The main object which induced the author to undertake this Work was, the hope of diffusing more generally, among gentlemen of landed property a taste for introducing a greater variety of trees and shrubs in their plantations and pleasure grounds." Apparently Loudon thought that they needed to be educated. The Duke's London residence, Syon Park, is virtually opposite from where I live and it still has several conifers that were planted in Loudon's time.

The legacy of all these efforts is great and imposes an obligation not only to preserve it, but to build on it. The United Kingdom is indeed fortunate to have "offered hospitality" to so many conifers from many parts of the world. Many conifers grow so well there, from *Pinus radiata* and *Cedrus libani* in the south and midlands, to *Abies grandis* and *Thuja plicata* in the wetter west, and *Araucaria araucana* and *Sequoiadendron giganteum* everywhere. Despite 200 years of planting, which seems long in human terms, it means that many of these trees are still youngsters. Will they grow old? Every owner of an arboretum or pinetum knows of the calamities that appear to visit planted trees more than those in natural woods. The great storm in the south of England in October 1987 levelled thousands, and a similar disaster happened in France in December 1999. Drought, sinking water tables from too much pumping, fungal attacks, and pollution have all killed trees on estates that were planted generations before. However, it seems that some introduced conifers can withstand all these threats. The giant sequoias at Wakehurst Place in Sussex and elsewhere still stood tall after the 1987 storm, with hardly a branch ripped off. We know, of course, that the giant sequoias lived here long before. In our endeavours to cloth our estates in Europe, we have only reintroduced them.

27 Conifers In and Out of Fashion

RECENTLY I WAS ON AN EXCURSION *with members of the British Conifer Society in Devon in the southwest of England. Our last visit was to a horticultural nursery for conifers. To me this was rather new, and, to be honest, I did not feel very inspired by what I saw during the first hour or so. As a botanist and a taxonomist, I am a "species man," and these were all cultivars. Some were, to my taste at least, positively ugly. With pale yellow new needles, some of the colour forms seemed to lack chlorophyll and would surely die, I thought. How can you want to do this to a tree? So I trotted along in the rear of the group, part of the time in discussion with another member about what I thought were the real conifers. But then we came to a field covered in poly-tunnels: long, half-round coverings of polythene, with a path through the middle. The members of the group were all standing at the entrance of one tunnel, taking turns to look inside, with the owner explaining. Realizing there must be something of interest in there, I interrupted our conversation and quickened my step. Inside were thousands of little square plastic pots, neatly in rows on either side of a narrow walkway. Each pot had a diminutive, round, bright green "tennis ball" conifer, a dwarf cultivar of Chamaecyparis obtusa. They were all identical, and the columns stretched to the end of the long poly-tunnel—an extraordinary sight indeed.*

▲ ▲ ▲

I knew the Dutch did this kind of thing with chrysanthemums and carnations, but I never realized it could be done with conifers, too. Some interesting biology must be behind this. I was now determined to find out more about this trade and its techniques, so I could write about it here. To get informed, I visited Derek Spicer, the chairman of the British Conifer Society and a botanist as well as a nurseryman, who kindly took me around his nursery at South Kilworth near Lutterworth in Leicestershire. I learned quite a lot that day. The following account is a review of the trade, the horticulture, and the fashions in gardening relevant to that trade. This book being about the natural history of conifers, there is that slant, too. The horticulture of conifers is much more interesting than I thought.

In recent years the horticultural trade appears to have been emphasising dwarf conifers, but the fashion is not new. One of the many garden crazes in the Victorian age was to build a rock garden in a park, with the plantings in it growing slowly and remaining moderate in size. In Britain dwarf conifers became popular from the 1850s onwards. Interest in garden conifers was renewed in the 1960s but this time it was a fashion to plant them with heathers in suburban gardens, and it affected Europe as well as the United States. Consequently, many arboreta and pineta followed suit and established heather gardens with small or medium-sized, preferably columnar or fastigiate conifers. When people began to be bored with this, seeing the same idea established everywhere, the heather garden went out of fashion again. One reason for the disillusion may have been that "dwarf" conifers, after a slow start, often grow bigger than they have been promised to do. Many people perhaps do not realize that trees cannot just stop growing because garden design requires it. Both the understanding and consequent development of growing dwarfs only slowly developed into what professional nurserymen can achieve in this *métier* today. The trade is influenced by the demand but

A poly-tunnel with thousands of dwarf conifers of various cultivars at the Kilworth Conifers nursery of Derek Spicer in Leicestershire, England. Photograph by Derek Spicer

Kilworth Conifers nursery, with conifer cultivars put out in beds in preparation for the trade

Chamaecyparis obtusa 'Chilworth', a so-called tennis ball dwarf conifer, is cultivated to remain very small.

Chamaecyparis obtusa 'Wissel' is another dwarf conifer that will assuredly not grow big.

also creates it by making new and better forms available. Many good dwarf and colour cultivar forms have been developed in the last decade or so.

Early on, divergent forms were probably found by nurserymen as either witches' brooms or seedlings differing from the parent plants. When grown on to maturity, these plants could produce offspring from seed, and in many of these offspring the new characters were again expressed. This provided material for the age-old method of selection that Darwin recognized when he wrote in the *Origin of Species*, "When a race of plants is once pretty well established, the seed-raisers do not pick out the best plants, but merely go over their seed-beds, and pull up the 'rogues' as they call the plants that deviate from the proper standard." Of course, the growers imitated natural selection without knowing it, which was Darwin's point.

To retain cultivar characters from seedling mutations, however, more rigorous propagation protocols and techniques are required. A divergent seedling or young plant is found as before. It is grown to sufficient size to take cuttings or scions, which are rooted as grafts or, if possible, grown on their own roots that they may develop. Genetically, the scions should be identical to the single parent plant from which they were taken. Rigorous new selections are made to retain only those rooted scions or grafts that develop according to the ideal the grower has formed in his or her mind about the cultivar to propagate and sell. These few become the stock plants, and propagation is by vegetative means only.

Another problem may still arise, however. Because selection occurred at the juvenile stage, the characters selected for are often only expressed in juvenile stages. Quite often, there is a gradual return to the common form of the species as such plants become mature; this is particularly common in seedling mutations involving juvenile fixation of foliage characters. Such plants are known among horticulturists as reversions. When I did verifications of plant labels in the collections of the Royal Botanic Gardens at their gardens at Kew and Wakehurst Place, I sometimes came across conifers with cultivar names in which I could see no difference from the normal variation that occurs in the species in natural populations. They could have been reversions, but if no documentation on provenance was available, even that could not be verified.

Despite the less rigorous methods of the past, gardens and parks abound with distinct older cultivars of conifers. To keep them for future generations, rigorous propagation methods would be necessary. That is less easy than it seems from what I described about the appropriate method so far. To germinate the seeds, if they are viable, does no good. Conifers are wind pollinated and chances are usually great that pollen from neighbouring trees of the same species, but not the same cultivar, is involved. Making well-rooting scions from the foliage of older trees often proves difficult, and grafting also works better with young material. To remain in the trade, a cultivar has to be mass-produced and requires large investments of labour and time. Without sufficient demand, this won't happen, and so many old cultivars disappear, they die out.

Probably the most diverse conifer in terms of numbers of cultivars past and present is *Chamaecyparis lawsoniana* (Cupressaceae), Lawson's cypress, known as Port Orford cedar in the United States. *Chamaecyparis lawsoniana* is restricted to mountains on the border between California and Oregon. In nature, its morphological variation is limited to foliage hues between dark green and glaucous green and more or less pendulous branches. The colour of seed cones before maturity may also vary, with more or fewer purplish markings or glaucous to green; in part, this correlates with leaf colour as the cone scales are derived from the leaves. In cultivation, this species mutates very easily, which has given rise to hundreds of cultivars since its first introduction in 1856. In Japan, *Chamaecyparis obtusa* has been the origin of almost as many cultivars, from stunted forms to tall trees. Japanese gardens require shrubs and trees

Foliage of *Chamaecyparis lawsoniana* (Lawson's cypress) with seed cones in two stages of development

The pollen cones of *Chamaecyparis lawsoniana* (Lawson's cypress) show bright red from the colour of the pollen sacs.

Chamaecyparis obtusa 'Caespitosa' is one of the smallest of the dwarf conifers. Photograph by Derek Spicer

with specific shapes and colours, and the art of selecting cultivars for these gardens is centuries old. Japan is now a major source of dwarf cultivars around the world. What may lie behind this extraordinary variation in horticulture of some conifer species that in nature show no such variation at all?

Mutations are alterations in the genetic code—the DNA sequence—that do not occur during fertilization. Rather, they are errors in the copying process that can occur when cells divide. Much of the DNA sequence in any organism has no direct influence on its development. In the DNA that does code for amino acids and hence proteins, most mutations that occur in third base positions of the triplet codons may also be passed on to the next generation without being expressed. Mutations in first and second base positions of the active DNA are different—they will lead to alterations in appearance or function. It is this kind of mutation that causes mutant plants with visible differences in their morphology. In natural populations there is a strong selection by the environment, which tends to weed out any mutants with disadvantageous traits (those maladapted to the environment). Most mutations in the coding parts of DNA are disadvantageous, and some are downright detrimental (like those causing yellow leaves lacking chlorophyll). Very few are advantageous, but these mutations can be selected for if they indeed increase fitness and overcome genetic drift, and over time they will gain dominance in the population. Natural selection is the main reason why much of the potential variation in *Chamaecyparis lawsoniana* is not realized in its natural habitat. The mutants are almost always weeded out. But under cultivation, they may be preserved.

This does not explain why some species seem to suffer mutations more frequently than others. Is there an inherent instability in the genome—the totality of the DNA sequence of an organism—that makes mutations more likely? Mutations can be artificially induced, with certain chemicals or x-rays, but that is not likely to happen in

Conifer cultivars are selected for colour as well as shape. Two contrasting colours in *Chamaecyparis* grow side by side in Kilworth Conifers nursery.

natural populations or even in gardens and nurseries under normal circumstances. Mutation rates are often considered to be fairly constant, at least in some parts of the genome, offering data for so-called molecular clocks to estimate divergence time in the phylogeny of species. That there may be substantial variation in mutation rates among conifer species is suggested by the lack of cultivars arising from mutants in some species or even genera. The truth is, we don't really know why different conifer species have different mutation rates. Both *Metasequoia* and *Taxodium* were, until recently, almost devoid of cultivars despite massive and widespread cultivation, in the case of *Taxodium* for more than 350 years. This cannot be blamed on difficulties with vegetative propagation in these two genera, as both grow easily from scions. However, they don't make good hedges, so there may also be economic reasons for the paucity of cultivars. *Pseudolarix amabilis*, of which only one or two cultivars were ever produced, may be much more difficult in this respect, although another limiting factor may have been its poor availability in the trade. That conservative monotypic genera are not necessarily devoid of cultivars is demonstrated by *Sciadopitys verticillata*, of which many cultivars have been developed in Japan as well as in Europe and elsewhere.

One of the most interesting mutations, both from a horticultural and biological point of view, occurs as a bud or shoot mutation, especially the one that forms witches' brooms. From a biological point of view, there are two types of witches' brooms. One type, most common in angiosperms but also occurring in conifers, is a tree's reaction to a parasite or pathogen. We have met with this phenomenon in chapter 17, where I discussed dwarf mistletoes in pines. The second type, however, involves genetic mutations. It has long been understood that there are witches' brooms, especially in conifers, of which there does not appear to be an external cause. In these cases, there is usually only a single broom in a tree. Parasites and pathogens operate in outbreaks, spreading out from an initial infestation, and the witches' brooms they cause in trees are not alone for long. Sometimes, the spontaneous brooms produce cones with viable seed. These cones and seeds are smaller, like everything else in the broom, than their counterparts elsewhere in the tree. When these seeds are germinated, something very interesting happens. On average, about half of the seedlings develop normally, but the other half remains dwarfish or grows decumbent or prostrate, not developing an erect leader. The pollen that produced these seeds came either from the parent tree or from other trees, but not from the broom if it has only seed cones. As the seedlings are further selected for dwarf traits, their offspring, now taken from rooted cuttings or grafts, remain truly dwarfish. This clearly demonstrates that a mutation occurred in a bud meristem cell nucleus that gave rise to the witches' broom twigs. The causes of such a mutation remain at present unknown, but as with all genetic mutations, it involves a copying error in DNA transcription. The mutation retards growth, so it occurs in a particular gene that determines the growth of shoots and everything that derives from these. With the genetic knowledge and techniques now available, that gene should not be too difficult to identify.

Meanwhile, these mutated witches' brooms present interesting implications for evolutionary biologists on the questions of individuality and genetics in trees. If a branch on a tree can mutate while the rest of the tree remains genetically the same as before, we end up with two different genomes in one tree. If that branch produces shoots genetically different from shoots from other parts of the tree, couldn't we then have a different individual? More disturbing still, if the offspring of the broom were substantially different from that of the remainder of the parent tree and sexually incompatible with it, perhaps due to size differences in the micropyle of the ovules and/or the length of the pollen tube, what would we have? We would have a new species! It would be a species of which the ancestor

A witches' broom in a Scots pine (*Pinus sylvestris*) growing in a hedge in England. Photograph by Derek Spicer

is a living tree. That is a very disturbing thought for cladists, who have to assume that ancestors are dead, because otherwise they create paraphyletic instead of monophyletic groups (see chapter 6). But it is not disturbing at all to Francis Hallé, who argued that trees are in fact colonies of individuals in his book *In Praise of Plants* (2002). In chapter 19 we learned how a tree such as the coast redwood (*Sequoia sempervirens*) through a process called reiteration grows trees of its own kind upon its branches. Here we discover that such growth could become genetically different from the parent tree. Yet they remain connected, linked to a single root system functioning for all, as in a colony. In nature, however, the chances of the broom's offspring to survive and build enduring populations are rather dim. The environment would indeed weed them out; they would be a short-lived species.

Nurserymen have used mutant witches' brooms for quite a long time to grow dwarf forms of conifers. The first cultivar derived from a witches' broom was probably *Picea abies* 'Clanbrassiliana' reported in 1836, and several dwarf forms of this species were derived from witches' brooms in subsequent years. In recent times, selections derived from witches' brooms have become a major source of dwarf conifers in cultivation, and a constant stream of new cultivars is entering the market. Dwarf pines seem to be particularly popular at present, and both in Europe and the United States many people are scouring the countryside to find that lone broom in a pine tree that may yield yet another cultivar. Sometimes witches' brooms occur on cultivars instead of on species trees in nature. When cones with good seeds are produced on a broom, an opportunity arises to select from seedlings and produce more than one form of cultivated conifer. Scions of these are clones, which should be more uniform in characters displayed. And so it goes on.

To an outsider like me, it would appear as if every newly found broom on a tree creates a new cultivar or two. But even voices within the trade are cautioning against too enthusiastic naming. A new cultivar should be unique, but how can one know that it really is that? Although there is an obligation to publish, the descriptions and illustrations of new cultivars are often highly individualistic. Publications with compilations of cultivated conifers rarely give explicit discriminating characters. Horticulturists are encouraged to register new cultivar names. The Royal Horticultural Society is the registration authority for conifers and their cultivars, and it is the task of its registrar to compile a list of registered cultivar names. This register should be consulted to avoid duplication of names, but it cannot avoid duplication of similar cultivars under different names. There is no scrutiny by monographers resulting in the placement of cultivar names under synonymy, and at any rate it is difficult to see how that could be accomplished when type specimens are nonexistent—not to mention the reluctance to accept such relegation to synonymy when trade is involved. Judgement by committee has been proposed, but that committee would have to be international and of high standing to be credible. It will be difficult to impose its ruling on someone whose ego and commercial interests are at stake at the same time.

Dwarf conifers are in fashion at present and so they are produced, the good ones along with the not so good. Survival in the garden is certainly one test to separate the bad from the good. At the beginning of this chapter I expressed my dismay at yellow

View of Cecil Franklin's garden at Reading, England, planted with dwarf conifers. Photograph by Derek Spicer

leaves in many cultivars. The good ones either have yellow leaves in the current season's growth and these leaves turn green later when shaded by new foliage, or there is some chlorophyll hidden in them. Most conifers retain leaves for a few years, so the older leaves restore the chlorophyll and keep the plant alive, while the new leaves display the colour. Our fancies and fashions may command weird colours and shapes, but certain requirements must be met for a conifer cultivar to stay alive and grow.

28 The Other Uses of Conifers

ARE CONIFERS FOOD *for humans? Some parts of some conifers are used for food or food flavouring, but we can't exactly list these among the staple foodstuffs for people. Are conifers medicine? Yes, some are, but this is an even more contentious subject. Medicine in traditional use for ailments in many cultures may or may not be medicine in science-based pharmaceutics. But one can take the view that if the patient gets better, the medicine had something to do with it, even if it was a placebo. In that broad sense, some conifers are medicine. At least one genus,* Taxus, *has recently proved to contain potent anti-carcinogenic substances. There is a lot of complicated chemistry in conifers, especially in the resin. These different substances—and there are thousands of them—have led to numerous applications, both traditional and industrial. Finally, there is the religious side of conifer usage, expressed in rituals and traditions that are often, but not always, intertwined with some of the more practical uses mentioned above as well as in previous chapters. All this adds to the human interest in conifers.*

▲ ▲ ▲

In 1894 John Muir, the naturalist, explorer, and conservationist, described how Native Americans used the seeds of *Pinus sabiniana* (grey pine), which grows abundantly in the foothills of the Sierra Nevada of California: "The men climb the trees like bears and beat off the cones with sticks, or recklessly cut off the more fruitful branches with hatchets, while the squaws gather the big, generous cones, and roast them until the scales open sufficiently to allow the hard-shelled seeds to be beaten out. Then, in the cool evenings, men, women, and children, with their capacity for dirt greatly increased by the soft resin with which they are all bedraggled, form circles around camp-fires, on the bank of the nearest stream, and lie in easy independence cracking nuts and laughing and chattering, as heedless of the future as the squirrels." The Americans despised both the natives and the pine, which was no good for timber and indeed only seemed to yield these edible seeds and, of course, resin. They called the natives "diggers" because they dug up certain plant roots for food, and the tree "digger pine," a name by which it was long known until more enlightened times emerged recently. The natives have long gone but the pine is still there, used now only for wildlife habitat.

Pine seeds of several unrelated species are nutritious and sometimes tasteful food, and some are of commercial value today. In Europe it is mainly the Mediterranean species *Pinus pinea* (umbrella pine) that yields seeds (Italian *pignolia*) of good size and taste for the food market, used in processed food as well as sold as whole seeds. The unrelated Asian pine *P. koraiensis* produces similar seeds and has become the leading species in the export market. *Pinus gerardiana* (chilgoza) and *P. bungeana* (lace-bark pine) are other Asian pines with good edible seeds. In the United States and Mexico there are several closely related species: *P. cembroides*, *P. edulis*, and *P. monophylla* are the most widespread and are commonly known as *piñones* or pinyon pines. Their seeds can be bought in shops and at markets in the southwestern United States and throughout most of Mexico. Its large edible seeds led to the discovery by botanists of the rare Mexican species *P. maximartinezii* (see the photos in chapter 23). In chapter 17 we met the extraordinary cases of mutualism with birds and pines involving *P. cembra* in Europe and *P. albicaulis* in North America. Humans could eat these seeds, too, but we find them not as good or easy to harvest; like the seeds of California grey pine, we leave them to the birds and squirrels. In Russia *P. sibirica*, which is closely related to *P. cembra*, produces seeds harvested for cooking oil extraction. No other taxa than pines in the family Pinaceae produce edible seeds.

A delicious conifer seed is produced by *Araucaria araucana*, the monkey-puzzle tree. This edible seed is much larger than most of the pine seeds and extremely nutritious. In the Andes of southern Chile and adjacent Argentina, native tribes have traditionally harvested the seeds as an important food crop. The seeds were stored as well as traded with tribes outside the range of the trees. They can be eaten raw but are better

Pinus pinea (umbrella pine) has been planted in many parts of the Mediterranean Basin since antiquity for its wood and edible seeds.

The closed seed cones of *Pinus pinea* require heating to be opened to release the edible seeds within.

The large seeds of *Araucaria araucana* (monkey-puzzle tree) are a delicacy in Argentina and Chile. Photograph by Edward Parker

lightly roasted. In recent years, a market has developed well outside the region, leading to a danger of overexploitation. Trees may grow in national parks or other reserves, but native people have rights to the seed resource, which makes the situation difficult. The species is listed in CITES Appendix I, which means no seeds can be exported. This restriction does not mean *A. araucana* seeds cannot be consumed elsewhere, as good seeds are produced on planted trees in several countries.

Another good seed for human consumption is produced by *Araucaria bidwillii* (bunya pine), which is native to a limited area in Queensland, Australia. Here the Aborigines used to meet in years of good seed crops (cones mature in three years) in large numbers for harvest and festivities. Each clan or tribe had jurisdiction over certain trees and their crop of seeds. Unfortunately, the Aborigines' traditional harvesting rights have not been upheld; their last great gathering for the *bon-yi* harvest was held in 1902, when the loggers took over. The last sawmill closed in 1945, and most of the remaining trees are protected in the Bunya Mountains National Park. Interest in Aboriginal foods, "bush tucker" as it is popularly called in Australia, is growing and the seeds of *A. bidwillii* are again on the menu for all Australians.

Beyond these seeds, there is not much else in conifers that one could eat or drink. The Maori of New Zealand traditionally ate the succulent "fruit" (receptacle of the cone) of the podocarp *Dacrycarpus dacrydioides* (see photo in chapter 17). Similar receptacles are found on all species of *Podocarpus*, but I have not come across references to people eating them. Perhaps these receptacles are left to the birds not because they are inedible to humans, but because these trees are scattered to rare in the forest and the receptacles are difficult to reach.

We are now down to flavouring. Perhaps the best known of the flavour-producing conifers is *Juniperus communis*, the common juniper. Its cones (often incorrectly called "berries") are small, globose, more or less succulent, and moderately sweet with sugars when ripe. My sister-in-law uses them in the traditional German *Sauerkraut mit Bratwurst*, but better known is their use in flavouring gin. The Dutch words for gin and for the shrub are *jenever* and *jeneverbes*, with the latter adding the word for berry. *Juniperus communis*, together with its varieties, is the most widespread conifer in the world and the various types of gin, like aquavit, jenever, and Schnaps, are all made with it. Some other species of *Juniperus* can be used, but none are as good as the common juniper. The resin

The cones ("berries") of *Juniperus communis* are used to flavour gin in many northern countries.

of the Mediterranean pine *Pinus halepensis* is used to flavour *retsina*, a Greek white or rosé wine popular with locals as well as tourists. Dioscorides proscribed the use of *retsina* in the first century for coughs and lung and stomach complaints. Perhaps resin was used to seal *amphorae*, the tall, pointed-bottomed earthen vessels in which wine was transported, giving it a slightly resinous flavour that the Greeks learned to like. In Canada, the shoots with needles and buds of *Picea mariana* (black spruce) are boiled to make spruce beer, as I recollect, a beverage with an acquired taste. The resin was used by native tribes as a chewing gum; we have learned of the same use of the resin of the sugar pine (*Pinus lambertiana*) in chapter 26. As with conventional chewing gum, when the sugary flavour has gone, the gum was spit out. Would this gum be less persistent on the pavement than conventional chewing gum?

Not very remote from flavour is scent. Most of us in the Northern Hemisphere have experienced the typical fragrance of a conifer forest, with subtle differences between pine, spruce, larch, hemlock, fir, and cedar. These fragrances are due to the volatile components of the terpenoid resins of these conifers, which are emitted with the transpiration of gases through the stomata in the leaves. The varied chemistry of these resins is responsible for the subtle differences in fragrance between species and genera. On a warm, sunny day a walk through a mixed conifer forest like that on the western slopes of the Cascade Range in Oregon can be an exhilarating experience to the olfactory senses. In modern cosmetics, these components are distilled from the resin and used in soap, both liquid and solid, and in deodorants. You can have a bath or shower and imagine a stroll through a pine forest.

Indeed, fragrance and scent play a major role in imagination, which leads us to incense and religious ceremony. On a journey to the northern parts of Yunnan Province in China in the early autumn of 2000, we crossed a mountain pass not far from the town of Dêqên. On the pass was a collection of small Buddhist *stupas* and what looked like stone ovens. Vendors behind crude tables on the side of the road were offering green boughs of a conifer for sale, and people were burning these in the ovens, creating a lot of fragrant smoke. I asked the driver to stop. Upon examination, the conifer foliage appeared to be from *Platycladus orientalis*, a tree native to northern China, a long way from here, but introduced and planted all over China and in other parts of Asia. From this encounter onwards, I began to see that wherever we passed Buddhist shrines or monasteries in Yunnan, this conifer was not far away, often covering mountain slopes but always in secondary vegetation. I saw plenty of evidence of foliage clipping on many small trees. This species and *Juniperus chinensis* are the two most commonly planted large conifer trees on temple grounds and around palaces—a good example is the Forbidden City in Beijing. The Aztecs called teocote pine (*Pinus teocote*) the pine of the gods, and to burn its rosin as incense was a privilege of priests and kings. In Mexico and Guatemala today the green boughs of *Abies religiosa* are taken into churches on important feast days of the Roman Catholic year, not for incense burning but for decoration. They give off a fragrant scent regardless, which is undoubtedly part of its significance in the local practices of that religion, perhaps together with the symbolism traditionally connected with evergreen plants in northern cultures and traditions.

This symbolism leads us into Christmas trees, a symbolic use of conifers introduced by Europeans to wherever they emigrated in the world. Today several conifers of Pinaceae are grown and used as Christmas trees, such as species of *Abies, Picea, Pseudotsuga,* and *Pinus,* depending on country and availability, although the choice was originally limited to *Picea abies* (Norway spruce). The tradition in its present form is originally German and coincides with the afforestation in that country, planting spruces from the 18th century onwards. Norway spruce is still the commonest species used for Christmas trees in Germany, the Netherlands, and England and probably elsewhere in northwestern Europe. Emigrants took the tradition to the United States and Canada.

The tradition to decorate the house, both inside and outside over the doorway, with evergreens at midwinter goes back a much longer time, and the Christmas tree is just a later version of it. This tradition does not belong to the Christian religion but to earlier, animistic beliefs. The Calvinist and Protestant ministers of the Reformation condemned it as furiously as the papist images of Mary and the Christian saints. They were hardly successful, as it turned out. In the darkest, shortest days of the year people were anticipating the return of light and life in spring. The evergreens in Europe's lowland woods are few and therefore symbolized that life, being carried on through the dark and death of winter. Holly (*Ilex*), ivy (*Hedera*), yew (*Taxus*), and mistletoe (*Viscum*) all provided this foliage and all were imbued with magical properties. Spruce (*Picea*), pine (*Pinus*), and fir (*Abies*) grow in mountains and in northern Europe, not naturally in lowland central and western Europe. Where they occur naturally, the woods are not bare but green in winter and a desire to decorate the house with their branches would be rather pointless under these beliefs. If Christmas trees are now taken into houses in

The green foliage of *Platycladus orientalis* (oriental arbor-vitae) is sold for incense burning on a high mountain pass in northern Yunnan, China.

Finland or Canada, it is because people do things like this out of tradition, not because it has a symbolic meaning or purpose. Few people seem to be aware of the origins of that tradition, which is apparent around Christmas time in Australia and New Zealand, which there falls in the middle of summer. It is also obvious from the sale of plastic, silver Christmas trees, which are missing the point altogether.

Conifers have been awe-inspiring to many cultures, especially when they are big, old, and mysterious. The Old Testament proclaimed, "Son of man, say to Pharaoh, king of Egypt and to all his subjects: To what shall I compare you in your greatness? Surely, to a cedar of Lebanon with noble branches" (Ezekiel 31: 2–9). The Haida, Kwakiutl, Nootka, and Tlingit nations of the Pacific Northwest certainly venerated the big conifer trees that clothe the shores of sounds and islands. These peoples used almost everything of *Thuja plicata* (western red cedar), as well as the wood and some other materials of other conifers. Perhaps most famous today is their use of conifer trees for religious purposes in the carving and erecting of huge totem poles. These depict a compilation of supernatural beings in animal or human form, which were related to clan ancestors to whom they had appeared or, sometimes, into whom they had transformed. These animal creatures, often recognizable as bear, beaver, eagle, or raven, are not really totems but clan symbols, comparable to the images of mediaeval European heraldry but of a supernatural nature and therefore symbols in a religion. The whole is carved from a single western red cedar, the most durable wood of the region.

In Ireland ancient yews (*Taxus baccata*) were venerated and feared at the same time, both before and after the conversion to Christianity. The yew features in many Irish tales and legends about kings, poets, and druids. The only evergreen conifer tree on that island in ancient times, the yew is also toxic, seems to live forever, and yields extremely hard and strong wood important in warfare—there are no better bows than yew bows. Yews were planted near the churches of Celtic saints and on old cemeteries by holy men, but few of these ancient yews survive in Ireland today. In Wales yews were planted at wells that were associated with early

Totem poles at Wrangell, Alaska, are each carved from a single tree of *Thuja plicata* (western red cedar).

Christian saints. Many mediaeval churches in England, Wales, Normandy, and Brittany have ancient yews, about the ages of which there is much more speculation than science. Because conventional methods of ring counts fail with hollow trees, which grow new wood on the inside as well as on the outside of the trunk, historical evidence may be better. This evidence points to an early Christian age for the oldest yews in this region, roughly 1300–1500 years old. Interestingly, recent findings in chemistry and pharmacology appear to confirm the extraordinary properties of the yew, which contains an anti-cancer drug known as paclitaxel (Taxol). The toxic diterpenoid alkaloids can kill a man as well as a horse if ingested in some quantity. These variable compounds are a combination of taxine alkaloids and volatile oils. However, the same taxine substances have been used to arrest advanced stages of breast and other cancers. In the first few years after this discovery a rush on the bark and leaves of certain yew species, especially *Taxus brevifolia* in North America and *T. wallichiana* in the Himalayas, threatened to deplete the natural resource, but the active compounds are now being synthesized by chemists. The story of Taxol shows that old beliefs in magical properties of trees should not always be discarded as mere folklore.

Another traditional use for conifers is the ancient art of bonsai in Japan, China, and Korea. Bonsai is an art form that attempts to manipulate a growing woody plant, usually a species of tree, into idealized shapes and forms very similar to those seen in Chinese and Japanese landscape paintings. It is also an imitation of how trees grow on rocks in mountains under adverse circumstances; in fact, the methods used in many ways imitate these natural conditions of constraint. For a start, the tree is planted in a

A *Pinus jeffreyi* (Jeffrey pine) blasted by a thousand snow storms into a natural bonsai high on Sentinel Dome in the Sierra Nevada of California

shallow tray with very little soil and its roots are not only constrained in this way but periodically cut back when the plant is transferred to a bigger container. Branches and twigs are clipped and stems bound with mesh or wire to deliberately create dead wood. This imitates the wind blasted, bare rock conditions at high altitude that some conifers endure in nature. A marvellous locality to see natural bonsai conifers is the Tioga Pass in the Sierra Nevada of California, where pines and junipers are contorted to fantastic shapes as they grow out of fissures in the bare granite.

Apart from wood, no other substance of conifers has more economic value than their resins. All conifers produce resin, albeit not in equal quantities. Resin in leaves can be distilled from them, resin in wood can be tapped as well as distilled, and there is even resin to be mined. Jean Langenheim has written a scholarly book on resins, and much in the following text owes credit to her *Plant Resins* (2003). The resins of conifers are mostly terpenoids, with some phenolic resins. Only two families, Araucariaceae and Pinaceae, produce copious amounts in the wood, stored in resin ducts or canals. There are usually also resin ducts in leaves (needles) and in seed cones. The cones of some species in *Abies* and *Pinus* (Pinaceae) and *Araucaria* (Araucariaceae) exude large amounts of resin, which flows out like dripping candle wax. The resin of conifers functions as a defence mechanism against intruders, from fungi to insects (see chapter 18).

The genus *Agathis* (Araucariaceae) is the most copious producer of resin. It has flowed from the trunks of large trees onto the ground and accumulated over centuries, forming large deposits of copal that can be excavated. In the 19th century the Northland region of New Zealand attracted not only loggers but also many "gum diggers" to the kauri (*Agathis australis*) forests. The activity resembled the digging for gold, but with a better chance of finding something of value, for this very hard resin occurred in great abundance and was priced for its special varnish qualities. Thousands from Europe, China, and Malaysia flocked to the copal fields from the 1880s to the beginning of World War I. Some conifers in Cupressaceae, such as *Callitris* in Australia and *Tetraclinis articulata* in North Africa, produce a resin called *sandarac* that is also good for high-quality varnish.

More commonly, resin is tapped from the trunks of pines. Major resin-producing species are or were *Pinus kesiya* in Southeast Asia, *P. massoniana* in China, *P. pinaster* in Europe (especially France), and *P. palustris* and *P. elliottii* in the southeastern United States. The resin tapped forms the basis of many industrial products, such as turpentine, rosin (pitch), oils, varnishes, printing inks, sealing wax, soap, plastics, and fireworks. Coarser products are obtained by destructive distillation of resinous wood; for instance, *P. sylvestris* wood is the source of Stockholm tar, which is a by-product of charcoal burning. In the age of wooden ships, pitch and tar were indispensable to keep them seaworthy by caulking the seams with pitch and by tarring the rigging. The term *naval stores* for these and similar products comes from the 17th-century English navy, where large quantities were required for an expanding fleet.

Amber is the fossil form of resin occurring as discrete pieces in sediment deposited at least 40,000 years ago. Most amber is derived from coniferous resin, and the oldest examples date from the beginning of conifers in the late Carboniferous (Stephanian, see chapters 9 and 11). The fossilization of resin to amber is a chemical process involving polymerization of diterpenes, forming complex compounds with a higher molecular weight. The chemical structures undergo slow changes over geologic time, known as maturation. Several characteristics of amber have made it a highly prized substance: its rarity and/or localized occurrence, its colour and transparency, its relative softness to work it into ornaments, its capacity to become negatively charged with electricity when rubbed, and its extraordinary preservation of encased organisms, especially insects.

Amber is found in several localities in the world, and an important source today is the Dominican Republic. The classical Greek word for amber is *elektron*, derived from *elektor*, the glare of the sun. The attractive properties of amber gave us the words *electron* and *electricity*. Most famous of all kinds is Baltic amber, which was traded all over Europe and beyond from Neolithic times to the present, a period of some 5500 years. The use of this amber for beads and other ornaments goes even further back to Late Palaeoli-

The necklace of Exloo discovered in Drenthe, the Netherlands. This Bronze Age necklace (ca. 3300 years old) was found under peat in 1881 and consists of 14 pieces of Baltic amber, with various other beads, some from Cornwall and Egypt. Reproduced by permission of Drents Museum, Assen, the Netherlands

thic reindeer-hunter camps. Late Neolithic and Bronze Age ornaments made from amber often have designs indicating cults worshipping the sun, and the colour of some light ambers would have made it an obvious choice. During the northwestern European Bronze Age, amber became an object of prestige that could be traded especially for metal wares from outside the Baltic region. Trade routes ran from the Baltic and Jutland south along river valleys and across the Alps to the head of the Adriatic Sea and beyond. The Roman Empire greatly accelerated the trade in amber from the Baltic shores under Nero (who reigned from 54 to 68 C.E.), once the Romans finally discovered the source of it. Amulets made of amber to protect children from evil as well as gladiators from defeat became very popular. With the fall of the Roman Empire in the fifth century, the trade of Baltic amber virtually ceased, not to be revived for 800 years. The conquest of the Baltic lands by the Order of Teutonic Knights in the 13th century revived the trade, and the conquerors assumed control of it. Paternoster or prayer beads were one of the main amber products of the Middle Ages, reflecting a belief that amber was a sign of the presence of God. The Roman Catholic rosary derived directly from these prayer beads. And so we are back to the spiritual importance of conifers, which in a wider sense is as important to society, secular or otherwise, as the economic uses.

Conifers and Conservation

29 Extinction Is Forever

EXTINCTION IS THE APPARENT FATE *of all species, just like death is the fate of all living beings—even though the causes are different. In a wider sense, nothing specific that exists within the universe is everlasting, matter or energy in one form changes into another form all the time. In that context, extinction of species is no cause of concern. It is commonly stated that of all the species that ever existed on our planet, 99 per cent have become extinct. Despite the fact that we have only a vague idea about the real numbers of both extinct and living species, I grant the validity of the principle. So why are we making a fuss about it? From a self-centred utilitarian point of view, humans could regret the demise of a species that was useful to us. But why worry about the demise of pests like mosquitoes, cockroaches, rats, nettles, and poison ivy or any species that seems to make no impact on our lives in any sense, negative or positive? Would it not be beneficial if some of these pests went extinct? Or in case of the species with no impact, what difference would it make?*

▲ ▲ ▲

It has often been argued that our knowledge about the usefulness to humanity of most species remains rudimental and that because extinction is forever, we might lose out on something without ever knowing it. Even a cockroach might one day fall into this category. I do not deny the truth of this observation, but to prevent extinction of some species on utilitarian grounds is not really different from exterminating others because we consider them dangerous, such as *Anopheles* mosquitoes, which transfer malaria. In order to be genuinely worried about the extinction of species, I believe more universal concerns than our own immediate benefits should have to be accounted for. Writers such as Edward Wilson, David Quammen, Jared Diamond, Peter Ward, Paul Ehrlich, Norman Myers, and others have expressed these concerns eloquently and with much detail. I shall briefly mention their ideas here, because they will provide the context for the next chapters, where conifers will again become the main subject. Here, I illustrate the main issues in the extinction debate that are currently topical. It is a fast-moving subject where much remains speculative, not least the exact rate and some of the more proximate causes of extinction.

The first issue that we must consider is extinction rates. If all species eventually become extinct, what is their life expectancy? How can we find out how long a species should exist on average? These questions even bring back the debate on speciation and how to define a species encountered in chapter 4. Does a species become extinct if it evolves into another species, that is, if through natural selection the entire population of individuals of the earlier form is replaced by those of the new form? Does it become extinct upon a phylogenetic branching event, as cladists will insist, or can a species live on after this, with the new species just a separated population without any evolutionary effect on the parent population? Ideas about extinction rates are obviously influenced by where you stand on these controversies about speciation.

Attempts have been made to estimate the duration of species by analysis of the fossil record. This gives valid estimates only for abundant, small marine organisms, as all other records are too fragmentary. Estimates vary between 1 and 5 million years for a species of this kind. It has been argued that species of insects in tropical rainforests, many of which have extremely limited distributions, may have a much shorter life, perhaps one or two orders of magnitude less. They will never leave an adequate fossil record to test this assumption. If a species lasts on average 1 million years and if there were 1 million species at any given time, then the extinction rate would be one species per year under normal circumstances. If its lifetime was shorter and there were more species, the extinction rate would go up accordingly. Taking the various estimates that have been made for these parameters into account, we may expect the normal (or background) rate of global extinction to be a figure between one and 100 species per year. If it was found to be much higher than that range, abnormal circumstances causing extinction should be suspected.

There have indeed been times in the geologic past when extinction rates were very much higher for relatively short periods. Five major extinction events and many lesser ones are documented in the fossil record. The most severe of these was the Permian–Triassic extinction, roughly 250–240 million years ago, followed by the Cretaceous–Tertiary (KT) extinction, 65 million years ago. Much of the direct evidence comes again from marine fossils, especially small and widespread organisms. Half of all the families of marine organisms became extinct at the end of the Permian. For a family to become extinct all its genera and species have to be gone, which leads to estimates of extinction of species amounting to 85–90 per cent of all those that existed. On land there were major extinctions, too. Many large animals of the Permian were no longer present in the Triassic, and extinctions of plant groups are apparent as well. The early conifer families became extinct and modern families evolved, perhaps from a single ancestor (see the evolutionary tree in chapter 9). It appears that this mass extinction was not a sudden event but happened over a period of perhaps 8 million years, with at least two episodes of very high extinction rates. There would have been many causes, ranging from drastic reduction of shallow seas to desertification and periods of massive volcanism. These can all be related to the results of plate tectonics at that time, when the continents coalesced to form the supercontinent Pangea.

The second largest extinction event is the more famous of the two, because it supposedly killed off the dinosaurs, even though it was by all estimates much smaller. Extinction seems to have been much more selective during this event, again with many marine organisms falling victim, but others carrying on as if nothing serious had happened. On land, no massive global extinction is apparent among plants, including conifers. The dinosaurs and other animal groups such as pterodactyls became extinct, but crocodiles and turtles continued as before. There is no evidence in the fossil record of a sudden mass extinction of dinosaurs on a global scale at the KT boundary. The fossil record is usually inadequate for large animals to record such events, mainly because these fossils are too rare. What the fossil record does show about dinosaurs is that they had become very rare or extinct in many parts of the world well before the KT event happened. Dinosaurs were probably also in decline in the few localities in the United States and China from where fossil evidence is present up to the KT boundary. It is more likely that the KT event was a coup-de-grace, but of course if this is true it spoils the sensational image we have of it. What actually happened? Few issues in modern science have been more hotly debated. The impact of an asteroid seems to have gained the upper hand, wholeheartedly supported by writers such as Stephen J. Gould (who had an axe to grind) and the popular science press, especially in the United States. In the 1980s, a time of acute fear about nuclear self-destruction and "star wars," it appealed to the imagination much more than prolonged volcanism, the other option, defended by Vincent Courtillot among others. Under such emotional pressure, one hardly dared to suggest the retreat of shallow inland seas caused by diminished activity of midocean ridges, which deepened the oceans under these circumstances. That would never reach the headlines, even though it explains many of the marine extinctions better than either an asteroid impact or volcanism could. The question is not whether an impact happened, as it apparently did (and so did the volcanism), but how to explain the selective extinction at that time. The answer must come from biologists, not from physicists, who can only give evidence of the impact.

Palaeontologists David Raup, David Jablonski, and Jack Sepkoski have done much to increase our understanding of extinction rates through geological time. They have demonstrated that extinction from time to time during the last 600 million years accelerated far beyond a background extinction rate of one to 100 species per year. They have used genera and families as units of taxa, because the fossil record never preserves all the species. Extrapolation to species numbers from these higher taxonomic ranks is tricky. There is no valid rule about the numbers of species in a genus or genera in a family, other than the general tendency in evolution to increase diversity over time. This tendency means that, on average, genera now contain more species than they did in the Cretaceous or Permian periods. The trend in biodiversity, as Edward Wilson put it, "has been consistently upward," despite major setbacks caused by the mass extinction events. There are at present (still) more species on Earth than at any time in the geologic past. Conifers demonstrate this tendency on a small scale with the radiation of species diversity in *Abies, Juniperus, Pinus*, and *Podocarpus*, most of which took place in the second half of the Tertiary or during the last 30 million years. There are also many relicts of genera that were presumably more diverse in the past. To know how many species these may have had is almost impossible because preservation in the fossil record is so chancy and biased towards certain types of environments and sedimentation. High estimates of past numbers of species, such as those of Anderson and Anderson (2003) and Debazac (1964) mentioned in chapter 12, are probably based on present-day species ratios and should be considered with caution. However, given the relict status of many conifer taxa and the dominance conifers had in the vegetation through much of the Mesozoic, diversity was probably substantially higher than the present 630 species. Conifers today may be an exception to Wilson's trend.

We now must ask the important questions: Are we experiencing another mass extinction event at the present time? If so, when did it start? What are the proximal and ultimate causes? If there is an extinction event, do we expect it to accelerate? What are the long-term consequences? There are in general two lines of evidence for extinction: direct observation and inference. The best evidence for increased rates of extinction, based on direct observation, comes from oceanic islands. There are many islands, both large and small, that only a few centuries ago had large numbers of species of animals and plants that are now completely gone. Because oceanic islands have higher rates of endemism than areas of similar size on the continents, if a species becomes extinct on an island it is less likely to be found elsewhere. Many of these extinctions have been directly observed in historic times, which means since the arrival of people who kept written records. Other extinctions are inferred from the occurrence of remains and/or anecdotal evidence, such as those of the giant flightless birds in Madagascar and New Zealand and the famous dodo in Mauritius. Biologists now closely observe these islands and find that the rate of extinction on almost all of them is accelerating. A great many species have recently become so rare as to waver on the brink of extinction. On continents recent extinctions are as yet less numerous, but we all know of the many cases of severe reductions in the ranges and numbers of individuals for many species, especially large animals and trees. These reductions have led to extinctions in recent times, and an increasing number of animals and plants on continents are now also down to critically low numbers.

This is all sound evidence, and we can conclude that the extinction rate is high and accelerating. But perhaps we are only seeing the tip of the iceberg, and much of the extinction is going on unseen. Can we learn about it by extrapolation? Ecologists have come to our help with the theory of island biogeography, first fully formulated by Robert MacArthur and Edward Wilson in 1967. Essentially, the theory explains numbers of species on islands in relation to the size of the island, its distance from other land, and the age of the island. Larger islands have more species than smaller islands,

Abies delavayi from the Sino-Himalayan mountains is a good example of increased species diversity in a genus, where differences between related species are slight and still evolving.

the other parameters being equal. Greater distance means fewer species, and older islands have more species. Based on MacArthur and Wilson's mathematical models, numbers of species, or biodiversity, can be predicted. For example, on the basis of area, an island ten times larger than another island will have twice as many species and vice versa. When a volcanic island emerges from the ocean, it has no land-based life, but natural immigrants will arrive in due course, at a rate determined by distance from other land (source) and size of that land, as well as of the receiving island (area). New arrivals and speciation on the island increase biodiversity, extinction checks it until a saturation level is reached, determined by size and availability of habitats and niches on the island. Disturbances such as volcanic eruptions or typhoons and hurricanes can cause perturbations from which the process will start anew, given enough time. Islands are in many respects natural laboratories of evolution, where these processes happen faster than on continents.

But when ecologists think of islands, these are not necessarily surrounded with water. To all land animals and plants, water is a barrier to overcome, but to a forest animal or plant, a steppe is the same as water. Isolated forests are islands. Isolated grasslands in forests are also islands for grassland species. There are many such ecological islands on continents, and due to habitat destruction they are rapidly increasing in number and decreasing in size. Forests reduced to islands surrounded by unsuitable habitat for forest species will have fewer species than before, when the forest was continuous. Forest fragments of the same size as parcels in the continuous forest will have fewer species. There are many proximal causes for this reduction in biodiversity, but it is strongly correlated with size and distance of islands, and so we can make these estimates about species numbers and hence extinction by extrapolation.

Another ecological reality from which we can infer extinction of species is what Paul Ehrlich has called "this utter dependence of organisms on appropriate environments." There are very few generalist species but very many specialists. Dependencies are not only on specific physical factors such as soil, water quality, or climate, but also and even more on other organisms. Trees like conifers are especially important, and many other species depend upon them. I shall return to this with examples in the next chapter. The extinction of one species inevitably means the extinction of other species, multiplying the extinction rate exponentially. It paints a bleak canvas. The reduction or alteration and fragmentation of habitats for millions of species can only mean a drastic reduction in biodiversity. The more species there were in a given area, the smaller their ranges, the more numerous their interdependencies, and the higher the losses. This is especially acute in the two most diverse ecosystems on Earth, tropical rainforests and coral reefs, but the principle applies to all ecosystems. Even generalists like humans ultimately depend on the myriad interactions in diverse ecosystems for a healthy and happy life.

The answer to the question of whether we are experiencing another mass extinction event is unequivocally yes. Estimates vary, of course, from 1000 times the background extinction rate to 10,000 times or more by those who try to calculate the consequences for all the myriads of insects in the tropics, most of which are not even known to science. When did it start? The first apparent mass extinctions involved large animals and began 40,000 to 35,000 years ago in Australia, followed by similar extinctions in North and South America between 12,000 and 11,000 years ago. Large animals became extinct on Mediterranean islands 9000 to 8000 years ago, in Madagascar 1500 years ago, in New Zealand less than 1000 years ago. All these extinctions coincide with the arrival and spread of humans in these areas and happened in a short time. In all cases, flora and fauna had evolved for millions of years without people. Where humans and large animals have evolved together for at least 1 million years, as in Africa and Eurasia, few if any such extinctions occurred. There were none in Africa, where humanity originated, but mammoth, woolly rhinoceros, and the giant deer of Ireland were probably helped to extinction in Europe at the end of the last ice age. These extinctions were selective, not general. Large, slow, and easily hunted grazing mammals and birds fell victim to cunning hunters with often wasteful methods. Both their natural predators and carrion eaters followed them into extinction. Climate change may have been a factor locally, but there were many climatic fluctuations earlier in the Pleistocene and very few of the extinctions can be correlated with these. Today we have little doubt who was the culprit—it was us. In fact, it is still us, but now on a global scale, and hunting is just one of many contributions to the extinction crisis.

Habitat destruction and fragmentation in montane forest in northern Vietnam is not only jeopardizing a relict population of the conifer *Taiwania cryptomerioides* but an uncounted number of other species as well.

"The primary cause of the decay of organic diversity is not direct human exploitation or malevolence, but the habitat destruction that inevitably results from the expansion of human populations and human activities." This is how Paul Ehrlich has summed up the cause of the present extinction crisis. He is an ecologist known not to mince words. Ehrlich calls the destruction inevitable, and that is what it is under those circumstances. He calculated that by the end of the 1980s humans had consumed, directly and indirectly, up to 40 per cent of the total net primary production of stored biological energy produced by plants from solar energy. One species is using two-fifths of all biological production on the planet. He warned that when the human population doubles again, that could become as much as 80 per cent. I would add, if human activities and economic growth also continue to rise, logically we will one day have to use it all. There will be no room for vegetation not in the service of humanity. If everyone in the world enjoyed a lifestyle similar to the one people have in Europe and the United States we would need at least three planets to sustain ourselves. With a world population double that of today, we would need six planets. Edward Wilson has put the ecological absurdity of our numbers succinctly, noting that we are now 100 times more numerous than the most abundant large animal that has ever existed. "There is no way that we can draw upon the resources of the planet to such a degree without drastically reducing the state of most other species." That state for most species means extinction.

What are the long-term consequences? In the past, it has taken 5–15 million years after the five major mass extinctions for biodiversity to restore itself to levels prior to the catastrophic events. After that long time, diversity gradually increased beyond these levels. Lesser extinction events caused shorter perturbations. In all cases, restoration began after the causes of mass extinction had disappeared or were ameliorated. These were rare but natural causes. Because humanity is now the cause of the present mass extinction, do we have to be removed first? Only if ultimately we had to be considered a natural cause, that is, one that cannot be avoided. We are the cause, but we can change that, at least in principle. It is going to be very difficult. Current remedies such as the setting aside of nature reserves will not be sufficient, nor will technological solutions. The current debate on climate change and its suggested remedies is in fact distracting from the real issues. We shall have to strive towards a substantially lower world population and moderated economic consumption or face the dire consequences. Biodiversity is our most valuable but least appreciated resource. Without it, human life will experience catastrophic destruction and the aftermath will be a bland experience, both materially and spiritually.

30 Why Conifers in Nature Are Important

ON A SUMMER DAY IN 1975, *I was sitting on the fringe of a small natural meadow in the Giant Forest of Sequoia National Park in the Sierra Nevada of California. It was the first time that the ecological importance of conifers had impressed itself upon me. The meadow was surrounded on all sides by the mixed conifer forest in which the giant sequoias (*Sequoiadendron giganteum*) towered above all other trees. I saw several of them, along with* Abies magnifica *(red fir) and* Pinus lambertiana *(sugar pine), a little distance behind the other trees at the edge of the forest. In the meadow itself, a young, sturdy sequoia stood alone. However, the most striking object was a huge, barkless, and mostly branchless tree that lay squarely across the meadow.*

▲ ▲ ▲

It was a giant sequoia that must have fallen who knows how long ago. The tree was buried for more than half of its great girth in the meadow. Against it, the meadow was very swampy, with tall herbs, but where I sat it was dry. Where it became moist the grass was dotted pink with the delicate flowers of *Dodecatheon frigidum* (shooting star). I realized that the tree may have created the meadow; several others were lying across it further down. The conifer forest will only succeed on dry ground, and the deer will keep the meadow free from seedling trees. In the big grey trunk was a small round hole, and a woodpecker arrived at it, eying me quickly before it disappeared inside. I then noticed a very small stream through the middle of the meadow that must have found a slow outlet under the tree. The sequoia had dammed it and created a habitat that was not here before it fell. How long before it will have decayed away? It was so big that I think it could be here another 300 years and may have laid across the meadow as long already. On the gently sloping terrain of this part of the mountain range, most ponds and meadows are caused by fallen giant conifers. They created habitats and increased biodiversity in an unexpected manner.

I slowly ascended a steep path through the mountain forest in the Valais Alps of Switzerland. My destination this summer day in 2006 was the Cabane du Trient, a mountain hut from where my companion and I planned to do some climbs above the glacier the next day. He waited for me at the top end of the chair lift to La Breya, while I walked the 800 m (2600 ft) elevation up from the valley. There were three conifer species in three genera: *Larix decidua* (European larch), *Picea abies* (Norway spruce), and *Pinus cembra* (Arolla pine) mixed together. The trail for some distance wound in and out of an open avalanche path where there were only shrubs and a few seedling trees. The lower slopes of the mountains were all forested and, getting higher, I could see across the deep valley several of these avalanche paths, some narrow, some wider. They all came down in a straight line to the bottom of the valley. As everywhere in Switzerland, the valley is inhabited with small clusters of houses and slightly larger villages,

In the forests of giant sequoias (*Sequoiadendron giganteum*), meadows are created by fallen trees that dam streams.

many built in traditional style with stone and logs and wide roofs to carry the snow, strategically situated well away from the avalanche channels under the protection of the trees. Above the tree line there was some grassy terrain and rocks, above that rocks and snowfields reaching to the summits. Long and hard experience has taught the Swiss not to cut trees here; the force of a large avalanche coming down over your village leaves no stone upon the other. But the overload of snow in some winters has to come down, so the avalanche paths are also strategically positioned. As you may expect from the Swiss, nothing is left to chance. Thanks to conifers, they can inhabit the remotest and steepest mountain valleys.

In Tule, near the city of Oaxaca in southern Mexico, we came to pay homage to The Tree, the largest specimen of *Taxodium mucronatum*. My Honduran helpers and I were after pines on this expedition in spring 1994. The Tree is not a pine, but it is a conifer and it is famous. It stands in a small fenced park next to a white church called Santa Maria del Tule and completely dwarfs the building. Its massive crown bulges out like a rising cumulus cloud of greenery, three times higher and four times wider than the church. We went through a gate and a crowd of visitors, among whom were school children in uniforms. Coming close-up, we met a wall of rising wood, branching into huge arms supporting the canopy. Walking round on a path marked by pebbles, we found deep recesses and protruding buttresses. Like all urban and roadside trees in warm countries, the locals had painted the lower part of the trunk white, but it was done some time ago and the paint had much faded. No one seemed to have a plausible explanation for this habit, and I hoped it would not be repeated on this tree.

Looking up from below into the crown, it was apparent that large branches were connected here and there; reiteration is rife. This tree is so big and complicated in comparison to other large specimens of its species in Mexico, that some have suggested that it is not a single tree but several grown together. But genetics appear to point to a single

A montane forest of larch, pine, and spruce across an avalanche path in the Swiss Alps

The Tree of Tule (Arból del Tule), *Taxodium mucronatum*, is the largest tree of its kind.

tree and, standing there, I had no problem with that. The Tree is weird but beautiful and impressive. Under its light shade, it was nice and cool on that hot day. Another school bus arrived and another herd of children was ushered through the church garden gate to see The Tree, touch it, and run around it. It was getting a bit full, so we had to go. We had paid homage.

These are just three examples from my experiences on journeys to show the varied ways in which conifers are important. For a natural group of plants with only 630 species, the importance is disproportionate, perhaps greater than of any other group of plants with comparable species numbers. I am not only thinking of economic value, as the examples show. First and probably foremost, there is the ecological significance. In earlier chapters much has been said about the ecology of conifers. Significant here are the habitats conifers provide for other organisms, which have become dependent on those habitats through a long process of evolution. The meadows in the giant sequoia groves of California are a peculiar example, for the same trees provide a very different habitat while still standing. When a single species of conifer forms the dominant, long-lived trees in a forest, it determines that habitat with the intricate networked relationships of species that live there. We collectively call this an *ecosystem*. Remove that conifer, partly or completely, and the ecosystem is seriously disrupted or destroyed. Much of this has to do with a complex spatial structure provided by the conifer in its various age and size classes. Its stages from juvenile to dead tree provide materials from young foliage to dead and decaying wood, each with its own specialist users. In the food chain, which is in fact a food web with a hierarchical structure, numerous other organisms follow on and are dependent on the conifer indirectly. The conifer is a keystone species in the ecosystem.

An example of this principle earned itself notoriety in the American West in the 1990s; it was the controversy around the spotted owl (*Strix occidentalis*). This owl lives exclusively in old growth conifer forest in the Pacific Northwest, and each

Old growth conifer forest in the Pacific Northwest, here with *Pseudotsuga menziesii* (Douglas fir) as the dominant species

pair of owls needs several square kilometres of forest at least 250 years old. Any manner of logging that removes the larger trees alters the ecosystem and also removes the owl. The fight was between conservationists and loggers, or as it was grossly oversimplified, between owls and jobs. What was overlooked in this simplification was that these old conifer forests are a complicated ecosystem, of which the owl is a minor component. Thousands of other species live in this ecosystem, most are unstudied, and many still unknown. If we decide to cut these forests, we must know what is being destroyed. Provided we leave enough old growth around, the logged areas will take at least 250 years to be restored to their full ecosystem function. It is doubtful that we can plan that far ahead with any guarantee of achievement.

With the worldwide distribution of conifers, their presence in most major biomes, their great sizes and longevity, it is not surprising if many would be found to be keystone species in forest and woodland ecosystems. We can assume this, but in reality few conifers have been studied ecologically with the question of their role as providers in mind. Especially in the tropics, our knowledge of conifers in this respect is rudimentary. Even in the tropics, where natural, undisturbed forests are formed by many tree species, conifers often occupy restricted localities and occur there in numbers. The ecosystem will be different in such places, and the conifers may be keystone species. Research is urgently needed where logging and deforestation threaten their existence, such as with the species of *Agathis* in Borneo and *Afrocarpus* in eastern Africa.

Much better known are the northern coniferous forests of Eurasia and North America, the taiga biome (see chapter 14). With far fewer species, these ecosystems are both simpler and more dynamic, with great oscillations in the numbers of individuals of many species of plants and animals. However, due to their vast extent and relatively intact status so far, they may become the last great forests after most of the temperate and tropical forests have been destroyed by human expansion. The global importance of such vast forest cover is primarily as a provider of oxygen and a regulator of climate. Conifers may regain the dominance they once had. A similar type of coniferous forest extends further south into the mountains of temperate latitudes. As I have demonstrated with the example in the Swiss Alps, these montane forests provide additional ecosystem functions. Their preservation is much less secure in many countries that are less affluent than Switzerland, while their destruction will have dire consequences. In the Southern Hemisphere, conifer forests are very different and more restricted in extent. Ecological studies in New Zealand and Chile have concentrated on forest dynamics, and much less is known about the role of

Cones and foliage of *Pseudotsuga menziesii* (Douglas fir)

particular species of conifer in the ecosystem. My impression is that with a different architecture and different dispersal mechanisms, especially podocarps will be found to differ substantially from northern conifers. Some podocarps are as rich in epiphytes as angiosperm trees can be, and their seeds are always eaten by birds (but which birds?).

Many species of conifer trees are well adapted to cope with episodic disturbances that destroy the forest cover. Indeed, they may be dependent on these events for their long-term survival in the succession (see chapter 16). By combining characteristics of pioneers and climax trees in one and the same species, their contribution to all phases of the forest ecosystem after disturbance is indeed significant. The conifers with these characteristics are predominantly found in the coniferous and mixed forests around the Pacific Rim, where we have seen in chapter 24 more than half of all conifer species occur. Unlike the situation in the northern conifer forests, these disturbances are widely spaced in time and location, allowing stable, species-rich ecosystems to develop, in which the dominant conifers act as the framework.

Conifers are important in nature in the sense that all trees are as providers of ecological services to a more stable environment. Climate regulation has already been mentioned. Protecting watersheds, preventing erosion, and assuring a steady supply of clean water in streams are other important functions of forests, especially in hilly terrain. That conifers provide these services in many parts of the world is the logical corollary of their dominant distribution in the Northern Hemisphere (see the map in chapter 21), where most of the landmasses and mountain systems are concentrated. The prevention or limitation of the effects of snow avalanches is obviously important in

Conifer forest in North Island, New Zealand, with various species of Podocarpaceae, a few small angiosperms, and emergent *Agathis australis* (kauri)

One of the veteran *Chamaecyparis formosensis* (Taiwan cypress) on the island much visited by tourists

valleys with human habitation. In nature, this allows more stable ecosystems to exist in which more species can evolve and thrive. On slopes where avalanche-stopping conifer forests have been removed, it is nearly impossible to restore them. In populated valleys artificial avalanche barriers need to be erected, and they are expensive and not as effective as the natural conifer forests. These environmental services of natural conifer forests, coupled with the creation of habitat for numerous species of animals, fungi, and plants and provision of material and immaterial goods to human society, are increasingly understood as vital.

The proper management of these forests aims at the perpetuation of the original ecosystem on large spatial and temporal scales. Those forestry approaches that tradi-

A giant *Juniperus occidentalis* (western juniper) high in the Sierra Nevada of California

tionally view the trees as a crop to be harvested and regrown over extensive areas are incompatible with this multiple-use forest. Tree-crop forestry is essentially a form of agriculture with relatively long harvesting cycles and is better practiced in plantations on fertile land suitable for agriculture. In many industrialized countries, forestry is developing in this direction, but in order to maintain this separation of functions and services in the future the growing demands on resources will have to be constrained. Wood production will compete with food production, and there is a limited and finite space available for either.

Finally, there is what I like to call the spiritual value of conifers. In chapter 28 I gave examples of traditional views and uses, often religious in nature, of conifers. Here I want to expand those views to include values developed in a secular society but based on older and universal notions about natural beauty and harmony. These values have led to the now-worldwide nature conservation movement. The Tree of Tule in Mexico is an example of the universal admiration of living things like trees that are much bigger and older than we are. Thomas Pakenham, in his books on remarkable trees, gave many examples from many countries, quite a number of which are conifers. The popularity of his books, illustrated with his similarly remarkable photographs, amply demonstrates the fascination people still have with large and ancient individual trees. I have already mentioned the giant conifers of the Pacific coast of North America, New Zealand, and Mexico and the ancient yews of Britain and France. In Japan, on Yakushima (Yaku Island, a World Heritage site) an old giant tree of the species *Cryptomeria japonica* called Jomon Sugi (Old Cedar) is an attraction drawing tourists. Likewise, a few ancient trees of *Chamaecyparis formosensis* in Taiwan have been protected from logging as natural monuments and draw crowds of visitors. Turkey has some very large and undoubtedly ancient junipers, as does California in the Sierra Nevada. That mountain range, of which praise has been sung by John Muir and many later nature writers, is richer than any other in great conifers. The national parks there were in large measure created about a century ago with several trees in mind: *Juniperus occidentalis, Pinus balfouriana, P. jeffreyi, P. lambertiana, P. ponderosa,* and *Sequoiadendron giganteum* among other conifers of only slightly lesser stature. And who fails to be deeply impressed when walking among the Methuselahs of trees, the gnarled bristlecone pines (*Pinus longaeva*) on the mountain heights of eastern California and Nevada?

31 A Pine in a Cage

OUT ON THE LAWN *in front of the Orangery in Kew Gardens, London, stands a cage of gleaming metal. Inside is a planted conifer, literally behind bars. Interpretive panels outside explain what the conifer is and why it is special, but not why it is caged. The young tree seems to have grown well after being planted out here, and by the summer of 2006 it had reached nearly 2.4 m (8 ft) in height. It is a specimen of* Wollemia nobilis *(Wollemi pine), a recent discovery from Australia belonging to the family Araucariaceae. (The name pine does not mean that it is a true pine. In Australia the word generally means conifer, and all species are called "pine" with different prefixes.) Why is this tree the only plant among many thousands at Kew around which they have built this unsightly metal protection? To explain this folly, which I think it is, I must briefly tell the story of the tree's discovery and its aftermath. You will probably agree that this is quite a remarkable story and one unusual for botany, which is known to arouse a keen interest but not normally high emotion or sensation.*

▲ ▲ ▲

Some distance to the northwest of Sydney, Australia's largest metropolis with over 4 million residents, is a very rugged section of the central tablelands of New South Wales known as the Wollemi Wilderness. It consists of elevated plateaus of Triassic sandstone that steeply drop off to the east in escarpments dissected by hundreds of erosion canyons. The area is free of roads simply because it is nearly impossible to build them there, so access is on foot or by helicopter. Much of the area was declared a national park in 1979. The area is visited by hikers and a few canyoners, an adventurous variety of hikers equipped with ropes and other gear for abseils into otherwise impassable canyons.

In September 1994 David Noble, who knows the Wollemi National Park as few others, was abseiling with two friends into a side canyon where he had not ventured before. The upper walls and slopes of these canyons, where they widen out, are covered in eucalypt forest and shrubs, as are the intervening plateau sections. By contrast, in the deepest, narrow canyon bottoms grows a dense warm temperate rainforest, especially if there is a permanent stream. The dominant trees are coachwood (*Ceratopetalum apetalum*) and sassafras (*Doryphora sassafras*). In such a bottom, Noble encountered a group of strange-looking, very tall trees. He took a small branch with leaves and later showed it to Wyn Jones, a naturalist who worked with the National Parks and Wildlife Service.

Jones involved a botanist friend, Jo Allen, but they could not identify the specimen. Jones went back to the canyon with Noble to collect more material, including an old pollen cone picked from the ground. Eventually Jones obtained the service of a helicopter to snatch a seed cone from the top of one of the trees. Earlier, they had shown Ken Hill, senior botanist at the Royal Botanic Gardens, Sydney, only Noble's twig. Hill had put them on the right path by saying it was a conifer, but by suggesting *Cephalotaxus* he implied an introduced species. This assessment was unacceptable to Allen and Jones, and they decided to work out the tree's identity alone, without further consulting Hill. It was the beginning of trouble. Eventually, they went back to Hill, because he was the gymnosperm specialist of Australia who was also in the position to pull a few strings with the authorities. The three concluded that it was a new genus in Araucariaceae, of which only two were known thus far, *Agathis* and *Araucaria*. Together, they published the new genus and species *Wollemia nobilis* in the botanical journal *Telopea* in 1995. Naming it had caused some further strife, because the species epithet *nobilis* only indirectly refers to its discoverer, David Noble. *Nobilis* is a Latin adjective

Wollemia nobilis (Wollemi pine), showing its unusual shoot apex, growing in the Royal Botanic Gardens, Kew. Photograph by Tony Kirkham, Royal Botanic Gardens, Kew

equivalent to the English *noble*, but naming the plant after a male person with that name would have created the Latinized adjective *noblei*. If pronounced quickly, that sounds like "knobbly," and for people not too literate in Latin it might seem to refer to the peculiar bark on the tree. Botanists do sometimes quibble over details. More disagreement of a more serious kind was soon to follow.

Allen and Jones embarked on field studies of the small grove of trees, which was soon discovered to be one of two, the other about 2 km (1.25 mi) upstream. Meanwhile, the Royal Botanic Gardens, after releases to the press that went quickly around the world in exaggerated articles and websites as if a living dinosaur had been spotted in the outskirts of Sydney, saw an opportunity. Its managers had agreed with the National Parks and Wildlife Service on a scheme to propagate the trees at one of its satellite gardens and sell them to the public. Botanic gardens around the world, though they may be partially funded by the taxpayer, are under constant and increasing pressure to generate additional income. It was also argued that it would safeguard the species, of which only about 50 trees were then known in the wild. Allen and Jones were barred from further visits to the trees, for the authorities had now taken over. More publicity followed, and soon the Wollemi pine became an icon. This placed a burden on the Wollemi National Park officials, who increasingly feared hordes of fanatics into the wilderness, trying to get a pine at any cost, while the Royal Botanic Gardens, Sydney bathed comfortably in the limelight of publicity.

Emotions were running pretty high, although largely behind the scenes, when I arrived in late October 1997. I met most of the early players, though not David Noble, who had apparently disappeared from the scene. I was given as much help and information as was in the power of these people and their bosses, but I could not see the trees in the wild. By then access was denied to anyone not crucial to a programme of monitoring the trees. The Wollemi pines in cultivation were shown to me; they were within a high-security compound, with no public access. Later, a few trees were displayed in security cages, in Sydney first and then in Melbourne. The Royal Botanic Gardens, Kew was given two seedling trees in 1997, but we were told to hide them.

The Australian government took charge of the matter and decided that not the Royal Botanic Gardens, Sydney, but a commercial nursery in Queensland should propagate the Wollemi pine and market it. This started in 2000, with the aim to grow 500,000 Wollemi pines, all derived from cuttings taken from the first batch propagated in Sydney. It was hoped that we would all soon be growing our own Wollemi pine. In October 2005 a highly media-covered auction was held by Sotheby's in Sydney to sell the first freely available plants, and they can now be ordered via the Internet. The good news is that a portion of the profits goes back to conserving the trees, of which now three little groves are known to exist, perhaps numbering 100 trees and their seedlings. The folly is that all the publicity and hype has compelled the management of botanic gardens to display their specimens in a cage, afraid that the trees may otherwise be rustled by criminals climbing fences or walls at night.

A lot of nonsense has been written about the Wollemi pine, hailed as the "botanical find of the century," "equivalent to discovering a living dinosaur," being a "relic of the Jurassic era," and more such hype. People, including scientists, tend to be forgetful. Just to stick to conifers, *Metasequoia glyptostroboides* (dawn redwood) was no less of a living fossil and was also found in the 20th century. The oldest fossils that *may* have belonged to the genus *Wollemia* are not Jurassic but Cretaceous in age, and a dinosaur would amount to the resurrection of a class, not just a genus. (The latter implication, of course, is true unless you agree with the cladistic puritans, who insist birds are dinosaurs. According to them, dinosaurs are alive and thriving in Sydney's city parks and do not need to be discovered.) The widely publicized photograph of Ken Hill with a slab of sandstone with plant fossils and a twig of the Wollemi pine was just for publicity. Neither he nor any palaeobotanist ever assumed that this fossil described as *Agathis jurassica* was identical with *W. nobilis*. As I have noted throughout this book, many conifers are living fossils and we have been discovering them all the time. For science, conifers are very important species because they allow us windows into the past by studying living plants, which are always better than fossils.

If we define a living fossil in its common and narrow sense as an animal or plant species believed to be extinct but, more or less unexpectedly, clinging on to life in some little corner of the Earth, there is no better example among plants than *Metasequoia glyptostroboides* from China. Unlike the Wollemi pine, this tree was first known to science as a fossil and was thought to have become extinct at the end of the Pliocene, several million years ago. Its living representative was found by a Chinese botanist in the village of Modaoxi in Hubei in 1941 and later identified by Wan Chun Cheng, the *Nestor* of Chinese botanists and an expert in gymnosperms. World War II and revolution in China prevented communication to the outside world, but in 1947 Cheng distributed seeds freely and in 1948 American scientists were able to visit the location. No impenetrable wilderness here, just villages and rice fields among which some old trees survived. Later inventories discovered more trees over a wider area, some in more natural settings, but still under pressure from an increasing rural population. Palaeobotanists revisited the fossils in museums and found that many specimens identified as *Sequoia* or sequoia-like in fact belonged to this genus. *Metasequoia* has occurred from the Cretaceous onwards in many areas in Eurasia and North America, even close to the North Pole. Some of its last fossil occurrences, Pliocene in age, had been described from Japan and now it was found alive in China. This discovery was also reported in the world press, but with less hype. Botanists and gardeners did not try to make fortunes, they just distributed the seeds.

In 1958 Chinese botanists described a new genus with two species, calling it *Cathaya* after Cathay, an ancient European name for China. Later, the two species were not considered distinct, so we now only recognize *Cathaya argyrophylla*. In the original Russian paper, the authors had also recognized that certain fossils from the European Tertiary belong to their new genus, so here was another living fossil. European palaeobotanists, not knowing about *Cathaya*, had ascribed these remains to other conifer

Cathaya argyrophylla, a monotypic genus in Pinaceae discovered in China in the 1950s and long kept a secret to the outside world.

genera in the Pinaceae. The living *Cathaya* was discovered in the mountains of Guangxi, but later explorations, largely by Chinese botanists, revealed its occurrence in other provinces of central China. For a long time, it was treated as extremely rare and, quite unlike *Metasequoia*, nothing, not even herbarium specimens, was allowed to leave the country. As late as 1990, when I published my book on Pinaceae, only two specimens were known from herbaria outside China, and there were no plants in any botanic gardens in Europe or the United States. There were rumours galore that private individuals had obtained specimens illegally, and some may have indeed succeeded. Only in recent years have the authorities in China relaxed the restrictions, for the species is now known to be not very rare or endangered and it does not have much horticultural value. Collectors would certainly want it, but the general public has not even heard of it. It makes you wonder about the real public interest in these conifers after the novelty aspect emphasized in the press dissipates.

In October 1999, a team of Vietnamese, English, and Russian botanists were looking for rare orchids in the karst limestone mountains of northern Vietnam, close to the border with Yunnan, China. My colleague and orchid specialist at Kew, Phil Cribb, noticed a cypress-like conifer while taking a break from the strenuous climbing on the sharp ridge of a mountain. No one in the party could identify it, and the tree seemed new for the Vietnamese flora. Once again it turned out to be a new genus and species, in the family Cupressaceae. We described it in the botanical journal *Novon* in 2002, and I named it *Xanthocyparis vietnamensis*. In that year, I was able to travel to Vietnam and visit the location myself (see chapter 4). The species is very rare and scattered, and to date between 500 and 600 mature trees have been counted.

What I also discovered was that its closest relative could well be a conifer from the western coast of North America, then commonly known as *Chamaecyparis nootkatensis* (Nootka cypress, the yellow cedar of foresters). The generic position of that species had been disputed for a long time, and there were researchers who considered that it should be classified with *Cupressus*, in which it had originally been placed. My cladistic analysis using morphological characters placed it with neither, but together with the new Vietnamese taxon in its own clade. This placement was later confirmed by other researchers in a similar analysis using DNA sequence data. No fossils are known of *Xanthocyparis*, but they may turn up in localities in Alaska or Alberta, where in rich strata with fossil conifers some possible relatives have already been found. What this discovery has done is provide new understanding of the phylogenetic relationships of some conifers. There is also an implication for botanical nomenclature. The Nootka cypress is the male parent of the cultivated hybrid conifer Leyland cypress, up to then known as *Cupressocyparis leylandii*. According to the rules of the Botanical Code, the name of a hybrid between two genera is a genus name constructed of elements of both parents. If the genus name of one or both parents changes, the hybrid name changes, too. I complied with this rule by renaming the hybrid genus *Cuprocyparis*, a change as the code requires, but as minimal as possible. Perhaps a shorter name will be a hint to grow shorter hedges?

These are all examples of new genera in conifers, described in roughly the last half-century, which can be called "living fossils" with greater or lesser justification. They are

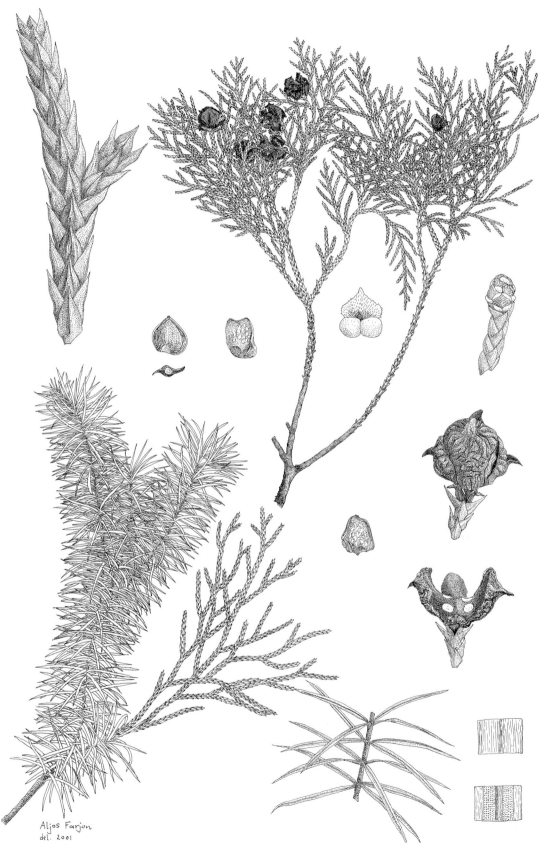

Xanthocyparis vietnamensis, a new genus and species described by the author in 2002

Aljos Farjon
del. 2001

not the result of taxonomic splitting, by which most new genera in conifers have originated (see chapter 7). They are genuinely new discoveries of rare conifers so distinct that botanists have placed them in new genera. All of these genera have just one or at most two species assigned to them. If there is a fossil record of relevance, it often indicates that there were more species in this genus in the distant past but that these have become extinct. The present species is the sole survivor of its genus and indeed, as we have seen, it is often extremely rare. The fossil record may indicate a wider distribution in the distant past. We cannot be sure, but the hunch is that even without human interference, these relicts are on the way to extinction, too. Extinction, remember, is the fate of all species. Why should we try to preserve them?

The extinction of too many species means a loss in overall biodiversity of ecosystems and the risk that these ecosystems become unbalanced and instable, leading to even more extinction. This perspective of extinction looks at the ecosystem and the function a species has in it. Species with key roles, dubbed keystone species, are more important. For conifers, these are usually the kind of trees we have looked at in the previous chapter. Here I am concerned with biodiversity represented by taxa—their distinctiveness, if you like. Biodiversity can be measured at different levels, from the population level up into the taxonomic scale from varieties and species via genera to families and even orders. The distinctiveness tends to increase up that scale, as can be expected from a hierarchical or nested classification system. Why is it important to conserve taxa that are more distinct?

It seems self-evident to a conservationist, but that question is not so easy to answer for a scientist. Genetic diversity is the material basis of evolution, its tool natural selection. But that mechanism operates at the population level, so distinctions between species or genera are irrelevant. Genetic diversity can be either very low in these distinct relict species, as in *Wollemia nobilis*, or quite high, as in *Metasequoia glyptostroboides*. These species were in decline before human actions played a part, for good or for bad. There can be all kinds of reasons for the decline, and it does not necessarily mean that these species are unfit. Many do very well when introduced to other continents, sometimes returning to where they once grew. Perhaps therein lies the main reason to conserve these relicts: we can restore something of a lost world. There is also an obvious scientific interest, a curiosity value if you like, in these distinct species representing the past. Given the threat of extinction to so many species, perhaps we want to prioritize our efforts to save at least some of these. Phylogenetic distinction seems to me a criterion well worth using to shortlist species for conservation action.

32 The Conifers that Grow on Nickel

IT WAS GETTING LATE in the afternoon when I passed an open gate on the brown dirt road that wound its way up the mountain, but there would be at least two hours of daylight left, so I pressed on. A little further, I started to encounter vehicles coming down; it looked like the crew was calling it a day and going home. The last one flashed its headlights, and we stopped. It was the crew boss of the mine. I explained what I was up to, and he said I could continue, giving me a set of keys to lock the gate when I returned. "When you come back tomorrow for your trees, leave them in the office you'll find up there," he said. I thanked him in my most cordial French and drove on. Awfully nice men, these miners, I thought.

▲ ▲ ▲

This was Mont Kaala in the northern part of New Caledonia, and I was here in November 2005 to make a field study of the 13 species of *Araucaria* known to exist on the island. According to my data, I should be able to find four species here when I returned the next day with my assistant, Alison Moore. I now only had time for a quick reconnaissance, so I drove the 4 × 4 as fast as safety allowed up the winding road that seemed to lead to the several summits of the mountain. From there I hoped to spot the trees and learn where we should go for collecting and fieldwork. But when I came up I was aghast at what I saw. The miners had dug up the mountain, and the summits I had seen from below were mere remnants. I drove and drove, from one large open pit mine to another, some still active with huge diggers in them, others seemingly abandoned, with large brown mud pools I knew I should better avoid. I saw some *Araucaria* trees, too, remnants of a forest clinging to the edges of the mine and on some steep slopes. It was time to go back to our campground on the beach, where Alison was waiting to hear where we should go the next day.

We spent that next day looking for the four species on the whole mountain. We even drove for three-quarters around Mont Kaala after we had left ahead of the miners. We found only one species, *Araucaria montana*, the common one. On the lower slopes, we found two trees of *A. columnaris* and some large figs and coconut palms. All were planted, the remains of an old settlement, so these did not count. It looked very much as if the other three species had disappeared, swallowed up by the mining operations since their herbarium specimens, now lodged in Paris, Kew, and elsewhere, had been collected and on which I had based my distribution data. Alison called it a depressing day, and in many respects it was, despite the sunshine and the helpful miners.

After Canada, New Caledonia is the second largest producer of nickel. Approximately 20 per cent of the world's nickel is found on the island, and nickel mining is its main source of income. In 1990, 4.9 million tons of ore were produced, nearly half of which was exported and the rest smelted locally near the capital, Noumea. The opera-

Nickel mines in New Caledonia are the greatest threat to the unique diversity of the genus *Araucaria* on this Pacific island. Photograph by Martin Gardner

tions are open-pit or strip mines. To reach the nickel-bearing rock, usually a cover of barren rock 5–6 m (15–18 ft) thick has to be removed first. There are two types of nickel ore, a rock type called garnierite and a softer one called lateritic iron stone. The nickel content varies but is around 2–3 per cent in garnierite and 1.3 per cent in lateritic iron stone. Mining of nickel in New Caledonia began in 1875 with the highest grades of around 13 per cent and expanded to the lower grades as techniques improved and demand rose, with ups and downs, to the present day. Currently, only garnierite is mined, but plans exist to exploit the laterite in the future.

Extensive basalt flows formed huge masses of peridotite in New Caledonia. In a later stage, these ultramafic rocks formed a nappe, an overthrust sheet covering much of the island. As a result of forces and pressures involved in this extensive displacement, the rocks were metamorphosed. The nappe was later disrupted and fragmented by faulting and erosion into isolated caps, interspersed by the underlying basalts and other formations. In the southeast (Massif du Sud) the ultramafic rock is continuous, in the lower parts largely eroded and decomposed to laterites. In the remainder of the island, the nickel-containing rock is a result of the overthrust movement concentrated on the higher slopes and summits of the mountains and hills. On the western coast, the majority of deposits are at 370–670 m (1200–2200 ft) elevation on the spurs of mountains overlooking steep sides of valleys or slopes down to the sea. On massifs away from the coast these elevations are higher. On the southeastern coast the ultramafics are in similar positions but somewhat lower than on the western coast. In several places ocean-

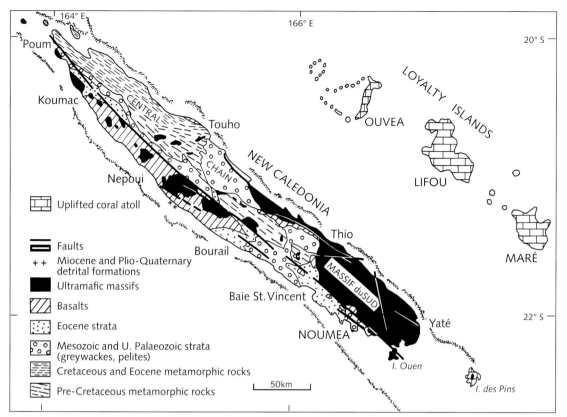

Generalized geological map of New Caledonia. From The Ocean Basins and Margins. Vol. 7B, The Pacific Ocean.
Reprinted by permission of Springer Verlag

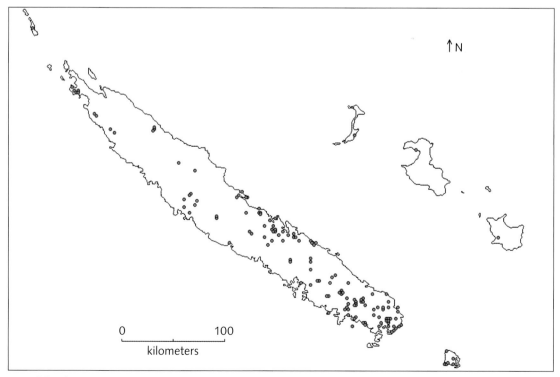

Natural distribution of the genus *Araucaria* on New Caledonia, where each dot represents a locality with one
or more species based on herbarium collections

going ore ships reach the mines in deep water near the shore through gaps in the coral reefs. The Société Le Nickel is the organization responsible for all nickel mining in New Caledonia and the largest producer, but many other companies are active. In Province Nord, the semi-autonomous government of the Kanak people, the first arrivals on the island, now has a stake in the mining operations there, with a majority share in the largest company and, of course, with jobs. Export of ore is mostly to Japan. Huge reserves are still untapped, especially when lateritic iron stone deposits are considered. Much of the land underlain by ultramafic rock of either type is under mining concessions.

By comparing the geological map of New Caledonia with the distribution map of the 13 species of *Araucaria*, we can see that there is much overlap with localities of the trees and ultramafic massifs, the geological formation that is the target of nickel mining. Mining operations in the Massif du Sud region are still limited, for several reasons. One I have already mentioned: in the lowlands much is laterite with the lowest grades of the metal. Another reason is that there are quite extensive nature reserves, such as Mont Humboldt, Mont Kouakoué, Mont Mou, and Montagne des Sources–Parc de la Rivière Bleue, as well as smaller ones. From a viewpoint of biodiversity conservation, elsewhere on the island the situation is often grave. There are no reserves in any of the ultramafic massifs along the western coast in Province Nord.

In Table 9 are listed the localities with populations of *Araucaria* that are mined. This list is based on my observations and those of other botanists who have visited New Caledonia on several trips in recent years with similar aims as mine, and it is not exhaus-

Table 9. Localities with nickel mines and populations of *Araucaria* on Grande Terre, New Caledonia

PROVINCE/LOCALITY	*ARAUCARIA* SPECIES
Province Nord	
Mont Poum	(*A. bernieri*), *A. scopulorum*
Dôme de Tiébaghi	*A. bernieri*, *A. montana*, *A. rulei*, *A. scopulorum*
Mont Kaala	(*A. biramulata*), (*A. laubenfelsii*), (*A. luxurians*), *A. montana*
Massif de Koniambo	*A. montana*
Massif de Kopéto	(*A. biramulata*)
Massif du Boulinda	(*A. montana*), *A. rulei*
Cap Bocage	*A. scopulorum*
Baie de Poro – RPN3	*A. montana*, *A. rulei*, *A. scopulorum*
Kouaoua	(*A. montana*), (*A. scopulorum*)
Boakaine	*A. laubenfelsii*, *A. montana*
(Mine Bwa Méyu)	*A. montana*, *A. rulei*, *A. scopulorum*
Province Sud	
(Mine Bogota)	*A. rulei*, *A. scopulorum*
Thio	(*A. bernieri*), (*A. luxurians*), *A. scopulorum*
(Mine Liliane)	*A. rulei*
(Mine du Marais Kiki)	*A. bernieri*

Note: Parentheses indicate mines that are not presently in use or species that have not been observed at the locality since 1980.

tive. The localities are listed from north to south under the two provinces of the main island, Grande Terre. Species that were not observed since 1980 are put in parentheses. There are also some old mines no longer in use, and these are also enclosed in parentheses. They may be reopened in the future if nickel deposits are not exhausted totally.

Substantial decline is certain to have occurred for all seven species, and several may have disappeared completely from these often extensively mined areas. It is difficult to estimate the losses in terms of numbers of trees because there are no records of population sizes prior to mining. Some mines have been exploited for a long time, and at Dôme de Tiébaghi, Mont Kaala, Cap Bocage, Baie de Poro–RPN3, and Thio almost all the habitat has indeed been excavated, leaving only marginal remnants of *Araucaria* forest or woodland standing. We did not see evidence of much consideration for these remarkable conifers—they are just vegetation to be stripped off to get to the nickel ore beneath. Yet the miners know about them, for on several occasions they led us to the last stands, which might have taken us some hours to find on our own. Environmental protection of land and amelioration and restoration of plant cover in abandoned parts of mines are minimal or nonexistent.

Of the 13 species of *Araucaria* native to New Caledonia, nine are virtually restricted to the ultramafic massifs: *A. bernieri*, *A. biramulata*, *A. humboldtensis*, *A. laubenfelsii*, *A. luxurians*, *A. muelleri*, *A. nemorosa*, *A. rulei*, and *A. scopulorum*. Two other species are indifferent, and occur on these and other rock types: *A. montana* and *A. subulata*. The strictly coastal *A. columnaris* does not grow on ultramafics at all, although it is not restricted to coral limestone, as I have seen it on basalt in undisputed natural settings. The Kanaks have also planted this species nearly everywhere. At least all occurrences

Araucaria montana is a fairly widespread and common species in New Caledonia. It occurs on ultramafic as well as other soils, and its survival as a species may therefore be relatively safe despite losses due to mining.

Araucaria rulei, here at Baie de Poro–RPN3, is restricted to ultramafic soils and uncommon, and it is therefore in danger of extinction due to nickel mining.

further than 100 m (300 ft) from the sea are not natural populations, and thus do not count. It seems *A. columnaris* has not been planted successfully or at all on the ultramafics. The other species not on ultramafic rock but on micaschist is the extremely rare *A. schmidii*, only known from the summit of Mont Panié, the highest mountain in New Caledonia at 1629 m (4965 ft). Three of the species confined to ultramafic rocks are not listed for the mining areas, *A. humboldtensis, A. muelleri*, and *A. nemorosa*, as these are all southern species (Massif du Sud) and mining is on a small scale or does not occur at present where they grow. They are also rare, especially *A. nemorosa*, which is restricted to one small area around Port Boisé at the southern end of Grande Terre and a small satellite population at Cap Reine Charlotte. *Araucaria subulata* is also rare and restricted to the south, but as mentioned not restricted to the dangerous ultramafic rock.

What is the conservation status of these species at present? The most recent assessment of conservation status for the World Conservation Union (IUCN) was done by its Conifer Specialist Group in the late 1990s and published in 1999. However, we have gathered a lot of new information, and the Conifer Specialist Group, which I have chaired since 1995, plans to do a reassessment before 2009. According to the IUCN Red List, one species, *Araucaria nemorosa*, is listed as critically endangered (CR) and three species, *A. luxurians, A. rulei*, and *A. scopulorum*, are endangered (EN); the others are near threatened (NT) or least concern (LC). I shall say some more about these categories in the next chapter. We believe that a reassessment is likely to move several species now listed as near threatened up the scale of threat categories to within the bracket for serious concern. This is especially suspected for the species restricted to ultramafics, which are all acutely or potentially affected by expansive nickel mining operations.

What needs to be done to protect the *Araucaria* species of New Caledonia? Unfortunately, there is much that needs to be done. Statutory protection under New Caledonian law at present includes only one species of conifer, *Parasitaxus usta*, presumably because of its interest as the only parasitic conifer rather than its level of threat, which is moderate at near threatened. Placing at least the endangered and critically endangered species of *Araucaria* under protection by the same legislation would of course amount to limitations for the mining industry. On the other hand, France is obliged under the Convention on Biodiversity to protect its biodiversity, including that in its overseas territories, of which New Caledonia is included. Reserves to protect flora and fauna are absent on the ultramafic massifs along the western coast in Province Nord; nearly all of these are designated for mining leases and, as shown in Table 9, many are being mined at present. Reserves to protect conifers were proposed on several of these massifs by Alistair Watt in the IUCN Conifer Action Plan (Farjon and Page 1999). To protect the 13 species of *Araucaria* in New Caledonia, an absolutely unique example of conifer biodiversity in what is perhaps the oldest conifer genus in the world, we need more reserves dedicated to their protection. With the data now available, it is possible to indicate where these additional reserves should be and how many are minimally needed to have at least several populations—if that many exist—of each species represented in nature reserves.

33 Numbers and Dots: Evaluation of Threats to Species

WHAT IS THE OVERALL STATUS *of biodiversity? At what rate is it being lost? Which are the species already extinct, and which are the ones at risk of becoming extinct soon? Which species are in decline, and what are the causes of decline? Where are the areas in which loss of biodiversity is most severe? These questions and their answers are becoming increasingly important as the world is finally beginning to respond to the present extinction crisis. The* IUCN Red List of Threatened Species, *known in short as the IUCN Red List, is one approach for assessing and monitoring the status of biodiversity. This information is crucial, for without it we are only guessing at the severity of the extinction crisis and cannot expect to be taken seriously by those in positions to take effective action.*

▲ ▲ ▲

The IUCN Red List has a considerable history, which I shall not relate here, but one aspect is of particular importance: the development of increasingly rigorous criteria used in red-listing species. This has proven to be an extremely complicated process that has only been achieved in several phases. As chairman of the IUCN's Conifer Specialist Group, I found it an interesting experience to be involved in, but at the same time frustrating when criteria had to change once again. The greatest challenge has been to find a formula that fits all organisms, from bacteria to giant sequoias. The IUCN (The World Conservation Union) does not want different criteria for different organisms and for good reasons. This dictum has obviously made the criteria somewhat complicated, but not so difficult to implement that they have become unworkable.

With a little training and experience, anyone with a basic knowledge of biology can apply the red-listing criteria, given that there are relevant data for a species. In the past, assigning a category of threat to a species was very much a matter of expert opinion. Because criteria were formulated in general terms, their interpretation could differ from one expert to another. The first set of explicit and rigorous criteria was published by the IUCN in 1994, and a major amendment followed in 2001. The categories are now as follows: Extinct (EX), Extinct in the Wild (EW), Critically Endangered (CR), Endangered (EN), Vulnerable (VU), Near Threatened (NT), Least Concern (LC), Data Deficient (DD), and Not Evaluated (NE). Evaluation (or assessment) follows the principle of worst scenario, that is, one assumes the worst category (Extinct) and if that is not found to be the case according to the criteria, one steps down a category and tries that one. Data Deficient applies to those species for which one has insufficient data to employ the criteria correctly. There are alternatives, so usually information of some kind about distribution, numbers, ecology, decline, exploitation, and habitat loss can be used. The categories Critically Endangered, Endangered, and Vulnerable together constitute the threatened species.

In the IUCN Red List all evaluated species are listed with their categories (status) and the criteria used to assign these, and both are given in coded form. This makes it possible to check and criticize the assessment, but also to compare results in case of reassessments and to determine trends. A good assessment nowadays has a data sheet behind it; IUCN has designed one that is recommended for use prior to assigning a status and should accompany a proposal to place a species on the IUCN Red List. Procedures have been developed to coordinate this activity, where possible through the specialist groups that act as Red List authorities, and to solve conflicting assessments from more than one source. It is a slow process—not least because the specialist groups have to work on a voluntary basis, so active involvement varies widely among groups as well as their members.

All the pre-1994 assessments are to be repeated with the 2001 criteria if these species are to be included in the IUCN Red List. Ideally, evaluations are repeated every 10 years, so many of the species that were assigned a category under the 1994 criteria are up for renewal, too. This is a daunting task, to put it mildly, but many more people are now working on it than before. In a major botanical institute, such as the Royal Botanic Gardens, Kew, it has been made routine that floristic and taxonomic publications on plant species are accompanied by an IUCN conservation status for each species. Several other major institutes are now similarly committed to the IUCN Red List.

Conifers, I am proud to say, are among the best-evaluated groups of plants in the world. A first attempt at a comprehensive assessment by the Conifer Specialist Group resulted in the publication of "A Preliminary World List of Threatened Conifer Taxa" (Farjon et al. 1993). This evaluation of species was done prior to the publication of the IUCN criteria in 1994, but with knowledge of the issues discussed in the formulation of those criteria. A few years after that publication and with the new criteria in hand, the Conifer Specialist Group revisited all conifer taxa from species to variety. The result was the "Global Red List of Conifers," published in the IUCN's *Conifers: Status Survey and Conservation Action Plan* (Farjon and Page 1999). The subcategory Least Concern, later elevated to a full category (LC) was not listed. A substantial number of conifer taxa, 80 in total, remained technically Data Deficient, even though a good number of them had been identified as Vulnerable or even Endangered in the 1993 list. Since 1999, only incidental assessments were made using the 2001 criteria, sometimes of species already assessed, because better information had become available. Early in 2006, a concerted effort was made by a small committee that I brought together to assess all the remaining Data-Deficient conifers. New developments in electronic data processing have made it possible to use data obtained from herbarium collections in a structured way to help the assessments. At present, only 22 Data-Deficient cases remain. Many of these are problematic because they are often based on one-off collections that were described as new species, while they cannot be relegated to synonymy off-hand. To revisit their localities to find out how rare or distinct these conifers really are is easier proposed than accomplished. The conservation status of conifers as of August 2006 is presented in Table 10.

The present situation is that 34 per cent of all conifers are threatened with extinction in the wild if current trends continue. For the first time, we can give these reliable

Table 10. The conservation status of conifers in the world as of August 2006

IUCN CATEGORIES	ALL TAXA	SPECIES	SUBSPECIES	VARIETY	FORMA
Not Evaluated (NE)	2	2			
Data Deficient (DD)	33	22	1	10	
Least Concern (LC)	389	287	16	84	1
Near Threatened (NT)	112	99	5	8	
Vulnerable (VU)	162	120	6	36	
Endangered (EN)	84	71	3	10	
Critically Endangered (CR)	30	26		4	
Total	**812**	**627**	**31**	**153**	**1**
Total threatened (VU, EN, CR)	**276** **(34%)**	**217** **(35%)**	**9** **(29%)**	**50** **(33%)**	**–**

figures for an entire taxonomic group of plants that is of great significance ecologically, economically, aesthetically, and as a subject for scientific inquiry. However, these figures will not remain static. As new and better information is obtained, new assessments will lead to changes (I have hinted at that in the previous chapter regarding the species of *Araucaria* in New Caledonia). Taxonomic changes will also have an effect. If you were a bit cynically inclined, you might observe that the easiest way to move a species out of danger is to declare it a taxonomic synonym of a species not in danger. But more importantly, the changing situation in the field will lead, on reassessment, to a changed status for conifer taxa. This is why the IUCN wishes evaluations to be done at intervals of about 10 years for all species. I called this a daunting task, and it is. On the other hand, for conifers it is now easier, with all the basic data already available, than it

The seed cones and foliage of *Pseudolarix amabilis* (Chinese golden larch), which is not a larch and not even closely related to *Larix*.

was when we pioneered back in 1993. We have not only better data but improved methods as well.

An example of a recent evaluation of a species that had remained Data Deficient at earlier attempts is *Pseudolarix amabilis* (Chinese golden larch). Why had it remained Data Deficient? Its taxonomy is in no doubt, for it is very distinct and the only species in its genus, a typical example of a relict species, another "living fossil." In China *P. amabilis* is a popular tree in ornamental plantings because its autumn colours are quite strikingly golden before it drops its leaves, which it does have in common with true larches (*Larix*). When *P. amabilis* became known in Europe, it was soon a sought-after tree as well, although it remains uncommon in cultivation. The Conifer Specialist Group knows it is native to China, but the problem was (and remains to some extent) to establish where it still grows in the wild. With that we mean in its original habitat, a certain type of mixed, partly evergreen forest that in its undisturbed state is extremely rich in species. If *P. amabilis* is found outside this habitat, it is not considered to be growing in the wild. Distribution maps and statements in Chinese Floras, even quite recent ones, do not adequately distinguish between the two types of occurrences. When, as is often the case, the tree was introduced long ago without records and grows in a temple sanctuary in which trees are protected, it has been recorded for that locality as if it was native. Such a locality does not count as an occurrence in the wild, not even if the tree appears to regenerate spontaneously. Without human interference, it would not have been there.

The IUCN rightly makes a distinction between extinction in the wild and extinction. If a tree species is widely planted, both in its native country and abroad, the latter calamity is unlikely to befall it anytime soon, but extinction in the wild could already be the case. How to resolve this if you cannot go on a trip to check all the localities? We know from some studies done by Chinese botanists years ago in undisputed localities in the northern part of Zhejiang Province what the forest type of *Pseudolarix amabilis* is like. This forest type only remains in isolated remnants on mountains in several provinces of southeastern China. If the forest is still present, *P. amabilis* may be there growing in the wild, if not, it is considered planted or absent altogether. A Chinese botanist in Beijing with whom I have studied conifers, Qiaoping Xiang, prepared data from specimens in the Herbarium of the Academy of Sciences in Beijing, with particular attention to habitat and locality notes. Western herbaria have hardly anything of this species collected in China, but I added the few I could find. The Internet is becoming a useful source, too, particularly

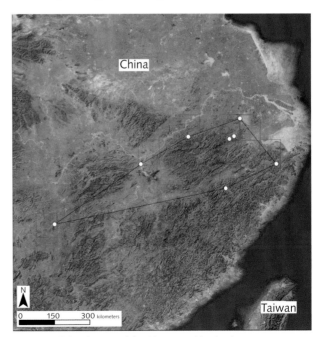

The natural distribution of the Chinese golden larch (*Pseudolarix amabilis*) in southeastern China. Background map 1-km resolution "Blue Marble" satellite image mosaic created by NASA/GSFC

with a species we can be fairly sure is correctly identified so we don't have to see the specimen. From all the specimens with locality data, we eliminated the ones that did not come from natural forest. A few were still doubtful, and a decision had to be made on the basis of the probable range of *P. amabilis* and if satellite imagery confirmed forest in that locality. This gave us the satellite image map shown on page 277.

The map is not complete, and one or two dots, in particular the one farthest to the west (left), remain uncertain. But it is the best we can get, and an evaluation can be made by looking at all that we know of *Pseudolarix amabilis* and the region. The first parameter to calculate is the natural range of the species, or in IUCN terminology, its Extent of Occurrence (EOO). We draw a line connecting the farthest dots on the map; inside that area the species may occur, outside it probably does not. Next is to determine how common the species is in that area. We take the dots to represent an area of a certain size in which the species actually occurs (red squares on the map) and add these up. This gives the Area of Occupancy (AOO). Calculating the distances between the dots gives an indication of the fragmentation into subpopulations, along with their number. With knowledge about frequency in its forest type, we may now make rough estimates about numbers of mature individuals. If certain dots do not coincide with forest reserves and we know there is ongoing destruction of forest habitat in the region, we may infer a decline of the species. All these criteria, following a protocol, lead to an evaluation of threat to the species. *Pseudolarix amabilis* turns out to be Endangered.

It is very important that several unrelated taxonomic groups of organisms with worldwide distributions (geographically and ecologically) are being assessed as completely as possible and as soon as possible. The Convention on Biological Diversity has recommended developing several indicators, including one based on changes in status of threatened species, to be able to monitor progress towards the target of reducing the rate of loss of biological diversity by 2010. The IUCN has therefore developed Red List Indices for two such groups: birds and amphibians. More taxonomic groups with complete assessments done more than once are urgently needed to provide data for the investigation of trends in the conservation status of biodiversity. The only taxonomic groups of plants with suitable baseline data at present are the cycads and the conifers. Conifers are more valuable for this purpose than cycads, of which the distribution, although wide, is much more restricted both in terms of geography and ecology. Conifers indeed occur worldwide and occupy nearly all the major biomes of the terrestrial world. With the first assessment completed, the Conifer Specialist Group has provided a baseline against which a second assessment in 2009–2010 would provide data to estimate a trend. The conifers could then become the first major group of plants—and one that would tell us a lot about the forests of the world—to be used in a Red List Index.

34 Invasions

IT WAS ONE OF THOSE WARM *midsummer days that can make you look for a space in the shade and a cool drink. Instead, I was standing in the middle of a large heathland, and the only shade of sorts was provided by a nearby pine tree. Cool drinks only existed in my imagination. This was a heathland in the Veluwe, an extensive sandy region in the Netherlands, and it was the summer of 1984. I was volunteering with students and others to pull young pines out of the heathland. It sounds easy, but with this heat it was hard and thirsty work, and I tried not to think too much of the beer in the pub we planned to have afterwards.*

▲ ▲ ▲

As I looked across this expanse of heathland, at first I could only see several widely scattered solitary pines and an occasional birch. In the distance, the edges of woodland were visible, with some birch, oak, beech, and abundant pines. However, as I walked into the heathland I could begin to see the pines nearly everywhere. They were mostly only about 30 cm (12 in) tall, some smaller, and a few larger ones among them. Very occasionally, I found one larger still, perhaps overlooked last time the volunteers had been out pulling them. These larger pines should be a priority now, because they soon would begin to have cones with seeds. The little ones were especially abundant near the solitary pines, concentrated on the eastern to northeastern side away from the tree. Obviously, the big pine was the parent tree of these little ones; the seeds had been blown a little distance with the prevailing westerly wind and germinated in the heathland. It seemed obvious to us that these source pines, themselves once seedlings, were the real problem, but we had no instructions to put a saw to them. They were seen as landscape features to be retained.

Under the pine tree near us there was no heather but grass, which does better in the shade and especially with the nitrogen made available by the decomposing needle litter. At lunchtime, we sat in this grass in the little shade the pine could provide. When we called it a day around five in the afternoon, we had pulled a sizeable heap of little pines from the heathland across 2 ha (5 acres). This was less than 0.5 per cent of the heathland we were trying to rid of its invasion of *Pinus sylvestris* (Scots pine). It seemed like removing a bucket of water from a lake, but our minds were now not so much on the results as on the beer we were promised as a reward for our labour.

In this final chapter I am going to turn the table on conifers. Throughout this book conifers were presented as admirable, a group of plants with a special place at least in my world. I am not referring to any dislike we may have of certain cultivars, of conifer hedges that grow too tall, or of monotonous plantations of radiata pine or Sitka spruce. I am going to talk of conifers as invasive weeds, destroying native natural or semi-natural vegetation and thereby causing extinction. Invasive species of animals and plants have become one of the most important issues in nature conservation, which aims at the preservation or restoration of biodiversity in ecosystems. After habitat alteration and destruction, invasive species are likely to become the second greatest threat to biodiversity on the planet. That is a big claim—and not mine—that needs some explaining of the basic ecology behind invasiveness and its effects. We humans are once again the cause behind the problems with invasive species, by introducing them to places where they do not belong. Let us look at that example on the Dutch heathland for a moment, so I can introduce some of the issues.

It has been estimated from topographical maps and historic records that at the beginning of the 19th century the Netherlands had about 600,000 ha (1.5 million acres) of heathlands, plus thousands of hectares of inland sand dunes eroded and blown from these caused by overgrazing and sod digging. This land had once been wooded, but even by the Bronze Age 3500 years ago extensive heathlands had formed after felling of the forests by farmers and pastoralists. The dominant heather species is *Calluna vulgaris*, also common is *Erica tetralix* on slightly moister soil, and certain grasses, mosses, and lichens. The vegetation is spontaneous and indigenous—nothing is planted or introduced—so it is semi-natural. This lowland heath community has a special flora and fauna. With less than 10 per cent remaining and that in trouble, the Dutch now want to preserve this ecosystem. In northwestern Europe, the Netherlands is the last bastion against the forces that threaten the heathlands. Of course, we did not always think of this ecosystem as special. As recently as the 1960s, projects to plough heathland into arable or dairy grassland helped by artificial fertilizer were still subsidized by the government. Across the border in northern Germany, virtually all heathlands disappeared over the course of the 20th century. For many centuries heathlands had a multiple function, grazing sheep for wool and manure, the latter going on the agricultural fields around the village. But during the 19th century, with cheap wool from Australia and chemical fertilizers being developed, the heathland became economically worthless. The sand dunes had expanded, threatening the fields and even some villages.

Then it was discovered that Scots pine would grow well on both heathlands and dunes, both of which have nutrient-poor soils, the former with poor drainage. This conifer had probably become extinct in the Netherlands, but its seed was brought in from Germany. It took nearly two centuries of sowing and planting, but after that effort *Pinus sylvestris* had restored forestry as an enterprise in the Netherlands and much of the heathland had been converted to pine plantations. The dunes were stabilized, only a few remained open, and these are now also nature reserves. But the pines did not stay in their plantations—they spread out into the remaining patches of heathland and sand. Of course, lowland heath being semi-natural vegetation here, it will not remain unless we do something. The natural vegetation is woodland or light forest, but without the Scots pine. Old stands of Scots pine, when not or only lightly managed for timber production, become ecologically valuable as well. Native trees and shrubs move in and eventually would outcompete the pines, which are not climax trees in this ecosystem. Forestry on these sandy soils has had its day, too, and is no longer economical. In a small, densely populated country such as the Netherlands, with a very long history of diverse land use, it is neither feasible nor desirable to let every nature reserve revert to

Planted forest of *Pinus sylvestris* (Scots pine) on a heathland in the Veluwe region of the central Netherlands

Scots pine has invaded the remaining heathlands, which the Dutch now want to preserve as a special and rare semi-natural ecosystem.

natural woodland, whatever that might turn out to be. Biodiversity here is best served by a mosaic of landscapes, from semi-natural to almost natural. With 360 inhabitants per square kilometre you cannot sensibly exclude people.

Invasive plants are a subset of naturalized plants. They are not only successful in establishing themselves in a foreign environment without further help by humans, but continue to spread aggressively, replacing native species and often dominating ecosystems. Some characteristics of invasive plant species are apparent from the example of *Pinus sylvestris* on the Dutch heathlands. Invasive species are not native to the area and in most cases never were. They have very good dispersal capacity, by mass-produced, small, winged seeds in the case of the pine. Invasive species grow faster than most native species and can reach reproductive age quickly. They are often pioneers or at least belong to early phases in a succession series. If a conifer species has all or most of these characteristics when it arrives, it has the potential to become invasive.

Marcel Rejmánek of the University of California at Davis has calculated a discriminant function Z using several of these parameters to predict the potential for invasive behaviour. If Z is positive, a species is more likely invasive given the chance, but not necessarily invasive. Ecological constraints may still stop it from invading an ecosystem (I shall return to that aspect later). Which conifer species have turned out to be invasive? Of all eight families, Pinaceae is the only one that can be called problematic in that it contains species that are extremely invasive. In particular, the genus *Pinus* has some invasive species that are as "bad" as any of the invasive angiosperms we know. They have become particularly troublesome in the Southern Hemisphere, where the five most invasive species are *Pinus contorta, P. halepensis, P. patula, P. pinaster*, and *P. radiata*, all of which exhibited the highest Z scores in Reymánek's studies. No species of *Pinus* occur naturally in the Southern Hemisphere, and all these species have been extensively used in plantation forestry. Other invasive species in the Pinaceae are *Larix decidua, L. kaempferi, Picea abies, P. sitchensis*, and *Pseudotsuga menziesii*, once again forestry favourites used in exotic plantations in many parts of the world. Most characteristics that make conifers potentially invasive are also those that make them good forestry trees. In chapter 22 I gave an example of invasion by Norway spruce (*Picea abies*) in the Belgian Ardennes, a case very similar to the Scots pine in the Dutch Veluwe region. The only other conifer family in which we find invasive species is the Cupressaceae. Here it is the genus *Juniperus* that has some particularly weedy species: *Juniperus bermudiana, J. communis, J. occidentalis*, and *J. virginiana*. This is interesting because junipers have a dispersal mechanism quite different from most pines, with the seeds transported by birds. This accounts for effective long-distance dispersal, but does not produce massive dispersal events, as is possible with wind-blown seeds. Perhaps recruitment of seedlings is more effective if the seeds are transported via the guts of birds, so fewer seeds are wasted. One other species in Cupressaceae with some notoriety is *Cryptomeria japonica*. Its small, light seeds are wind dispersed even though the wings are tiny strips, and in high winds they can undoubtedly travel quite far from the parent tree. Like the pines, *C. japonica* is also an important tree in plantation forestry.

Where have these conifer species become invasive? Obviously this happened in countries where they have been widely planted and especially when their first introduction was a considerable time ago. There is usually a time lag between introduction, establishment, and invasion, the causes of which are complicated and often poorly understood. In many regions, invasions by conifers have become rampant only in the last few decades. Cases of invasive pines are particularly common and often severe in Australia, Chile, Madagascar, Malawi, New Zealand, and South Africa. Of these, South Africa was the first country where pines were introduced, some as early as the late 17th century. Trees and forests are naturally scarce in the Cape Provinces, where fynbos, a natural dwarf shrub community, predominates in winter-rain areas both in lowlands and mountains. European settlers were in need of timber, and pines would grow on the extremely poor soil of the fynbos biome. This habitat is in many respects equivalent to the situation with the heathland in the Netherlands; the vegetation is heath-like and even the settlers were mostly Dutch. The main differences, however, are that fynbos is entirely natural, its biodiversity is extraordinary rich, and it occurs nowhere else. The pines invade the fynbos as easily and rapidly as they do the heathland, but in South Africa five species are presently involved (Richardson 1998): *Pinus canariensis, P. halepensis, P. pinaster, P. pinea,* and *P. radiata.* Of these, *P. halepensis, P. pinaster,* and *P. radiata* now have invaded large areas in the region. All five come from regions in the world with a similar Mediterranean climate, summer drought and fires, winter rains, and skeletal, nutrient-poor soils.

In the Cape Peninsula, an area covering 470 km2 (185 mi2), the indigenous flora of vascular plants comprises 2285 species, more than in the whole of the British Isles. Ninety (about 4 per cent) of these are endemic to the peninsula. This area includes the famous Table Mountain above Cape Town. When I climbed this mountain in late

Invasion of pines (*Pinus pinea*) on a slope with species-rich fynbos vegetation above Villiersdorp in the Cape region of South Africa. Photograph by Colin Paterson-Jones

spring 1995 from its eastern side, starting in the Kirstenbosch Botanic Garden, I came to a gully with forest that led steeply up not to a flat top, as I had expected, but to an undulating landscape with valleys, hollows with water reservoirs, and small peaks. The flat table is an optical illusion seen from the ocean to the west, looking at the seaward side. Over large areas, pines once planted here had been felled years earlier, the bleached trunks still lying around everywhere. The vegetation in most places was very impoverished and disturbed compared to what I had seen in areas where no pines had existed. These had been plantations of *Pinus radiata* now eradicated in an attempt to save the fynbos of Table Mountain and restore the water reservoirs for the city. These and other pines had been planted for timber, which turned out to be a failure, and to improve the "bleak and naked appearance of these bare and stony slopes" above Cape Town. Eradicating the invasion of seedlings proves much more difficult. In 1994 these pines, many then mature trees, covered some 3300 ha (8250 acres) of the Cape Peninsula. *Pinus pinaster* and increasingly *P. radiata* have become the most widespread and difficult to eradicate of the woody alien species threatening the fynbos biome. Nobody knows how many extinctions these invaders may have caused already.

Similar disasters are happening due to invasive pines in Australia, New Zealand (probably the worst-affected country when it comes to invasive pines), New Caledonia (where *Pinus caribaea* invades the *maquis minier* on ultramafic soil), and Chile. The New Zealanders seem to have tried many of the world's species of *Pinus* for plantation forestry, with the result that 13 species are now naturalized. They have also recorded naturalization and invasion rather well, so we can perhaps use this information in the future to understand the phenomenon of invasion better.

Island biotas appear to be particularly sensitive to invasions, especially on remote oceanic islands. These islands derived their biodiversity from rare events of immigration and, over time, also from evolution, but in many cases the diversity is still very limited. New arrivals with the characteristics of invasive species—a positive Z factor—turn out to be even more destructive than on the mainland. It was not a good idea to take *Juniperus bermudiana*, endangered on its native island of Bermuda, to St. Helena off the west coast of Africa. In the absence of both competitors and natural enemies, this juniper had the island to itself and behaved accordingly. Eradication will be costly but has to be done if the already-battered and greatly depleted biodiversity of this little mid-Atlantic island is to be preserved.

The case of *Juniperus occidentalis* in eastern Oregon is very different. While the U.S. Forest Service has recorded a fivefold expansion of its range in a little more than 50 years, most ecologists would not accept what is going on there as an invasion. First of all, the species is indigenous to Oregon, including much of the area it is now expanding into. Its spread is closely associated with changes in land management and use since the arrival of European settlers, especially of the livestock-raising variety. Suppression of fires led to lower frequency of fire on any given site, allowing junipers to grow and establish denser stands of larger trees, providing seed trees in twice as large an area as before. Long-term overgrazing increased the density of sage brush (*Artemisia tridentata*), a woody shrub not eaten by cattle and sheep. Protected by these bushes, juniper seedlings can succeed undetected by the same animals to a stage where they are no longer palatable. Junipers establish less easily from seed in a dense grass sward. With changing agro-economics, many ranges are now less intensively grazed and fields once cultivated are being left fallow or are abandoned permanently. All of these areas are invaded by junipers, but in this case it is merely a first stage in a succession back to an ecosystem that probably occupied the region in the past. The species' limits are set by climate, particularly precipitation, with shortgrass prairie and scattered sage brush on the dry limit and open pine-juniper woodland merging to ponderosa pine (*Pinus ponderosa*) on the wetter side. Human disturbance may have enlarged the potential range of *J. occidentalis* at most for a few centuries. Future climate change may also influence this, of course.

Are there natural limits to invasion set by the environment? Charles Elton, in an early book about the subject (Elton 1958), discussed what he called the balance between populations. A substantial number of potential invasions never happen. The ecosystem puts up an effective resistance, and the would-be invader has no chance to become numerous. The keys are complexity of habitats and diversity of tree species. In a complex forest ecosystem, any newcomer has to compete with numerous other species for light, water, and nutrients. They will find few spaces unoccupied and will not succeed to gain dominance—at best they may find a mode of coexistence. The first fact to observe is that almost all invaders, or any aliens for that matter, live in drastically simplified habitats. With a constant influx of introductions, sooner or later a species will arrive to take up the niche in the ecosystem vacated by an indigenous species or created anew by human interference. With competition removed and natural enemies absent, that newcomer may become invasive. Oceanic islands often have naturally simple habitats, as time may not have been sufficient for the evolution of more complex ecosystems. Second, some ecosystems may be complex in terms of species diversity, such as the South African fynbos, and be able to resist newcomers with similar characteristics and requirements. But in that ecotype no species of trees evolved to cope with its poor nutrient conditions, summer drought, and frequent fires. If such trees exist somewhere else, all that has to happen is introduction by humans. For millions of years this was not an option, and the native flora and ecosystems developed without any defences against trees. Here lies the main reason why pines have been so disastrously invasive in the Southern Hemisphere in recent times, threatening diverse plant communities dominated by small or medium-sized shrubs in which no tree-forming conifers existed.

This chapter and this book should end with a positive note on conifers, which are often portrayed as evolutionary losers when compared with woody angiosperms. Having arrived at the end of this book, you will agree that this negative picture needs amendment. Perhaps the invasive power of some conifers will even educate those champions of the flowering plants. Although very inferior in numbers of species, conifers have fully earned their space on Earth and are definitely here to stay.

Appendix: A Classification of Extant Conifer Families to the Genus Level

The conifer families are here given in alphabetical order. For their hypothetical relationships, see chapter 9. The hypothetical relationships of genera within families are indicated by their groupings; some of these groupings have been named at the rank of subfamily, while others are here presented as informal and separated from each other by a blank line. The relationships in Podocarpaceae are most tentative, as they are based on phylogenies derived from recent cladistic analyses of molecular and morphological data, which are not in agreement for several clades. The DNA-based analyses tend to place Phyllocladaceae within Podocarpaceae. The names of families and genera are given with their abbreviated authorities. For more detailed recent classifications down to species, for Cupressaceae see Farjon (2005b); for Pinaceae excluding *Pinus* see Farjon (1990), for *Pinus* see Richardson (1998) and Farjon (2005a); and for Taxaceae see Cope (1998).

Araucariaceae Henkel et W. Hochst.

Agathis Salisb.
Wollemia W. G. Jones et al.

Araucaria Juss.

Cephalotaxaceae Neger

Cephalotaxus Siebold et Zucc. ex Endl.

Cupressaceae Rich. ex Bartl.

Cunninghamioideae (Zucc. ex Endl.) Quinn
Cunninghamia R. Br. ex Rich. et A. Rich.

Taiwanioideae L. C. Li
Taiwania Hayata

Athrotaxoideae L. C. Li
Athrotaxis D. Don

Sequoioideae Saxton
Metasequoia Hu et W. C. Cheng
Sequoia Endl.
Sequoiadendron J. Buchholz

Taxodioideae Endl. ex K. Koch
Cryptomeria D. Don
Glyptostrobus Endl.
Taxodium Rich.

Cupressoideae Rich. ex Sweet
Thujopsis Siebold et Zucc. ex Endl.
Thuja L.

Calocedrus Kurz
Chamaecyparis Spach
Cupressus L.
Fokienia A. Henry
Juniperus L.
Microbiota Kom.
Platycladus Spach
Tetraclinis Mast.
Xanthocyparis Farjon et Hiep

Austrocedrus Florin et Boutelje
Libocedrus Endl.
Papuacedrus H. L. Li
Pilgerodendron Florin

Actinostrobus Miq.
Callitris Vent.

Diselma Hook. f.
Fitzroya Lindl.
Neocallitropsis Florin
Widdringtonia Endl.

Phyllocladaceae Bessey

Phyllocladus Rich. ex Mirb.

Pinaceae Lindl.

Pinoideae Pilg.
Pinus L.
Cathaya Chun et Kuang
Picea A. Dietr.

Laricoideae Melchior et Werdermann
Larix Mill.
Pseudotsuga Carrière

Abietoideae Pilg.
Abies Mill.
Cedrus Trew*
Keteleeria Carrière
Nothotsuga Hu ex C. N. Page
Pseudolarix Gordon
Tsuga (Endl.) Carrière

*The genus *Cedrus* has come out as basal (sister group to all other genera) in some recent DNA-based cladistic analyses. Morphological evidence, however, places it firmly within Abietoideae, and a basal position is not corroborated by the fossil record. Its position is tentative.

Podocarpaceae Endl.

Saxegothaea Lindl.

Podocarpus L'Hér. ex Pers.
Retrophyllum C. N. Page

Afrocarpus (J. Buchholz et N. E. Gray)
   C. N. Page
Nageia Gaertn.

Acmopyle Pilg.
Dacrycarpus (Endl.) de Laub.
Dacrydium Sol. ex G. Forst.
Falcatifolium de Laub.

Halocarpus Quinn
Lagarostrobos Quinn
Lepidothamnus Phil.
Manoao Molloy
Microcachrys Hook. f.
Parasitaxus de Laub.
Pherosphaera W. Archer
Prumnopitys Phil.
Sundacarpus (J. Buchholz et N. E. Gray)
   C. N. Page

Sciadopityaceae Luerss.

Sciadopitys Siebold et Zucc.

Taxaceae Gray

Amentotaxus Pilg.

Austrotaxus R. H. Compton
Pseudotaxus W. C. Cheng
Taxus L.

Torreya Arn.

Glossary

abaxial in a position removed from an axis or stem

adaxial in a position nearest an axis or stem

allopatric speciation the evolution of species from geographically separated populations

angiosperms flowering plants

apex (adj. apical) in plant morphology, the terminal point of a growing structure like a shoot or a leaf; a conifer cone that is apical grows at the apex of a shoot (but very few are)

arboretum (pl. arboreta) a park or garden dedicated to a living collection of planted trees and shrubs

arborist a tree technician involved in maintenance and tree surgery of individual, usually planted, trees

aril (Latin *arillus*) a fleshy or succulent cup-like structure that partially envelops a seed

axillary positioned in the axil, being the crotch between an axis or stem and an appendage, such as a leaf

binomial a name consisting of two separate words; in biology it refers to the names of species, which are always the name of a genus written with a capital first letter followed by an epithet written in lowercase

biodiversity the total number of **taxa** (or sometimes genetic diversity) known to exist in a given area; the greater this figure, the higher the region's biodiversity

biogeography the study of the geographical distribution of organisms as well as its causes and history

biota (Latinized form of Greek *biotē*, "life") the totality of life (plants, animals, fungi, etc.) in a region

boreal (Greek Boreas, "god of the north wind") of northern regions of the world

canopy the upper crown level in a closed forest, where the crowns of the tallest trees meet to form a more or less continuous cover

chlorophyll a usually green substance, contained in **chloroplasts** in leaf or sometimes stem tissue of plants, responsible for photosynthesis

chloroplast a microscopic body (organelle) inside a plant cell that contains **chlorophyll**

clade a section of a **cladogram** that represents a **monophyletic** group of taxa

cladistic referring to a methodology first developed by the German entomologist Willi Hennig to analyze **phylogenetic** relationships among taxa; its adherents are sometimes referred to as cladists

cladogram a two dimensional, tree-like (branching) representation of the **phylogenetic** relationships of taxa inferred from **cladistic** analysis

climax a supposedly terminal stage in the succession of vegetation types from pioneer colonizers to mature vegetation; in fact, all stages in the succession are temporary because they are all subjected to natural disturbances, including the climax stage

codon the triplet of **nucleotides** or bases in **DNA** consisting of a base pair (adenine and thymine or cytosine and guanine) plus one other base

congener a species in the same genus as another species

conifer a gymnospermous plant belonging to the order Coniferales

convergence the evolution towards similar morphology not as a result of common descent but of adaptation to similar environments or life strategies

288

coppice regrowth from the stump of a tree after cutting (or burning), producing new stems and branches; the stump after cutting is called coppice stool; in many species the stems will regrow even after repeated cutting

cultivar a form of a plant in cultivation, the characteristics of which are perpetuated by vegetative propagation; see **variety**

cycad a gymnospermous plant belonging to the order Cycadales

decumbent (Latin, "lie down") growing low over the ground or surface of a rock

decurrent running down a stem from a leaf base

dendrological of dendrology, the study of trees

dichotomy a branching habit in which a single branch divides in two equal branches

disjunct (of distribution) occurring in areas widely separated from each other

dispersal the spreading of organisms to areas other than where they originated

DNA (deoxyribonucleic acid) the macromolecule in cells of organisms that contains the genetic code acting as a template to build new cells; parts of DNA are not involved in transcription to the **RNA** (ribonucleic acid) that builds proteins and cells but preserve character changes (copying errors or **mutations**) passed on to descendants and useful for **systematics**

ecology the study or science of **ecosystems**, or of the functional relationships of organisms with their environment and with each other

ecosystem the supposed totality of the functional relationships of organisms with their environment and with each other living in a given area and **habitat**

ecotype a plant form with morphological characters that are modified by the environment in which the individual plant grows; such characters are not inherited and therefore are not a good basis for taxonomic distinction

emergent in the context of trees, referring to individuals rising above the forest **canopy**

endemic (n. endemism) referring to the occurrence of a **taxon** in a limited area (for example, on a single island or mountain range); taxa limited to a single country are also considered endemic, although the term becomes fairly meaningless biologically for widespread species limited to countries that cover nearly half a continent

epimatium the outer layer of tissue that (partly) covers a seed in many species of the family Podocarpaceae; it is derived from the seed scale

epiphyte a plant that grows upon another plant (usually a tree) using it for support only

figure in sawn and planed or turned and polished wood, the decorative patterns and shapes caused by growth rings and other structures in relation to the plane of sawing or turning

gamete reproductive cell with one set of chromosomes (haploid) that combines with a gamete from the opposite sex at fertilization to form the zygote with two sets of chromosomes (diploid); sperm or **pollen** in males and egg in females

gene a bit of **DNA** (sequence of nucleotides) coding for a protein or part of a protein

genetic drift random changes in **gene** frequencies in a population; these are not caused by natural selection, which is not a random process

graft the artificial growing connection of two parts of different plants, involving a root stock and the grafted cutting or **scion** with foliage; the resulting "plant" minus the rootstock is also referred to as a graft

gymnosperms nonflowering seed plants

habitat the type of place an organism lives in, characterized by both abiotic and biotic environmental factors, such as substrate, microclimate, and vegetation

hardpan a compact soil surface inhibiting percolation of rain water to deeper levels where tree roots could take it up

heartwood the inner section of the wood of a tree, with dead wood cells through which no water is transported

helical arranged or formed in an upwards spiral (helix)

holotype the one specimen or illustration used by an author in publishing a new name

homeotic genes (Greek *homeos*, "same or similar") **genes** that determine when, where, and what kind of organs or parts are formed in a developing organism; the term was originally coined by William Bateson for abnormalities that seemed to transform one body part into the likeness of another

homologous referring to shared characters in two or more species due to common descent, or to modifications evolved from such commonly inherited characters (such as fingers in humans and wing bones in bats)

homonym a name of an organism spelled exactly the same as the name of another organism; homonyms within the jurisdictions of the several codes of biological nomenclature are not allowed and the rule of priority dictates that the name shall be applied to the earliest named plant or fungus (in case of the Botanical Code) and that the other plant or fungus must be renamed

igneous referring to rock that was formed from molten material (magma) in the interior of the Earth; it may have solidified below as well as on the surface

incertae sedis (Latin, "place uncertain") a heading under which taxonomists place names of taxa for which the original description is unclear in the context of present knowledge and of which no good original material exists to determine their identity

indigenous naturally occurring in an area or a country, without having been transported there (intentionally or unintentionally) by people

inflorescence a branching system supporting flowers but usually not leaves

inverted a position turned about 90° from an earlier position; inverted seeds have turned their **apex** back towards their attachment point

karst a deeply eroded formation of marine limestone, of which surfaces are partly dissolved by rain water containing carbon dioxide and where acidic groundwater dissolves caves; drainage in karst landscapes is largely underground; in tropical climates karst landscapes develop tower hills or mountains

keystone species a species in an **ecosystem** upon which many species depend that characterize that ecosystem and make it function; removal of the keystone species destroys that particular ecosystem

knot in sawn wood the remainder of a branch in the stem of a tree, visible as a darker, rounded bit of wood with a different grain

lanceolate of a shape reminiscent of a lance point, commonly used to describe the shape of a leaf

laterite (Latin *later*, "brick") a chemically weathered, earth-like type of rock rich in oxidized metals

lectotype the type specimen of a species chosen from various original material when no **holotype** was designated, to serve as the nomenclatural type by which the application of the name of the species is fixed

lignite an organic deposit from plant remains in an intermediate phase of being transformed from peat to bituminous black coal

lignotuber an outgrowth or swelling on the basal root system of a tree, forming excess wood and capable of initiating new aerial stems with foliage and reproductive organs

meristem the active growing point of a plant consisting of dividing cells

mesa (Spanish, "table") a flat-topped mountain resulting from processes of erosion in ancient sandstone or other sedimentary formations

mesothermic referring to a relatively warm climate with moderate seasonal fluctuations in temperature

metamorphic of a rock type that has been substantially altered due to high pressure and/or heat generated by movements of the Earth's crust

micropyle the opening in an **ovule** through which **pollen** enters, in most conifers with the aid of a pollination drop of fluid

molecular analysis in the present context, a **phylogenetic** analysis using **DNA** sequence data as characters and **cladistic** methodology

monograph in biology, the comprehensive taxonomic description of a natural group of species, usually a genus or a family, including all aspects pertinent to the **systematics** and classification of that group

monophyletic in **cladistic** terms, referring to a taxonomic group consisting of a hypothetical ancestor and *all* its descendants; in evolutionary terms, referring to a not necessarily inclusive group of taxa that share a common nearest ancestor; the term is now almost always used in its cladistic (i.e., narrower) sense, as I do in this book

monotypic referring to a **taxon** containing only a single taxon of lower rank, such as a genus with only one species

morphology the detailed study of form; in systematic research of taxa this involves investigations into anatomy and development as well as comparison among individuals and taxa in order to understand characters and their states

mutant an organism that obtained a genetic character change (**mutation**) not present in other individuals of its species

mutation a change in the genetic properties of an organism; it involves a change in the **DNA** sequence code that is not due to sexual recombination of DNA in the zygote

mutualism an ecological or behavioural relationship between two species that is beneficial to both

mycelian of the mycelium, the threadlike, usually underground network of hyphae of fungi

mycorrhizae the thread-like hyphae of certain fungi that form intricate connections with the roots of plants and live in **symbiosis** with these plants

natural group a group of taxa that is based on a hypothesis of common descent from a nearest ancestor

nucleotide any of the unit building blocks or bases of **DNA and RNA**, commonly represented by the letters A (adenine), C (cytosine), G (guanine), and T (thymine); in RNA U (uracil) replaces T; in the DNA chain, A links with T and C with G, forming sequences of nucleotides

nutrient in the context of plants any of the basic elements such as nitrogen, potassium, and phosphorus necessary for growth and physiological processes

ontogenetically referring to the process of development or growth of an organism or its parts from fertilized egg to adult

ovule initial stage in the development of a seed before fertilization and subsequent growth

palaeobotany the study of fossil plant remains

palaeontology the study of fossil organisms

palynology the study of **pollen** and spores, both of recent and fossil plants

paraphyletic referring to a group of taxa that share a nearest common ancestor but not all the descendants of that ancestor

pathogenic referring to a pathogen, an agent or organism that causes disease

paucitypic (Latin *pauci*, "a few") referring to a **taxon** containing only a few taxa of lower rank; I coin this term here in analogy to **monotypic**

pectinate arranged in two rows along an axis, spreading sideways

peltate shaped like a shield, with an attachment more or less close to the centre

phyllotaxis the arrangement of leaves on a shoot or stem and their position in relation to each other

phylogenetic (n. phylogeny) referring to ancestor-descendant relationships between extant species or taxa of higher ranks

phylogeny a hypothetical "tree" or formula that shows **phylogenetic** relationships; it does not show ancestors. (The meaning of *phylogeny* has changed with cladistic methods; originally it referred to the evolutionary history of a lineage, including ancestors, and their morphological change through time.)

pinetum (pl. pineta) a park or garden dedicated to a living collection of planted conifers

pinnate having the arrangement of a feather, with a single rachis from which leaflets arise on either side

plate tectonics the formation and dynamics of the plates into which the crust of the Earth is divided

podzolic (Russian *podzol*, "under ashes") referring to an infertile, sandy and acidic soil with minerals leached from its surface layers and deposited in a lower stratum; the leached part of the profile is ash grey

pollen the nearly microscopic unit or "grain" in seed plants that contains the male **gamete** enclosed by a hard and usually multilayered wall and is dispersed to meet an **ovule** for fertilization

pollen tube a hollow extension that grows from a **pollen** grain upon entrance through the **micropyle** towards the egg and through which the contents of the male **gamete** are transferred

polyphyletic referring to a group of taxa that do not share a nearest common ancestor

provenance information about the source of a plant or its seed used in forestry or horticulture

radiation in biology, referring to the spread and taxonomic diversification of a species into new **habitat** or territory

receptacle a fleshy or succulent structure subtending a free-standing seed in *Podocarpus* and some other genera of the Podocarpaceae; it is formed from all remnants of the seed cone after fertilization of usually a single egg developing into the seed

refugium (pl. refugia) a geographical area into which one or more species have retreated (or where they remained) from a much wider distribution in the past

reiteration (Latin *reiterare*, "to say or do repeatedly") the secondary initiation of branching from a primary branching system (or from the trunk) of a tree, usually as a response to damage

rheophyte a plant that completes its life cycle in streams but is not aquatic; a rheophyte germinates out of water when the stream falls temporarily dry or recedes from normally higher levels

RNA ribonucleic acid; see **DNA**

ruderal referring to plants or vegetation growing in and adapted to continuously or repeatedly disturbed sites (dynamic **habitats**)

saprophagous feeding or subsisting on dead organic matter, thereby decomposing it to inorganic and organic compounds

sapwood the outer section of the wood of a tree, with living wood cells through which water is transported

scarification slight chemical and/or mechanical damage done to the seed coat, facilitating germination by enabling the embryo to break through

scion a vegetative shoot cut from a plant and caused to produce roots or grafted onto a different rootstock

sensu lato (Latin, "in a wide sense") in **taxonomy**, this term follows a **taxon** name to indicate that it includes another taxon at the same rank which some may recognize as distinct (abbreviated as s.l.)

sister group a **clade** in a **cladogram** that is nearest in relationship to another clade, or a **taxon** represented by such a clade; the term usually (but not necessarily) refers to the clade below the next one in a cladogram

speciation the formation of new species through evolutionary processes

speciose having many species

sporophyll literally a leaf bearing spores (as in ferns); in **gymnosperms** it refers to leaf-like appendages bearing male (i.e., microsporophyll) or female (macrosporophyll) reproductive organs, the **pollen** (in pollen sacs) or **ovules**

strobilus the technical term for the reproductive unit of a **gymnosperm** that bears male or female organs, regardless of whether it forms a cone or not

succession in ecology, the gradual and successive replacement of plant species by others in one locality due to development of the vegetation from a pioneer phase to a **climax** phase

symbiosis a mutually beneficial physiological relationship between two or more different species

sympatric speciation the evolution of species from populations with overlapping geographical ranges

synapomorphy a shared derived character, present in an ancestor **taxon** and its descendants

synplesiomorphy a shared ancestral character, present in a **taxon** and (some of) its ancestors

systematics the science of the diversity and relationships of taxa based on evolutionary principles, including (or sometimes seen as synonymous with) **taxonomy**

taiga (Russian, "forest") northern coniferous forest ranging between tundra in the north and steppe in the south

taxon (pl. taxa) any group of organisms that is recognized at any of the ranks of classification used by taxonomists, such as family, genus, species

taxonomy the science of classification of organisms and the identification and naming of taxa

terrane the area or surface over which a particular rock or group of rocks is prevalent

tracheid a cell in the wood of **gymnosperms** distinct from the equivalent cells in **angiosperms** (**vessels**) and characterized by lateral pits allowing fluid transport

ultramafic (also ultrabasic) referring to rock or soil poor in silica but extremely rich in iron and magnesium minerals and with a high pH value

vademecum (Latin, "go with me") a handbook or guide constantly carried with you

variety the category of taxa intermediate between subspecies and forma, the characteristics of which are perpetuated by sexual reproduction

vessel (in wood) a cell in the wood of **angiosperms** (and some **gymnosperms**) with closed lateral walls and distal openings allowing fluid transport

vicariance (Latin *vicarius*, "substitute") in **biogeography** referring to the distribution of taxa explained by the history of the separation of the areas in which these taxa occur; the term originally referred to a method of analysis in which area **cladograms** were substituted for **taxon** cladograms

xerophyte a plant adapted to withstand drought conditions in its natural **habitat**; in wet but salt conditions plants often have xerophytic adaptations because water intake with dissolved salt must be minimized

References

Alvin, K. L. 1983. Reconstruction of a Lower Cretaceous conifer. *Botanical Journal of the Linnean Society* 86: 169–76.

Anderson, J. M., and H. M. Anderson. 2003. *Heyday of the Gymnosperms: Systematics and Biodiversity of the Late Triassic Molteno Fructifications*. Strelitzia 15. South African National Biodiversity Institute, Pretoria.

Beck, C. B., editor. 1988. *Origin and Evolution of Gymnosperms*. Columbia University Press, New York.

Benzing, D. H. 1990. *Vascular Epiphytes: General Biology and Related Biota*. Cambridge University Press, Cambridge.

Briggs, J. C. 1995. *Developments in Palaeontology and Stratigraphy*. Vol. 14, *Global Biogeography*. Elsevier, Amsterdam.

Burns, R. M., and B. H. Honkala, technical coordinators. 1990. *Silvics of North America*. Vol. 1, *Conifers*. Agriculture Handbook 654. Forest Service, U.S. Department of Agriculture, Washington, D.C.

Cope, E. A. 1998. Taxaceae: the genera and cultivated species. *Botanical Review* (Lancaster) 64(4): 291–322.

Debazac, E. F. 1964. *Manuel des Conifères*. Ecôle Nationale des Eaux et Forêts, Nancy.

de Laubenfels, D. J. 1972. *Flore de la Nouvelle-Calédonie et Dépendances*. Vol. 4, *Gymnospermes*. Muséum National d'Histoire Naturelle, Paris.

Elton, C. S. 1958. *The Ecology of Invasions by Animals and Plants*. Methuen, London.

Elwes, H. J., and A. Henry. 1906–1912. *The Trees of Great Britain and Ireland*, Vols. I–VI. Published by the authors, Edinburgh.

Engler, A. 1926. Verbreitung der Coniferae. In A. Engler and K. Prantl, editors. *Die natürlichen Pflanzenfamilien*, 2nd ed., Vol. 13, pp. 180–90. W. Engelmann, Leipzig.

Farjon, A. 1984. *Pines: Drawings and Descriptions of the Genus Pinus*. E. J. Brill & W. Backhuys, Leiden.

Farjon, A. 1990. *Pinaceae: Drawings and Descriptions of the Genera Abies, Cedrus, Pseudolarix, Keteleeria, Nothotsuga, Tsuga, Cathaya, Pseudotsuga, Larix and Picea*. Regnum Vegetabile 121. Koeltz Scientific Books, Königstein.

Farjon, A. 1998. *World Checklist and Bibliography of Conifers*. Royal Botanic Gardens, Kew.

Farjon, A. 2001. *World Checklist and Bibliography of Conifers*. 2nd ed. Royal Botanic Gardens, Kew.

Farjon, A. 2005a. *Pines: Drawings and Descriptions of the Genus Pinus*. 2nd ed. E. J. Brill, Leiden.

Farjon, A. 2005b. *A Monograph of Cupressaceae and Sciadopitys*. Royal Botanic Gardens, Kew.

Farjon, A., and C. N. Page, compilers. 1999. *Conifers: Status Survey and Conservation Action Plan*. IUCN/SSC Conifer Specialist Group. IUCN, Gland, Switzerland.

Farjon, A., and B. T. Styles. 1997. *Pinus (Pinaceae)*. Flora Neotropica Monograph 75. The New York Botanical Garden, New York.

Farjon, A., C. N. Page, and N. Schellevis. 1993. A preliminary world list of threatened conifer taxa. *Biodiversity and Conservation* 2: 304–26.

Farjon, A., Nguyen Tien Hiep, D. K. Harder, Phan Ke Loc, and L. Averyanov. 2002. A new genus and species in Cupressaceae (Coniferales) from northern Vietnam, *Xanthocyparis vietnamensis*. *Novon* 12(2): 179–89.

Florin, C. R. 1963. The distribution of conifer and taxad genera in time and space. *Acta Horti Bergiani* 20(4): 121–312.

Gould, S. J. 1985. Of wasps and WASPS. In *The Flamingo's Smile*. W. W. Norton, New York.

Grauvogel-Stamm, L. 1978. La flore du Grès à *Voltzia* (Buntsandstein supérieur) des Vosges du Nord (France): morphologie, anatomie, interprétations phylogénique et paléo-géographique. Université Louis Pasteur de Strasbourg, Institut de Géologie. *Science Geologique Mémoirs* 50: 1–225.

Hallé, F. 2002. *In Praise of Plants*. Trans. D. Lee. Timber Press, Portland, Ore.

Hawksworth, F. G., and D. Wiens. 1996. *Dwarf Mistletoes: Biology, Pathology, and Systematics*. Agriculture Handbook 709. Forest Service, U.S. Department of Agriculture, Washington, D.C.

Hennig, W. 1966. *Phylogenetic Systematics*. University of Illinois Press, Urbana.

Hernandez-Castillo, G. R., G. W. Rothwell, R. A. Stockey, and G. Mapes. 2003. Growth architecture of *Thucydia mahoningensis*, a model for primitive Walchian conifer plants. *International Journal of Plant Science* 164(3): 443–52.

Hill, R. S., and T. J. Brodribb. 1999. Southern conifers in time and space. *Australian Journal of Botany* 47: 639–96.

Kunzmann, L. 1999. Koniferen der Oberkreide und ihre Relikte im Tertiär Europas: Ein Beitrag zur Kenntnis ausgestorbener Taxodiaceae und Geinitziaceae fam. nov. *Abhandlungen des Staatlichen Museums für Mineralogie und Geologie zu Dresden* 45: 1–134.

Langenheim, J. H. 2003. *Plant Resins: Chemistry, Evolution, Ecology, and Ethnobotany*. Timber Press, Portland, Ore.

Lara A., and R. Villalba. 1993. A 3622-year temperature reconstruction from *Fitzroya cupressoides* tree rings in southern South America. *Science* 260: 1104–6.

Li, H. L. 1953. Present distribution and habitats of the conifers and taxads. *Evolution* 7: 245–61.

MacArthur, R. H., and E. O. Wilson. 1967. *The Theory of Island Biogeography*. Princeton University Press, Princeton, N.J.

Mayr, E. 1988. *Toward a New Philosophy of Biology: Observations of an Evolutionist*. Harvard University Press, Cambridge, Mass.

McIver, E. E., and J. F. Basinger. 1999. Early Tertiary floral evolution in the Canadian High Arctic. *Annals of the Missouri Botanical Garden* 86: 523–45.

Mill, R. R., M. Möller, F. Christie, S. M. Glidewell, D. Masson, and B. Williamson. 2001. Morphology, anatomy and ontogeny of female cones in *Acmopyle pancheri* (Brogn. & Gris) Pilg. (Podocarpaceae). *Annals of Botany* (London) 88: 55–67.

Millar, C. I. 1993. Impact of the Eocene on the evolution of *Pinus*. *Annals of the Missouri Botanical Garden* 80: 471–98.

Oliver, W. R. B. 1930. New Zealand epiphytes. *Journal of Ecology* 18(1): 1–50.

Richardson, D. M., editor. 1998. *Ecology and Biogeography of Pinus*. Cambridge University Press, Cambridge.

Rothwell, G. W., and G. Mapes. 2001. *Barthelia furcata* gen. et sp. nov., with a review of Palaeozoic coniferophytes and a discussion of coniferophyte systematics. *International Journal of Plant Science* 162(3): 637–67.

Rothwell, G. W., G. Mapes, and G. R. Hernandez-Castillo. 2005. *Hanskerpia* gen. nov. and phylogenetic relationships among the most ancient conifers. *Taxon* 54(3): 733–50.

Rothwell, G. W., L. Grauvogel-Stamm, and G. Mapes. 2000. An herbaceous fossil conifer: gymnospermous ruderals in the evolution of Mesozoic vegetation. *Palaeo* 156: 139–45.

Schmidt-Vogt, H. 1987. *Die Fichte: Ein Handbuch in zwei Bänden*. Band I. 2nd ed. Verlag Paul Parey, Hamburg.

Sillett, S. C., and R. Van Pelt. 2000. A redwood tree whose crown may be the most complex on earth. *L'arbre/The Tree* 2000: 11–18.

Stewart, W. N., and G. W. Rothwell. 1993. *Paleobotany and the Evolution of Plants.* 2nd ed. Cambridge University Press, Cambridge.

Stockey, R. A. 1994. Mesozoic Araucariaceae: morphology and systematic relationships. *Journal of Plant Research* 107: 493–502.

Stützel, T., and I. Röwekamp. 1999. Female reproductive structures in Taxales. *Flora* 194: 145–57.

Tomlinson, P. B., and T. Takaso. 2003. Seed cone structure in conifers in relation to development and pollination: a biological approach. *Canadian Journal of Botany* 80: 1250–73.

Van Pelt, R. 2001. *Forest Giants of the Pacific Coast.* University of Washington Press, Seattle.

Xiang, Q. P., A. Farjon, Z. Y. Li, L. K. Fu, and Z. Y. Liu. 2002. *Thuja sutchuenensis*: a rediscovered species of the Cupressaceae. *Botanical Journal of the Linnean Society* 139(3): 305–10.

Index